Four Anthropologists:
An American Science in its Early Years

Frank Hamilton Cushing in Zuni dress

4 Anthropologists:

An American Science in its Early Years

Joan Mark

Science History Publications
New York
1980

Published in the United States of America by
Science History Publications, New York
a division of Neale Watson Academic Publications, Inc.
156 Fifth Avenue, New York, N.Y. 10010

Library of Congress Cataloging in Publication Data

Mark, Joan.
    Four anthropologists.

    Bibliography: p.
    Includes index.
    1. Anthropology—United States—History.
2. Anthropologists—United States.   I. Title
GN17.3.U6M37   301′.092′2   80-25414
ISBN 0-88202-190-7

Designed and manufactured in the U.S.A.

To E.L.M.

Contents

Illustrations

Introduction

In this study I have attempted to show two things. The first is that American men and women in the nineteenth century played a far larger role in the development of the science of anthropology than has generally been recognized. The second and related thesis concerns the continuity which exists between nineteenth and twentieth century anthropology in the United States.

Thomas Jefferson began anthropology as we know it at the beginning of the century by showing how questions about the nature of man and his relation to the rest of the natural world might be approached scientifically. From Jefferson there was a continuing tradition of anthropological inquiry in the United States culminating in a burst of activity after 1875. By 1900 anthropology was one science in which the United States led the rest of the world. What anthropologists were doing between 1865 and 1900 and what happened to their work is the subject of this book.

When Franz Boas came from Germany in 1886, he joined—he did not create—an ongoing science of anthropology in the United States. Yet a legend has been built up around Boas, partly at his own instigation, which has tended to obscure the contributions of his American predecessors and contemporaries. Boas found his own intellectual forerunners in Europe, as American anthropologists ever since have tended to do. Yet during the middle and late nineteenth century there were many ideas going in the other direction, from the United States to Europe. American anthropology in the nineteenth century, its methods, concepts, and institutional forms, had a profound impact on European scholars, and to an unrecognized extent it has continued to shape the science of anthropology.

This is a study of four of the most important anthropologists in the United States in the late nineteenth century: F. W. Putnam, Alice Fletcher, Frank Hamilton Cushing, and William Henry Holmes. Lewis Henry Morgan is included peripherally, rather than as a major figure, because the general outline of his work is already well known and also because he died in 1881 and so belongs to an earlier generation. John Wesley Powell is the other conspicuous omission, but his importance has likewise been generally recognized. Powell appears here mainly as a strong force behind the work of Cushing and Holmes. Untold numbers of native Americans made various kinds of contributions to anthropology, and some of them, such as J.N.B. Hewitt, Arthur C. Parker, Louis Shotridge, and Francis La Flesche, became anthropologists.[1] La Flesche, a member of the Omaha tribe, is included here as Alice Fletcher's adopted son and coworker. There are other anthropologists who deserve further study, including Cyrus Thomas, who worked on the mound builders, O.T. Mason, who wrote studies on *The Origin of Invention* (1895), *Woman's Share in Primitive Culture* (1895), and the classic *Aboriginal American Basketry* (1904), James Mooney,[2] who studied the Ghost Dance, and W J McGee, Powell's deputy and later a leader in the conservation movement, but none of them rank with Putnam, Fletcher, Cushing, and Holmes as major formative influences in the development of the new science.

F.W. Putnam, Alice Fletcher, Frank Hamilton Cushing, and William Henry Holmes together were responsible for the establishment of anthropology in Cambridge, Massachusetts, New York, Chicago, and California, the founding of the School of American Research in Santa Fe, New Mexico, the resort to field work in ethnography and to stratigraphy in archaeology, and the formulation of the modern concept of culture. They gathered materials and made studies of native American music, arts, ceremonies, folktales, social organization, and material culture.

Putnam, Fletcher, Cushing, and Holmes all knew one another, and they knew John Wesley Powell and Franz Boas. Together they made up a complex and interlocking scientific community. They worked with an eye on one another in ways which will be apparent throughout this account. In the last chapter I have attempted to suggest the long-term results of their work and of their interactions. The first chapter traces the development in the United States of the new science which came to be called anthropology, from the beginning of the nineteenth century up to the time when first Putnam, and then nearly simultaneously Fletcher, Cushing, and Holmes entered the field.

The history of anthropology has, over the last fifteen years, become a flourishing discipline. I would like to acknowledge in particular the papers by Jacob Gruber and Nancy Lurie in *Pioneers of American Anthropology*, edited by June Helm (Seattle, 1966), George W. Stocking, Jr.'s *Race, Culture, and Evolution* (New York, 1968) and subsequent publications,[3] the doctoral dissertations and recent work of Regna Darnell[4] and Curtis M. Hinsley, Jr.,[5] and the encouragement given to so many of us working in this field by Stephen Williams and William C. Sturtevant. I was well along in this project when I reread Jacob Gruber's "In Search of Experience: Biography as an Instrument for the History of Anthropology" and was surprised to find how firmly his suggestions had lodged in my subconscious, particularly his comment that someone ought to do a comparative biography of Boas, Holmes, and Putnam. Similarly it was Stocking's comment that Cushing had used the word "cultures" in the plural before 1900 that led me to explore Cushing further and to take finally a position on the development of the concept of culture quite different from Stocking's own. Nancy Lurie found so much valuable work done by women in anthropology in the late nineteenth century that it seemed the men too might have been doing more than we had thought. To all of them I am grateful.

I write of the importance of institutions keenly aware of those which have nurtured me, including the History of Science Department at Harvard University, the Radcliffe Institute (now the Bunting Institute of Radcliffe College), the Peabody Museum of Archaeology and Ethnology, and the Charles Warren Center for Studies in American History at Harvard University. Donald Fleming has been for a long time my exemplar in matters of American intellectual history. He as well as Stephen Williams, William C. Sturtevant, George W. Stocking, Jr., Helen Swick Perry, and Edward Mark have all been kind enough to read this manuscript and offer comments and criticisms for which I am very grateful.

I have used letters and other materials from the Archives of the Peabody Museum of Archaeology and Ethnology, Harvard University Archives, the National Anthropological Archives at the Smithsonian Institution, the Archives of the Smithsonian Institution, the Library of the National Collection of Fine Arts and the National Portrait Gallery, the Library of the American Philosophical Society, the Rush Rhees Library at the University of Rochester, and the Schlesinger Library at Radcliffe College.

Chapter Three has appeared previously in *Perspectives in American History*, X (1976).

Notes and References

1. Recently scholars have begun to give native Americans some of the credit due them for their many contributions to anthropology. See Margot Liberty, ed., *American Indian Intellectuals*. 1976 Proceedings of the American Ethnological Society (St.

Paul, West Pub. Co., 1978), and Hazel W. Hertzberg, "Nationality, Anthropology and Pan-Indianism in the Life of Arthur C. Parker (Seneca)," *Proceedings of the American Philosophical Society*, 123 (1979), 47–72.

2. Mooney is the subject of two recent dissertations: William Munn Colby, "Routes to Rainy Mountain: A Biography of James Mooney, Ethnologist," Ph.D. dissertation, University of Wisconsin—Madison (1977) and Lester George Moses, "James Mooney, U.S. Ethnologist: A Biography," Ph.D. dissertation, University of New Mexico (1977).

3. These include "What's In a Name? The Origins of the Royal Anthropological Institute (1837–71)," *Man*, n.s. VI (1971), 369–391; *The Shaping of American Anthropology, 1883–1911: A Franz Boas Reader*, ed. by G.W. Stocking, Jr. (New York, Basic Books, 1974); "Ideas and Institutions in American Anthropology: Thoughts Toward a History of the Interwar Years," in Stocking, ed., *Selected Papers from the American Anthropologist, 1921–1945* (Washington, American Anthropological Association, 1976), 1–53 and "Anthropology as Kulturkampf: Science and Politics in the Career of Franz Boas," in Walter Goldschmidt, ed., *The Uses of Anthropology*, Special Publication of the American Anthropological Association (1979), 32–50;

Stocking also edits *The History of Anthropology Newsletter*.

4. Regna Darnell, "The Development of American Anthropology 1879–1920: From the Bureau of American Ethnology to Franz Boas," Ph.D. dissertation, University of Pennsylvania (1969); "The Emergence of Academic Anthropology at the University of Pennsylvania," *Journal of the History of the Behavioral Sciences*, 6 (1970), 80–92; Regna Darnell, ed., *Readings in the History of Anthropology* (New York, Harper and Row, 1974); "Daniel G. Brinton" in John Murra, ed., *American Anthropology: The Early Years*. 1974 Proceedings of the American Ethnological Society (St. Paul, West Pub. Co., 1976); "History of Anthropology in Historical Perspective," *Annual Review of Anthropology*, 6 (1977), 399–417.

5. Curtis M. Hinsley, Jr., "The Development of a Profession: Anthropology in Washington, D.C., 1846–1903," Ph.D. dissertation, University of Wisconsin (1976); "Amateurs and Professionals in Washington Anthropology, 1877–1903," in Murra, ed., *op.cit.*; "Anthropology as Science and Politics: The Dilemmas of the Bureau of American Ethnology, 1879 to 1904," in Walter Goldschmidt, ed., *op. cit.*, 15–32; with Bill Holm, "A Cannibal in the National Museum: The Early Career of Franz Boas in America," *American Anthropologist*, 78 (1976), 306–316.

Chapter One
Towards an Organized Community of Anthropologists

Anthropology as a science, rather than as an outgrowth of philosophy or a compendium of travel literature, had its beginnings in the nineteenth century. In the United States it was shaped by a uniquely American situation. Here was a vast, rich country, relatively unexplored by the Europeans who had settled along the East coast and inhabited by Indian peoples whose origins, history, and ways of life had thus far only been guessed at. Anthropology grew out of the broad science of natural history, a generalized study of the plants, animals, mountains, rivers, minerals, archaeological remains, and native peoples of the New World.

Thomas Jefferson, Louis Agassiz, and Joseph Henry were among those most responsible for organizing scientific activity in the United States in the early and middle years of the nineteenth century, and they each helped to shape what became by the end of the century an organized science of anthropology.

Jefferson was interested in the misnamed "Indians" as well as in the Africans and Europeans who had come or been brought forcibly to the New World. He wondered where the American aborigines had come from and how their languages were related to other languages. He wondered about the relative capacity for civilization of Indians, slaves, and slave-holding Virginians. In seeking answers to these questions in natural history rather than in social philosophy, Jefferson took a momentous step forward. In *Notes on the State of Virginia*, first published in 1785, Jefferson wrote:

> To our reproach it must be said, that though for a century and a half we had had under our eyes the races of black and of red men, they have never yet been viewed by us as subjects of natural history.[1]

This he proposed to change.

Jefferson's personal contributions to the natural history of man are well known: his excavation of an Indian burial mound, collections of Indian vocabularies, and studies of Indian customs. Far more important in the long run, however, were his organizational activities for science, in particular, for the study of the American Indians. Jefferson encouraged private scientific societies to collect information on the Indian nations and on ancient mounds and fortifications; he began the use of questionnaires for gathering data in anthropology;[2] and with the Lewis and Clark expedition he established the precedent for government support of anthropological inquiry.

Under Jefferson's leadership the American Philosophical Society in Philadelphia became a major repository for materials for study of the American Indians. Other societies were soon organized specifically to do archaeological and ethnological work. The American Antiquarian Society was founded in Worcester, Massachusetts in 1812 by a printer, Isaiah Thomas, who wanted to encourage study of the earthworks and mounds in the Mississippi and the Ohio River valleys. In New York Albert Gallatin, who had been secretary of the treasury under Jefferson, founded an American Ethnological Society which was active in the 1840s and 1850s. All three societies published volumes of "proceedings" or "transactions," and all attempted, through foreign and corresponding members, to keep their home members informed of what was going on elsewhere in the world.

One of Jefferson's first acts as president of the American Philosophical Society in Philadelphia was to have widely distributed a "circular" which solicited information for the society on four topics: mammoths and other hitherto unknown animals; ancient fortifications, tumuli, and other Indian works of art; the natural history of the earth and the changes in mountains, lakes, rivers, and prairies; and "the Customs, Manners, Languages and Character of the Indian nations, ancient and modern and their migrations."[3] By 1804 when he sent Meriwether Lewis and William Clark to explore the Louisiana Purchase the questions had been refined and elaborated,[4] and subsequently questionnaires on the history, customs, and languages of the Indian tribes were used by Lewis Cass, Albert Gallatin, Henry Rowe Schoolcraft, and Lewis Henry Morgan.

Government expeditions also continued to gather information on Indian tribes and archaeological remains. George Brown Goode, writing in 1886, listed forty-two explorers between Lewis and Clark and the great surveyors of the 1870s who were responsible for "a vast amount of good scientific work,"[5] some of it anthropological. All of this activity, however, was occasional and pursued by amateurs. The results were haphazardly preserved and of varying quality, for no self-correcting community of anthropologists existed which could exercise some measure of judgment and control. The lavish publication by the federal government of Henry Rowe Schoolcraft's six large volumes, *Historical and Statistical Information Respecting the History, Condition, and Prospects of the Indian Tribes* (1851–1857) became a near scandal when reviewers pointed out that the volumes were so poorly organized as to be useless and even contained many blank pages, charts with no data.[6]

A change began in the 1840s, which have been described as "the formative years" and the "take-off" period for the organization of American science.[7] Two events in particular were important: the founding of the Smithsonian Institution in 1846 under the leadership of Joseph Henry and the establishment of the American Association for the Advancement of Science in 1848. From their first tentative beginnings both of these institutions grew to be powerful instruments for the organization of American science, and they both had an impact on anthropology.

Joseph Henry was a physicist, but he wanted the new institution which he headed to raise standards generally in American science. Almost from the beginning of his tenure at the Smithsonian Institution, he was interested in promoting ethnology, archaeology, and linguistics. He saw in these fields a broad opportunity, not just to "diffuse" but to "increase" knowledge, which he took to be the intent of James Smithson's bequest. Henry encouraged research on a wide range of anthropological topics and published reports when they met his high standards. He also gradually accepted the heterogeneous collections which accumulated in Washington and became the nucleus of the United States National Museum. It was Henry who took the first steps toward making the Smithsonian Institution a coordinating center for anthropological research, a tradition later continued by John Wesley Powell.[8]

The American Association for the Advancement of Science was an outgrowth of the earlier Association of American Geologists and Naturalists. Although by no means the creation of one man, it became one of the agencies through which Louis Agassiz made his presence felt in American science. The eminent Swiss naturalist helped to organize the new, more comprehensive association soon after his arrival in the United States in

1846 and dominated its annual meetings. At the Cambridge meeting in August of 1849 Agassiz presented twenty-seven papers on topics including marine biology, botany, insect life, comparative embryology, and geology; and the following year he was elected president of the Association.[9]

The AAAS gradually became the leading gathering place for scientific men in the United States. Lewis Henry Morgan attended the tenth meeting of the AAAS in 1856, and it was a decisive event in his life, for he found himself in the company of Louis Agassiz, Asa Gray, Jeffries Wyman, James Dwight Dana, and Spencer Baird and was inspired by their example to take up again his Indian studies.[10] Three years later at the annual AAAS meeting he appealed to Joseph Henry for the aid of the Smithsonian Institution in sending out his kinship questionnaires, and within a few months Henry had made the necessary arrangements.[11] The AAAS called off its meetings during the Civil War but resumed them immediately afterward and for the remainder of the century they were where people interested in anthropology, as well as the other sciences, met. Section H (Anthropology) was formally established in 1882, and within fifteen years its meetings drew the largest attendance of any section.[12]

Agassiz, along with Alexander Dallas Bache of the United States Coast Guard, also organized a more elite group, the National Academy of Sciences, founded in 1863 to offer advice to the federal government on scientific questions. The National Academy of Sciences was modeled on the Royal Society of London and the French Academy of Sciences. Its founding was in part a patriotic gesture, an offer of help to the government in the midst of the Civil War, but Agassiz intended it also as a signal to Europe that American science had come of age. Agassiz had immersed himself in the science of his adopted country, and he wanted two things for it. He wanted it to be as professional as European science but more democratic. He wanted it to be open to all and its results freely available to the public.[13] The AAAS, the National Academy of Sciences, and the museum-building tradition which Agassiz began in founding the Museum of Comparative Zoology all reflected these goals.

The Agassiz tradition was carried into anthropology by F.W. Putnam who made Cambridge, Massachusetts one of the organizational centers of the new science. In Cambridge was located not only the Peabody Museum of American Archaeology and Ethnology, which sponsored expeditions and published annual reports, but also after 1879 the Archaeological Institute of America, which, at Putnam's urging, undertook to do work in American archaeology. Putnam was for many years Permanent Secretary of the AAAS and in that capacity planned the annual meetings at which anthropologists gathered and edited the *Proceedings*, in which they published papers. From his post at the Peabody Museum, Putnam organized the anthropology section of the World's Columbian Exposition at Chicago in 1893 and subsequently directed the anthropological departments of the American Museum of Natural History in New York City and the University of California. Cambridge under Putnam became the center for one of the kinds of anthropology which Jefferson had encouraged, that which could be done by private scientific societies and organizations.

The second center of anthropology in the United States in the late nineteenth century was Washington, D.C. There it grew out of the tradition established by Joseph Henry and more immediately out of the federal geographical and geological surveys of the 1870s. Post–Civil War Congresses were willing to spend money for western exploration, and they financed four large and sometimes overlapping surveys: the United States Geological Survey of the Fortieth Parallel begun under the War Department in 1867 and led by Clarence King; the United States Geological and Geographical Survey of the Territories also begun in 1867 but under the Interior Department and led by Dr. Ferdinand Vandeveer Hayden; the Geographical Surveys West of the 100th Meridian begun in 1869 by the War Department and led by Lieutenant George M. Wheeler; and the Geographical and Geological Survey of the Rocky Mountain Region begun in 1870 with John Wesley Powell in charge and put by a clerical error under the jurisdiction of the Smithsonian Institution instead of the Department of the Interior.[14] Three of these, the Hayden, Wheeler, and Powell surveys, had included anthropological work. When the surveys were consolidated in 1879, John Wesley Powell made the involvement of the federal government in anthropology official by providing for a Bureau of Ethnology. Henceforth the Bureau of Ethnology, along with the newly established National Museum, was the center of Washington anthropology. There was also an Anthropological Society of Washington, founded in 1879 with John Wesley Powell its first president, and a Women's Anthropological Society, active from 1885 until 1899 when it merged with the men's group.[15] The Bureau of

Ethnology published monumental annual reports, and beginning in 1888 the Anthropological Society of Washington sponsored a journal, the *American Anthropologist*.

Anthropologists after 1879 had what they had not had before in the United States: numerous institutions, publications, meetings, and in general enough activity so they could begin to judge one another's work. Philadelphia, the home of the American Philosophical Society, was still a reference point, for Daniel G. Brinton lived there; and around 1891 a museum and university department of archaeology and palaeontology was established by William Pepper, provost of the University of Pennsylvania.[16] Most anthropological work, however, was directed from Washington or Cambridge.

The two centers were nearly equal in resources and prestige. They were competitive, but generally in a friendly way, and individuals moved back and forth between them. Alice Fletcher was officially and loyally associated with the work of F.W. Putnam in Cambridge, but she lived in Washington and in 1903 served as president of the Anthropological Society of Washington. Frank Hamilton Cushing was employed by the federal government during most of his life, but he had patrons in Boston and Cambridge and was a warm friend of F.W. Putnam's. In material resources each of the two centers held its own. John Wesley Powell received from the government annual appropriations of up to fifty thousand dollars a year for the Bureau of Ethnology, while in Cambridge Putnam worked with a much smaller steady income but was able to appeal to private philanthropy for funds for special projects.[17] No single person or place was able to dominate anthropology in the United States in the late nineteenth century, and the result was an intensely creative period for the new science.

One observer who recognized the uniqueness of the American situation was the French anthropologist Paul Topinard, who traveled in the United States in 1893. Topinard commented on the two centers, Washington, D.C. and Cambridge, which "grouped around themselves a multitude of workers and competed in sending out every year exploring parties to all regions of the country to dig, to collect Indian artifacts, and to record customs, beliefs, dances, and languages."[18] Although to a Frenchman the situation seemed to be, at best, inconvenient, Topinard concluded that in fact this friendly rivalry contributed to the great prosperity of anthropology in the

United States. He called Putnam and Powell high personifications of the remarkable "American genius" for building organizations.

The two centers of anthropology had in common a self-conscious return to the natural history tradition which had been pushed aside briefly during the years of Samuel G. Morton's more physical and mathematical approach to the study of mankind.[19] F.W. Putnam had been trained in natural history. John Wesley Powell and others founded the Anthropological Society of Washington "to encourage the study of the natural history of man, especially with reference to America."[20] On this basis a science of anthropology was established in the United States.

Notes and References

1. Thomas Jefferson, *Notes on the State of Virginia*, Edited and with Introduction and Notes by William Peden (Chapel Hill, University of North Carolina, 1955), 143.

2. A. Irving Hallowell, "The Beginnings of Anthropology in America," in Frederica de Laguna, ed., *Selected Papers from American Anthropologist, 1888–1920* (Evanston, Illinois, Row, Peterson and Co., 1960), 26. George W. Stocking, Jr. describes two more complex memoirs written by the French scientists Cuvier and Degérando in 1800 in "French Anthropology in 1800," *Race, Culture, and Evolution* (New York, The Free Press, 1968), 13–41. In 1839 the British Association for the Advancement of Science appointed a committee to prepare a questionnaire for use by travelers, missionaries, and others who might be able to contribute to ethnology, and beginning in 1874 the BAAS published *Notes and Queries on Anthropology*, a guide to investigation.

3. The circular was printed in Vol. IV of the *Transactions* of the American Philosophical Society. See also Gilbert Chinard, "Jefferson and the American Philosophical Society," *Proceedings of the American Philosophical Society*, 87 (1943), 263–276.

4. See Verne F. Ray and Nancy O. Lurie, "The Contributions of Lewis and Clark to Ethnography," *Journal of the Washington Academy of Sciences*, 44 (1954), 358–370.

5. George Brown Goode, "The Origin of the National Scientific and Educational Institutions of the United States," *Annual Report of the Smithsonian Institution*, 1897, Part II (Washington, D.C., 1901), 263–354, 292. Another good summary of early work is Samuel F. Haven, *Archaeology of the United States, or, Sketches, historical and bibliographical, of the progress of information and opinions respecting vestiges of antiquity in the United States*, Smithsonian Contributions to Knowledge, VIII (Washington, D.C., 1856).

6. One review still well worth reading for its indignant and pungent comments is F. Bowen's in *North American Review*, 77 (1853), 243–62.

7. Sally Gregory Kohlstedt, *The Formation of the American Scientific Community: The American Association for the Advancement of Science, 1848–1860* (Urbana, University of Illinois, 1976), x.

8. Wilcomb E. Washburn, "The Museum and Joseph Henry," *Curator*, 8 (1965), 35–54; Curtis M. Hinsley, Jr., "The Development of a Profession: Anthropology in Washington, D.C., 1846–1903," 23, 39–70. See also Howard S. Miller, *Dollars for Research: Science and Its Patrons in Nineteenth Century America* (Seattle, University of Washington Press, 1970) and A. Hunter Dupree, *Science and the Federal Government* (Cambridge, The Belknap Press of Harvard University, 1957.)

9. Edward Lurie, *Louis Agassiz: A Life in Science* (Chicago, University of Chicago Press, 1960), 132, 162, 179. For Agassiz's and Henry's activities in the early years of the AAAS, see Kohlstedt, *op. cit.*

10. Carl Resek, *Lewis Henry Morgan: American Scholar* (Chicago, University of Chicago Press, 1960), 69.

11. *Ibid.*, 79.

12. W J McGee, "Anthropology at Detroit and Toronto," *American Anthropologist*, X (1897), 317.

13. Lurie, *op. cit.*, 179.

14. Wallace Stegner, *Beyond the Hundredth Meridian: John Wesley Powell and the Second Opening of the West* (Boston, Houghton Mifflin, 1953, Sentry ed.), 123–126. On the surveys see William H. Goetzmann, *Exploration and Empire* (New York, Knopf, 1966) and Richard A. Bartlett, *Great Surveys of the American West* (Norman, University of Oklahoma Press, 1962). In his excellent "Brixham Cave and the Antiquity of Man" Jacob W. Gruber stresses the importance of geology in shaping the methodology, point of view, and status of anthropology (in M.E. Spiro, ed., *Context and Meaning in Cultural Anthropology*, Glencoe, Illinois, The Free Press, 1965, 373–402).

15. Daniel S. Lamb, "The story of the Anthropological Society of Washington," *American Anthropologist*, 8 (1906), 564–579. Nancy O. Lurie has a good account of the Women's Anthropological Society in "Women in Early American Anthropology," in June Helm, ed., *Pioneers of American Anthropology* (Seattle, University of Washington Press, 1966), 29–81. See also Mrs. J.C. Croly, *The History of the Woman's Club Movement in America* (New York, 1898), 341–343 and J. Kirkpatrick Flack, *Desideratum in Washington: The Intellectual Community in the Capital City 1870–1900* (Cambridge, Schenkman Publishing Co., 1975).

16. A. Irving Hallowell, "Anthropology in Philadelphia," in Jacob W. Gruber, ed., *The Philadelphia Anthropological Society* (Temple University Publications, 1967), 1–31, 19. Daniel G. Brinton (1837–1899) was a medical doctor and editor who wrote twenty-three books and many pamphlets, articles, and papers on various topics in anthropology, especially myth and religion. *Brinton Memorial Meeting* held Jan. 16, 1900 (Philadelphia, American Philosophical Society, 1900) includes papers and letters commemorating him and commenting on his work by W J McGee, F.W. Putnam, Alice Fletcher, and F.H. Cushing.

17. See the *Annual Reports* of the Smithsonian Institution and of the Peabody Museum of American Archaeology and Ethnology.

18. Paul Topinard, "L'Anthropologie aux Etats-Unis," *L'Anthropologie*, (1893), 301–351, 304, 334.

19. Samuel George Morton, a Philadelphia physician and professor of anatomy, collected and measured human crania and published the results of his work in *Crania Americana* (1839) and *Crania Aegyptiaca* (1844). His disciples Josiah C. Nott and George R. Gliddon popularized in *Types of*

Mankind (1854) an "American school" of anthropology which claimed that human races were the result of separate creations and innately unequal. Their polemical "school" soon collapsed under the dual impact of Darwinism and the Civil War. A recent and excellent critique of Morton's work is S. Gould, "Morton's Ranking of Races by Cranial Capacity," *Science*, 200 (May 5, 1978), 505–509. For this whole episode in American anthropology, see William R. Stanton, *The Leopard's Spots: Scientific Attitudes Toward Race in America, 1815–1859* (Chicago, University of Chicago Press, 1960).

20. Lamb, *op. cit.*, 566.

Chapter Two
Frederic Ward Putnam
(1839–1915)

Chronologically, in American anthropology Frederic Ward Putnam follows Lewis Henry Morgan, the great nineteenth century amateur, and precedes Franz Boas, the German university trained scientist who dominated early twentieth century anthropology in the United States. Little attention has been paid historically to Putnam, and even in his own time, he worked during the early years of his career in the shadow of Lewis Henry Morgan and found himself eclipsed by Franz Boas, who had been his protege, at the end. Yet Putnam did more than either Morgan or Boas to create the profession of anthropology in the United States. He gave the new science of anthropology its name. He established many of its major institutions, including three museums and two university departments of anthropology.

Putnam was an organizer, an energetic and genial man who did not dominate others, for he preferred to work alongside them. He gave advice and friendly counsel to nearly everyone who entered the field. Putnam was also a scientist, trained in the natural history of Louis Agassiz, and he brought into anthropology some of the approaches and the careful, painstaking methods he had learned in biology. He left anthropology a major legacy in the standards he set, the genial way in which he worked, and the organizations he created.

Putnam was born in Salem, Massachusetts on April 16, 1839 to a family which had been in America since the arrival of John Putnam from England in 1640. There were Appletons, Fiskes, Wards, Higginsons, and other names important in New England history in his ancestral line. His parents were Eben and Elizabeth Appleton Putnam. Putnam was educated in "the old style of private schools,"[1] but he left them at an early age and spent his time exploring the natural history of Essex County and helping his father cultivate plants in the conservatory. The family was fairly prosperous, but Putnam was by no means independently wealthy. The need to have an additional paying job alongside his position at the Peabody Museum in Cambridge runs through his life history. An older brother of his went to sea at the age of fourteen and after many foreign voyages eventually became a river-boat captain.

Putnam wrote his first scientific papers, a list of the fishes and a catalogue of the birds in Essex County and a study of the fish in Salem harbor, when he was sixteen years old. On the strength of these he was named Curator of Ornithology in the Essex Institute of Salem.[2] In 1855 he met Louis Agassiz, who was visiting Salem, and the famous zoologist promptly invited the young man to become his student in Cambridge, Massachusetts.[3] Putnam put aside his plan to enroll at West Point and in the spring of 1856 moved to Cambridge.

Louis Agassiz had established himself as a major force in American science in the ten years since he had come from Switzerland. In 1856 he was in the midst of founding his Museum of Comparative Zoology. From his post as professor of zoology and geology in the Lawrence Scientific School, a part of Harvard University, he had persuaded Massachusetts lawmakers, university officials, and private benefactors that there should be in Cambridge a great museum of natural history to equal the British Museum and the Jardin des Plantes in Paris. Putnam moved with the other students into the basement of the building as it was completed and began a course of study unique in the United States, for Agassiz was building the first research-oriented museum in the country. Putnam learned a scientific method from Agassiz, and he also learned principles of museum direction which were to serve him well for the rest of his life.

Putnam's first assignment in the museum was to prepare the skeleton of an old turtle. He spent more than six weeks at the task, and several years later he claimed he could still see every scale and bone that turtle had.[4] It was a lesson in careful observation and in the ways of this museum where they would learn by handling specimens—where they would learn, in sum, from nature and not from books. It was a lesson, too, in the value of every specimen, no matter how common or small. Alfred Kroeber later described Putnam as a true natural historian, a man who knew how to use books but who read few of them, for he much preferred to learn directly from the specimen or phenomenon.[5] This was the Agassiz legacy.

Agassiz also impressed his students with his view that the primary purpose of a museum was the furthering of scientific investigation. There should be explorations, collections of materials for study, and publication of the results of study.

Putnam was put in charge of fish and invertebrates in the Museum of Comparative Zoology.[6] His first foray into anthropology came almost by accident. He was attending a meeting of the American Association for the Advancement of Science in Montreal in 1857 when he happened on a shell heap which he stopped to investigate, unearthing bones and tools. Soon afterward a collection of tools and other objects was brought to Agassiz's museum from the recently discovered prehistoric Swiss lake dwellings,[7] but Putnam did not really begin his archaeological work until after he left the Museum of Comparative Zoology in 1864.

There were two reasons for the dissatisfaction which led to the exodus from the museum in 1864 of most of Agassiz's first group of students. One was Agassiz's autocracy and his refusal to let students publish, as their own, work which they had done in the museum. The second problem was Agassiz's continuing and vehement opposition to the theory of evolution by natural selection. Agassiz had been a student of Cuvier's in Paris, and he continued to accept Cuvier's doctrine of special creationism, which held that distinct and immutable species of plants and animals existed in their geographical areas by virtue of special acts of creation.[8] He arranged his museum on this idea of zoological provinces, an arrangement which was continued after his death by his son, Alexander Agassiz. At the end of the nineteenth century it was the only large natural history museum in the country arranged by geographical areas rather than by animal families.[9] Although Putnam became a convert to the biological theory of evolution, he did not accept any scheme of social evolution. He arranged his museums of anthropology according to the scheme he had learned from Agassiz, that is, by geographical areas. Although Putnam rebelled against Agassiz, he came to speak of him with increasing gratitude, as the man who had had more influence on his life than any other.

When Putnam left Agassiz's museum, he returned to the Essex Institute in Salem where he became superintendent in 1866, and he induced his former fellow students, A.S. Packard, Alpheus Hyatt, and Edward S. Morse to join him there as curators. Another fellow student, Albert S. Bickmore, left Agassiz and within six years had been instrumental in founding the American Museum of Natural History in New York City.[10] Soon

Frederic W. Putnam on a mound

Putnam's own genius for building institutions was apparent. He and his friends founded a popular journal of natural history, *American Naturalist*, established their own printing office, and set up an agency for the sale and exchange of books and specimens. In 1867 they persuaded George Peabody, a wealthy London philanthropist who had come originally from Essex County, to endow a Peabody Academy of Science in Salem.[11] There they brought together the natural history collections of the Essex Institute and the ethnological curiosities picked up around the world by the merchants and sea captains who belonged to the East India Marine Society.

Putnam was made director of this new institution in Salem, the Museum of the Peabody Academy of Science, and he began immediately to practice some of the principles of museum work he had learned from Agassiz. The staff made excursions to local shell heaps and sponsored a collecting expedition to Central America. They published a series of *Memoirs* and began to build up a library. Underlying this was Putnam's conviction that the purpose of a museum was not entertainment or education for the general public, although these were important, but the furthering of scientific investigation. This was done in two ways. The staff pursued certain problems and investigations, but they also tried simply to collect for future study ethnological materials which might otherwise be lost forever.[12]

Meanwhile a new kind of museum, one devoted solely to the study of man, was established in Cambridge.[13] Agassiz had refused George Peabody's offer of a large endowment for his museum because of the stipulation that the museum then bear the Peabody name,[14] so George Peabody continued to consider how he might endow a museum at Harvard. The right idea came to his nephew, the paleontologist Othniel C. Marsh, in 1856 while he was digging in an ancient mound in Ohio. Marsh suggested a museum for American archaeology to his uncle, and President Walker of Harvard, although he thought it "unusual," was persuaded to accept it. The Peabody Museum of American Archaeology and Ethnology was formally established in 1866, and Jeffries Wyman, a professor of comparative anatomy best known for his scientific description of the gorilla, became the first curator.[15]

Putnam later described this period as one in which great impulse was given "to archaeological and ethnological research in all directions."[16] Charles Lyell's uniformitarian geology, based on the principle that the earth has always been shaped by the same slow geological processes now at work, resulted in a greatly expanded time scale for life on earth. This was a necessary prerequisite for the theory of evolution which Charles Darwin published in 1859. It was also necessary for the acceptance in the same year by the Royal Society of evidence found by Boucher de Perthes in the valley of the Somme in France (human tools associated with the bones of extinct animals) that man had a much longer history than had been thought possible. The Smithsonian Institution, whose first volume of *Contributions* in 1848 had included the work done by Squier and Davis on ancient monuments in the Ohio Valley, published in 1861 an article by a Swiss geologist popularizing the discovery of kitchen-middens or shell heaps in Denmark, of remains of ancient lake dwellers in Switzerland, and the Danish system of classification of artifacts by Stone, Bronze, and Iron ages. That article, according to Joseph Henry, the secretary of the Smithsonian, aroused great interest in the remains of the ancient inhabitants of the North American continent.[17] Sir John Lubbock's *Prehistoric Times*, first published in 1865, went through many editions, popularizing the term *prehistoric* and Lubbock's own creations, the terms *Palaeolithic* and *Neolithic*. Apart from archaeology, there was what Putnam called "Morgan's great ethnographic study," *The League of the Iroquois* published in 1851 and E.B. Tylor's *Researches into the Early History of Mankind and the Development of Civilization* in 1865 followed by *Primitive Culture* in 1871. A great impetus was being given to what would later be called physical anthropology by the work done by Samuel G. Morton in Philadelphia, Anders Retzius in Sweden, and Paul Broca in France.

Putnam had studied comparative anatomy with Wyman during his days at Agassiz's museum. He and Wyman worked closely together in these last years before Wyman's death in 1874. Together they visited shell heaps in Maine and Massachusetts, and Wyman published accounts of his work there and in Florida in *American Naturalist* and in the *Memoirs* of the Peabody Academy of Science at Salem. Wyman made careful excavations, discovering distinct strata, indicating occupation at various periods of time, and the bones of animals no longer found in the area. He thought that the bones, shells, bone implements, and cord pottery found were not as old as those found in Denmark but did perhaps go back several centuries.[18] Wyman was searching for the bones of a "truly primitive man" who, according to the theory of evolution, would be passing out of the animal into the human state and would not yet have tools of any sort. The only knowledge that could be acquired "must come through the remains of his own body, older than his inventions."[19] Shellfish seemed to provide a more primitive source of food than hunting and agriculture, which require tools and long experience. But Wyman was disappointed in the results of the search. The skull found in California by J.D. Whitney, even if its authenticity were not in doubt, showed that man to be a maker of tools and with essentially the same anatomical features as contemporary man. The flint tools found in the gravels of the Somme in France and in localities in England showed that even then man was far from being primitive. Wyman wrote that a traveler could now meet in Borneo, Australia, the Straits of Magellan, or the Andaman Islands men as primitive as those of whom there was prehistoric evidence. In other words, prehistoric studies had so far been able to go only a very slight distance back into the human and protohuman past. This long view of human history was absorbed by Putnam, whose lifelong search for evidence of the antiquity of man in America was a continuation of the quest of his gentle friend.[20]

In 1873 Putnam accepted a position which he would hold for twenty-five years, that of Permanent Secretary of the American Association for the Advancement of Science. It was the one nonrotating office in the Association and surely was, as Kroeber later suggested, "more deeply influential upon the destiny of scientific endeavor in the New World than is generally recognized."[21] The AAAS increased greatly in size during the years Putnam ran its affairs. It was his responsibility to plan the large annual meetings and to gather and publish the annual reports. One change was immediately apparent. The small subsection of Natural History previously called "Ethnology" appeared in the Proceedings of the AAAS meeting in 1873 as "Anthropology."[22] The previous year Joseph Henry had written in his annual report for the Smithsonian Institution that the Smithsonian had from the first given much attention to anthropology, for that was a common ground between science and "letters."[23] Putnam, by his use of the term in the AAAS in 1873, tipped the scales in favor of science, and Joseph Henry acquiesced four years later, noting in the annual report of the Smithsonian for 1877 that "anthropology, or what may be considered the natural history of man is at present the most popular branch of science."[24] Putnam had named the new discipline and defined its nature.

In 1875 Putnam was appointed to succeed Jeffries Wyman and Asa Gray, who had had a temporary appointment, as curator of the Peabody Museum of American Archaeology and Ethnology. He began immediately to emphasize the importance of publications, to build up a library, and to seek new collections. Under Putnam the museum pioneered both in its methods of collecting and in its manner of arranging the materials. As Putnam wrote in 1889:

> the collections have been largely made by trained explorers in the field . . . each object is authenticated and the exact conditions under which it was obtained and its association with other objects fully recorded. In this way the larger part of the collections has been obtained from the systematic and thorough exploration of burial-places, caves, shell-heaps, village-sites, mounds and ruins in many parts of North, Central, and South America.[25]

The collections were accompanied by field notes, drawings, plans, and photographs which Putnam felt were an essential part of thorough exploration.

Putnam advocated a method of archaeological research he called trenching and slicing, trenching to find the bottom of the site and then vertical slicing, "cutting down about a foot at a time, always keeping a vertical wall in front, the whole width of the mound."[26] He acknowledged that this was an expensive and laborious method, but it was the only way the work should be done.

Putnam included ethnography also and wrote that the Peabody Museum had "taken its full share in the work of introducing scientific methods of arrangement into the heterogeneous collections of antiquities and of curios from uncivilized peoples."[27] Pitt-Rivers in England and O.T. Mason at the National Museum in Washington were arranging their culture materials in presumed evolutionary sequences, as of baskets or weapons, but Putnam insisted that the collections be kept together as wholes and put in geographical sequence. Any visitor could go from case to case and get an impression of a particular people. Nearby cases would show neighboring peoples, and similarities in cultural goods would indicate probable contact between the groups. The visitor could also go from room to room making comparisons between whole geographical regions.

Putnam was a member of the United States Geographical Survey West of the 100th Meridian, led by First Lieutenant George M. Wheeler from 1876 to 1878. He studied archaeological and ethnological materials in Arizona, New Mexico, and the vicinity of Santa Barbara, California.[28] In the summer of 1878 both Putnam and Major John Wesley Powell made extensive explorations among the earth mounds and burial places in Tennessee. For two weeks they worked together with a united force of nearly fifty workers.[29] Later there would be rivalry between Putnam's museums and Powell's Bureau of Ethnology, but at this early date they were more interested in the seemingly unlimited possibilities which lay ahead of them.

Another frequent visitor in Cambridge was Lewis Henry Morgan, now nearly at the end of his long career. Both Putnam and Morgan realized that they were at a transition point in American anthropology.

Lewis Henry Morgan was a lawyer and student of the classics who had written three major works in ethnology, each of which was a pioneering achievement: *The League of the Ho-de-no-sau-nee, or Iroquois*, published in 1851, *Systems of Consanguinity and Affinity of the Human Family*, published in 1870, and *Ancient Society*, published in 1877. Morgan had first sought out the Iroquois Indians who lived near him in New York state when he was searching for rituals for the literary club he had founded. His initial romantic interest in the Iroquois was transformed as a result of a chance friendship formed with Hasaneanda (Ely Parker), a young Seneca Iroquois and the son of a chief, who had been chosen by his people to study law in order to defend them against imminent and illegal forced removal beyond the Mississippi.[30] Morgan made a trip to Washington in 1846 to plead the Seneca cause, and Ely Parker helped him learn about Iroquois life and political organization. Morgan collected knives, tomahawks, pipes, and other material objects for an Indian museum sponsored by the regents of the University of New York,[31] and in 1851 he published *The League of the Ho-de-no-sau-nee, or Iroquois*, a study of their religion, government, and customs. It was, in John Wesley Powell's words, "the first scientific account of an Indian tribe given to the world."[32]

Morgan's next two projects grew out of a trip he made in the summer of 1858 to the iron-rich Upper Peninsula of Michigan to check on the progress of a railroad in which he had invested. He found himself on the edge of the largest beaver district in North America, and his initial mild curiosity turned into a ten-year study of that animal. In 1868 Morgan published *The American Beaver and His Works*, a compendium of everything he had been able to learn about beavers.[33] Putnam later wrote that "Jeffries Wyman remarked that it came the nearest to perfection of any work of its kind he had ever read."[34] There were only a few works, including Réaumur's study of insects in the eighteenth century and François Huber's books on bees, with which it could be compared; for a monograph on a single animal was as unusual a work in biology as *The League of the Iroquois* had been in ethnology.

Morgan began *The American Beaver* with quotations from Cuvier and Louis Agassiz, and the book is remarkable in that it was shaped throughout by the same pre-Darwinian biology in which Putnam had been trained. In 1816 Georges Cuvier had set out in his *Règne Animal* a classification system which divided the animal kingdom into four great branches. Morgan suggested that what was needed next was a monograph on each of the principal animals, and so he had done his small part by writing one on the beaver.[35] Eventually enough would be known to make possible comparative studies, as of animal psychology, in which Morgan was keenly interested.

Morgan also was surprised to discover on his trip to Michigan in 1858 that the Ojibway kinship system was the same as that of the Iroquois. He got out the Indian materials, which he had put aside when he married in 1851 and had begun to establish a law practice in Rochester, New York, and began a ten-year study of kinship systems. He speculated that perhaps all of the American aborigines had a similar kinship system, one which had originated sometime before they had migrated across the Bering Strait from Asia into the Americas. Based on this speculation, he began a comparative study and classification on kinship systems which he gathered from around the world. It is possible that he saw himself doing for kinship systems what Cuvier had done for the animal kingdom, for Morgan believed at this time that kinship systems were nearly as fixed and unchanging as Cuvier had thought species to be.[36] Morgan's massive and technical study, *Systems of Consanguinity and Affinity of the Human Family* was published by the Smithsonian in 1870.[37]

Morgan next began to consider the hypothesis that the different kinship systems reflected stages in the evolution of human society, from an original primal horde through various limiting forms of marriage to finally the monogamous pair.[38] Perhaps inventions, social institutions, forms of marriage and the family, and what Morgan called "the idea of property"—the desire to accumulate property—all developed together as a society evolved. This is the theory he spelled out in 1877 in *Ancient Society, or Researches in the Lines of Human Progress from Savagery through Barbarism to Civilization.* Morgan began to be sympathetic toward Darwin's theory of evolution at the same time, but nowhere in *Ancient Society* did he mention Darwin. Their theories were essentially unrelated for Morgan was concerned, not with the evolution of species, but with what he thought was the evolution of society within a single species. The mechanism he envisioned was not unexplained variation and then competition in nature but rather human intelligence and learning accumulated through language.[39]

Morgan drew one conclusion from his theory of particular importance for American anthropology. From kinship systems and other evidence, he decided that none of the American aborigines, including the Aztecs, had advanced beyond Middle or Upper Barbarism to the "ethnical period" of civilization. All American Indian societies, according to Morgan, lived communally, held their property in common, and had democratic forms of government. In 1876 he published in the *North American Review* a strongly worded attack on the American historian H.H. Bancroft whose account of the Aztec monarchy Morgan considered "delusive and fictitious."[40]

"How you have gone for Bancroft, you have taken his scalp off down to his neck," Putnam wrote his friend, but Putnam also questioned whether there was adequate evidence for some of Morgan's claims.[41]

Lewis Henry Morgan and F.W. Putnam had met at the annual meetings of the American Association for the Advancement of Science, which Morgan had been attending since 1856. Morgan helped establish and then presided over a special subsection for anthropology in 1875, and from then until his death in 1881 he and Putnam were in frequent communication.

They wrote often about AAAS matters. There were forty papers for the meeting of the anthropology subsection in 1876, a meeting about which Putnam had earlier admitted:

I don't know about presenting one myself. With all you Indian men about I should feel afraid to bring my little contributions forward.[42]

The section continued to grow, as did Morgan's prestige, and in 1879 Morgan was elected president of the AAAS. "You will have the honor,"

Putnam wrote him, "of being the President of the largest and most important meeting of scientists ever held in the U.S."[43]

At first Morgan conceived of the Peabody Museum largely as a place that
might make "a fine collection" of objects, such as he had gathered for an
Indian museum in New York.[44] As he grew to know Putnam better, however, Morgan began to reveal to the younger man his hopes for the science of
American ethnology, as Morgan still called it. He wrote in 1876:

> There was never a time in our country as I believe when the interest
> was stronger in the Indian subject than now; but as heretofore the work
> is nearly all done by amateurs. Inflation and imaginary magnificence
> is the bane that infects all these efforts. But a better time is coming. At
> this moment we have no science of American Ethnology. The reason is
> the American material is enormous and it requires, as the materials of
> any other science, twenty years of uninterrupted work in the field—
> and of thought and reflection to master it.[45]

But Morgan was confident that if a few young men went into the field, not as
amateurs, but determined to know all about it, the results in a few years
would be "splendid."

One young man whom Morgan clearly had in mind was his disciple, a
Swiss-American businessman in Illinois, Adolph Bandelier, who had made
himself an expert on the Spanish chronicles of the New World. At Morgan's
urging, Putnam arranged to publish Bandelier's studies, reinterpretations
of Aztec society in the light of Morgan's theories, in annual reports of the
Peabody Museum.[46]

Morgan was very grateful, for it was a tribute to himself as well as to Bandelier, and he began to look with increasing interest at the Peabody
Museum. George Peabody's endowments for anthropology at Harvard and
natural history at Yale were remarkable for their "wisdom and sagacity",
Morgan thought, for Peabody had made possible not just a professorship but
the "essential" thing, which was original investigation in the field. In a long
letter to Putnam in 1876 Morgan ruminated on the importance of field investigations and of institutions and in effect passed the mantle of American
anthropology on to Putnam at the Peabody Museum. He wrote:

The Harvard Professor . . . ought to spend six months of every year among the Indian tribes studying the structure of their society, their plan of life, their institutions, usages, and customs, their arts, and inventions, their languages and their religion. . . . America when discovered was more opulent than any other continent in anthropological materials . . . but this material is now perishing before our eyes. . . . What we need at this time is at least ten endowments equal to that of Harvard in as many of our principal institutions, and the ten professors at work in the field collecting, verifying, and systematizing this anthropological material. . . . In the mean time this Herculean work rests upon the Harvard foundation alone. . . . The work has hitherto fallen upon amateurs like myself, an unstable class, who work fitfully and spasmodically, and have neither the learning nor the proper sense of obligation resting upon them.[47]

Morgan then gave Putnam some practical advice: he should prepare a twenty-five year plan of research, he should publish memoirs for these help to raise interest in the subject, and above all, he should not be afraid to ask for money.

Two months later Morgan reemphasized his position:

Around institutions especially the highest and best work has been done. These have been grievously neglected in American Ethnology.[48]

Morgan's interest was encouraging to Putnam, but it was short-lived. Within two years his attention had been drawn to a new and, to some extent, rival organization.

In 1879 Charles Eliot Norton, professor of the history of art at Harvard and an ardent supporter of classical knowledge as the foundation of the education of a gentleman, called together a few of his friends in Boston to discuss the furthering of archaeological work in the United States. Out of this gathering was born the Archaeological Institute of America. From the beginning there was a tension built into the organization between the avowed purpose, as expressed by Norton, of contributing to classical knowledge, and the practical conviction that American scholars might make their best contribution by turning first to what was near at hand, namely, an exploration of the antiquities of the Americas. Norton himself was torn between these alternatives. He wanted to send expeditions to Greece, yet felt that America ought not be neglected. [49] At the organizational meeting F.W. Putnam and the American historian Francis Parkman argued in favor of American explorations, but their choice for the name of the new group, the Society for American Exploration, was passed over in favor of the Archaeological Institute of America, and the classicists controlled the council which was elected. Plans were made for an expedition to Assos in Asia Minor and for a school in Greece. The Germans had had an archaeological institute of one form or another in Athens since 1829. The Ecole française d'athènes was founded in 1848, and the English were trying to start a similar school. Norton and his colleagues felt that the United States should not be left behind, and in 1882 they formally established the American School of Classical Studies in Athens. [50]

But Norton did not let the matter of American work drop. For advice on how to pursue American archaeology, he turned to the foremost anthropologist in the country, Lewis Henry Morgan.

Early in 1880 Morgan wrote to Putnam:

I am having some correspondence with C.E. Norton of Cambridge, Ch. of the Executive Com. of the Archaeological Institute of which you are a member. Will you write me who Mr. Norton is and his status at Cambridge. Is he in the university [sic]. I can't quite make him out though I quite like him as a correspondent. [51]

Later in the month Morgan asked him again:

Why don't you write to me [and] tell me something about Mr. C.E. Eliot [sic] and the Archaeological Institute, for whom I am now attempting to write an extended article and a scheme for exploring New Mexico, Arizona and the San Juan region; and after that Yucatan and Central America. . . . I like Mr. Norton's views. He is a man quick to apprehend and well qualified to stand at the head of the Institute, I should think. [52]

Thus prodded, Putnam poured out his feelings in a long letter to Morgan. He described the original meeting which had led to the establishment of the Archaeological Institute of America and added:

> From that day (now over a year) I have not heard a word about the Institute from headquarters until you wrote me what you were doing. So you see, notwithstanding I was the only person present who had done anything in American exploration and was at the head of the only Museum in the country devoted entirely to that work I was left out in the cold.

Putnam urged Morgan to come to Cambridge to see what he was doing:

> For several years now I have been quietly at work carrying on a systematic series of explorations in order to show by the distribution of certain objects and characteristic works of art over N. and S. Amer. the several centres of development and distribution of nations from these centres. As a result of this work I have brought together at the Museum the *largest* and *most important* and in every way *authentic* collection relating to the antiquities of America that has been made. This may seem a pretty strong statement for me to make, but *I know* the collections in other Museums and those that I have are now to be seen by any one who will take the trouble to call at the Museum. Our two (yours and *mine*) methods of work *will tell* the story in time, but it will tell it all the sooner if you will come and see what I have been doing and take advantage of some of the facts *shown* in the Museum. Now why not come on and see if what I say is not true and stay with me.[53]

Putnam wanted the AIA to give his museum one or two thousand dollars annually, but Lewis Henry Morgan had another idea. Morgan sent Charles Eliot Norton his proposed plan for American explorations, and he arranged to have Adolph Bandelier sent by the AIA to New Mexico to study the house life of the Pueblos. Both Morgan and Norton took pains to sooth Putnam's feelings as much as possible, but Bandelier felt a little guilty about what they had done. As he set out in 1880 he wrote to Morgan:

At all events, I leave behind me at Cambridge one true friend whose name is *F.W. Putnam*, although the Archaeological Institute has not treated him right. But *our* relations to him lie beyond any organization, and I shall do my best to dispel the cloud which at present floats between the Peabody Museum and Prof. Norton.[54]

Even without Bandelier's mediations, Putnam bore no grudges. He continued his membership in the AIA for several more years, and he continued a warm friendship with Lewis Henry Morgan. Morgan, on his part, although his main concern at the end of his life was to find support for his disciples, continued to appreciate the value of what Putnam was doing at the Peabody Museum. Bernhard Stern in his biography of Morgan quoted from a diary of F.W. Putnam an entry dated March 6, 1895:

In relation to Mr. Morgan: He and I were the best of friends and for several years after 1874 he was in the habit of making me a yearly visit and staying at my house for a week or more at a time, and I also visited him several times in Rochester. At these visits we always discussed anthropological matters and his views and theories were often the special subject of our discussions. During one of these visits as I distinctly remember he stated that he was living a generation too early and got founded in his beliefs before he had the facts now in hand, but that it was too late to renew his work and do it all over with the knowledge of late discoveries and that I must take the matter up and show where he had made mistakes and also what of his would stand. He died December, 1881.[55]

For a brief time around 1878 Putnam proposed to arrange one of the many rooms in the Peabody Museum in accord with Morgan's scheme "to illustrate the development of Man toward civilization, as shown by his inventions, arts, and manufactures from remote times";[56] but he apparently gave up the plan, for it was not mentioned in subsequent annual reports of the museum. Putnam was too aware of the rise and fall of what he liked to call "nations" and of their diversity to carry through for long on any unilinear scheme.

Putnam wrote an obituary sketch of Morgan in 1882 in which he declared that, although some of Morgan's theories would be criticized as new facts were gathered,

> the great principles which his researches have brought out are so apparently beyond controversy that they will ever stand as . . . . foundations upon which to build in the further study of American archaeology and ethnology.[57]

A last word was added many years later by William Henry Holmes who called Morgan a heroic figure, not because he gave the last word on any subject but because he said the first word on so many.[58]

One last event in the middle period of Putnam's career was significant for the future of American anthropology, and that was his efforts resulting in the passage of the first legislative act in the country for the preservation of archaeological monuments. Squier and Davis in 1848 had described the Serpent Mound in Adams County, Ohio, a massive earth mound more than twelve hundred feet long, made of banks of earth arranged in a serpentine figure. Putnam visited the site in 1885 and found that the area was being cultivated and that the Serpent Mound might soon be gone. He made arrangements to purchase the site and, with the help of Alice Fletcher, an assistant in ethnology at the Peabody Museum, raised the necessary money. Putnam spent three seasons at the site, exploring the area, protecting the serpent, and laying out the grounds for a public park. Subsequently it was given by the Peabody Museum to the state of Ohio, which passed the necessary protective legislation. Putnam was enormously proud of this act of preservation, an act he considered the most important thing he had done in anthropology to date.[59]

Frederic Ward Putnam's long career as a university professor began in 1887 when, after a two-year delay by the Harvard Board of Overseers, Putnam was appointed Peabody Professor of American Archaeology and Ethnology. The delay meant that the honor of having the first academic appointment in anthropology in America went to Daniel G. Brinton, who in 1886 was appointed professor of American archaeology and linguistics at the University of Pennsylvania. They were soon joined in the academic world by Franz Boas who began lecturing at Clark University in 1889.

Putnam first met Franz Boas in 1886 when the young German scholar sought him out at the annual meeting of the AAAS. Putnam saw to it that Boas was made a foreign associate and shortly thereafter helped him get a job as assistant editor of *Science* magazine,[60] the first of several positions which Putnam would find for Boas. Putnam was at the time forty-seven years old; Franz Boas was twenty-eight. Born in 1858, Boas had spent the first nineteen years of his life in Minden, Westphalia, where his father was a prosperous businessman and his mother a liberal activist in civic affairs. Boas studied physics and geography at the universities of Heidelberg, Bonn, and Kiel, receiving a doctorate from Kiel in 1881. There followed a year of military training in the German army, during which time he wrote several articles in the psychophysics tradition of Gustav Fechner. George Stocking has suggested that Boas felt alienated from the Bismarckian Germany in which he lived and that, after 1882, he repeatedly considered emigration.[61] In 1883 he made a trip to Baffinland to study geography and the Eskimos, a trip financed by articles he wrote for a Berlin newspaper. He spent some time in New York with his maternal uncle, Dr. Abraham Jacobi, who had come to the United States in 1851 and established himself as a professor of children's diseases, and then returned to spend a year trying to qualify as privatdocent at the University of Berlin while working for Adolf Bastian preparing exhibits at the new Royal Ethnographic Museum. But he was restive. As soon as he had qualified as docent, he left on a field trip to British Columbia. On the way he met Putnam, and when he returned he went to work for *Science*. He was casting his lot with the New World.

One event stands out in Boas's term on the staff of *Science*. That is the controversy he aroused in its pages over methods of museum arrangement. Boas began it with "a letter to the editor" in which he objected to the way in which O.T Mason at the National Museum was arranging objects in supposed evolutionary sequences. Boas insisted that the meaning of objects could not be understood if they were removed from their surroundings, and he recommended geographical arrangements based on the "geographical province" idea of Adolf Bastian.[62] This was, of course, although Boas did not yet know it, the method which Putnam was already using.

Mason replied in a later issue of *Science* that any system of arrangement was somewhat arbitrary and that it was good for different museums to use

Franz Boas c. 1906

Professor F.W. Putnam with George Byron Gordon

different systems.[63] Boas responded that although Mason's plan might suggest scientific problems, Boas's plan was the only way to solve them. He thought that Mason overemphasized technology and material objects. Boas was concerned with the meaning of the objects to the people using them. He wanted ethnological collections to show "that civilization is not something absolute, but that it is relative, and that our ideas and conceptions are true only so far as our civilization goes."[64] Boas also wanted to show to what extent every civilization was the result of its geographical and historical surroundings. After these variables were allowed for, attention could be given to a "common psychical cause."

Here in a remarkably complete form is the spelling out of the method, and implicitly of the theory, that was to guide Boas through almost sixty years of work in anthropology. Boas began where Putnam did; that is, he rejected evolutionary sequences, preferring to trace the actual historical paths of migration and contact. But he went beyond Putnam in his emphasis on the meaning of this to the people involved and in his hopeful search for universal psychic causes or laws. What entered American anthropology with Franz Boas was a tendency to see anthropology at bottom as psychology. He also brought in a dogmatism about method. Arguments from analogy such as Mason used, Boas wrote, "are the foundation of most errors of the human mind."

Finally, John Wesley Powell, the foremost spokesman for government work in anthropology, stepped into the controversy to defend Mason. Groupings of tribes were arbitrary. There had been thousands of tribes in America when the Europeans began to arrive, and since then there had been a great deal of absorption, interchange, and movement. Powell thought that classification by geographical provinces as advocated by Bastian was interesting and commented that the Bureau of Ethnology was giving much attention to grouping arts in this way, but it did not yield valid groupings of peoples for quite different tribes sometimes inhabited the same area. There was no proper way to divide the peoples of the world into groups: neither geography, nor race, nor language, nor arts and institutions. Powell concluded, "The unity of mankind is the greatest induction of anthropology."[65]

Boas insisted on having the last word. He wrote that there was little difference between Powell and himself, but he still thought that for ethnological, not archaeological materials, geographical arrangement was possible. It had been done by many museums.[66]

In 1889 Boas left *Science* to join the faculty at Clark University. When he and others left three years later as a result of disagreements with G. Stanley Hall and Jonas Clark, respectively the president and the founder of that university, Putnam was again able to get him a job. Putnam had been appointed chief of the Department of Archaeology and Ethnology of the World's Columbian Exposition to be held in Chicago in 1893 in commemoration of the four hundredth anniversary of Columbus's voyage. Putnam invited Boas to become his chief assistant in Chicago with special responsibility for the work in physical anthropology. Boas accepted the position, and the two men worked closely together through fourteen months of feverish activity. Putnam's plan for the building which he labeled the "Hall of Anthropology" was an enlargement of the plan for the Peabody Museum. There were ethnological exhibits arranged geographically with emphasis on early life in America down to the time of Columbus, and sections on archaeology and physical anthropology. Putnam repeatedly emphasized that he did not want to waste his time setting up a temporary exhibit, and it was he who first suggested that the exhibits become the basis for a permanent museum in Chicago. This was done when Marshall Field provided a million-dollar endowment. Putnam was an incorporator of the museum, but in the power plays for control he was not made a trustee.[67]

Putnam returned to Cambridge at the end of 1893, leaving Boas in Chicago to finish the dismantling of the exposition and its transformation into the Field Columbian Museum. They both expected that Boas would be named curator of anthropology in the new museum. Boas wrote to Putnam on January 4, 1894:

> I hope, my dear Professor, that as long as I am here, you will kindly help me with your advice and your experience. . . . Let me tell you once more that it has been a great pleasure to me from beginning to end to work under your direction and to do my best to help carry out your broad plans.
>
> With kindest regards to Mrs. Putnam, your daughter and the "department Family"
>
> > Your orphan boy,
> > Franz Boas[68]

Boas was not an orphan in the usual sense, for he had parents in Germany. His self designation may have been wryly intended, but it is nevertheless an indication of the dependent relationship he had with Putnam.

Immediately there was disappointment, for events in Chicago did not go as planned. There were months of intrigue and rumors that a new anthropologist might be brought in. In April, Putnam had personal good news to relate, but he broke it to Boas gently:

I am wondering how things are going with you and what is the latest development in connection with the Columbian Museum. Of course I wish to do everything I can for you and shall keep my eyes open for another place for you if you are to leave Chicago. I have been so driven of late with all my duties that I have not had the opportunity to write to you of what is going on. An interesting matter has developed in New York which may be the means of my doing something for you by and by. The Trustees of the American Museum have placed the Anthropological Department of that Museum under my charge, and for the present I am to go there one week in four with the understanding that I shall have such assistants as may be required. As soon as their new wing is completed, which will be some time this year, there will be a good deal of arranging to be done, and if you are not in Chicago I shall hope to have you with me in New York for some special work which may lead to something more.

I shall see Mrs. Stevenson here in Cambridge in two weeks from now and will find out how things are drifting in Philadelphia. Dr. Pepper's resignation as President of the university leaves things rather doubtful there.

Of course my great wish is to have you here in Cambridge, but I see no chance of bringing that about at least for some time. We are all so poor that it is difficult to get a living salary for anyone. However, keep me posted, and believe me,

> Ever your sincere friend,
> F. W. Putnam[69]

Within a week Boas had to report to Putnam that William Henry Holmes from Washington, D.C. had been hired to head the Department of Anthropology at the Chicago museum. Boas was upset, and he wrote Putnam:

I immediately packed up and have left the Museum for good. . . . I am now, of course, adrift and shall appreciate whatever you may be able to do for me. You know that I have nothing to fall back upon.[70]

Boas, married and with a family, was without steady employment for the next year and a half. He spent the fall months of 1894 in British Columbia. Then he did anthropometric work in California, supported by a grant from the AAAS which Putnam helped him get. Early in 1895 Boas worked for O.T. Mason at the National Museum for two months, setting up exhibits of ethnographic groups.[71]

Meanwhile Putnam had not put Boas's plight nor his abilities out of mind. He was trying to arrange a position for Boas at the American Museum of Natural History as well as a series of lectures or some more definite position at Columbia College. There Livingston Farrand and William Ripley, professors of philosophy and political science, were beginning work in anthropology. In October Putnam gave up a trip to Mexico in order to plead Boas's case before President Seth Low of Columbia.[72] In November he was able to hire Boas at the museum for two months to set up a display of the North Pacific Coast tribes. Finally, on December 9, 1895 Boas accepted the position offered "yesterday and the day before" of special assistant in the American Museum of Natural History. He was to have charge of the ethnological and somatological collections and to work under the personal supervision of Putnam alone. If he took a paid position as instructor in a college in New York the following fall, his museum salary would be reduced accordingly.[73]

The long months of unemployment were over, but Boas soon found his position not at all to his liking. Within a week he was suggesting that his title and position should be that of assistant curator. He complained that he was not personally in contact with Morris K. Jesup, the president of the museum, and that he was not consulted about plans for the department. Boas felt that he should be able to make suggestions and initiate plans, after consultation with Putnam, and not merely be expected to carry out orders. On December 18, 1895 he wrote to Putnam:

I believe you can make it clear to Mr. Jesup that my position in science is such that I can demand that much as a simple matter of courtesy.[74]

Boas's title was changed, and he did begin to meet with Jesup directly, but he continued to feel slighted on occasion and undervalued.

Through 1896 Boas's disgruntlement surfaced occasionally despite Putnam's attempts to keep things running smoothly. In October Boas protested bitterly that he had not been told of the forthcoming opening of the department's exhibit halls but had learned of it only by chance.[75]

In a reply sent immediately and marked "Personal," Putnam asked his assistant to try please to be more patient. He wrote:

My dear Boas

I have been so driven ever since the first of this month owing to the opening of my courses here with 8 students taking 13 courses, all but 4 under my special instruction, and also my assoc. work, getting the vol. out in nov. if the printers do their part; *on top* of my setting up housekeeping after boarding for seven years, that I have had to let all other matters go unless imperative—I have however done a lot of Am. Mus. work, writing letters, looking after the labels. . . . When I am absent I expect that you and Saville will take my place for all matters to be attended to at once and I shall see that it is done in future so far as possible. But go slow and don't get disturbed. Remember the old saying "that it is the quiet pig that gets the most milk." We will get our milk all right in the end. Let the others do the talking; we will do the work. . . . I leave here Wed. a.m., go to the meeting of the Am. Ant. Soc. in Worcester, leave there on the midnight train for N.Y., and will be with you early in the morning on Thursday.

In haste
Yours faithfully,
FW Putnam[76]

Putnam's long efforts to get Boas a job at Columbia were also successful. In 1896 Boas was appointed lecturer in physical anthropology, and he was made a full professor in 1899. Meanwhile Boas continued to press for a more permanent position at the museum.

In February of 1897 Morris K. Jesup instructed Boas to consult with Putnam and then prepare a plan of work for an exploration of the North Pacific

Coasts of both Asia and America, to be financed by Jesup himself. Boas's experience in this ethnographically rich area coincided conveniently with Putnam's search for the routes of early man. Boas attacked this new project with his usual energy and used it also in his job negotiations. He asked Putnam to tell President Low about it, and he described to Putnam his own conversation with Jesup:

> I told Mr. Jesup that this expedition practically tied me to the Museum and that I did not want to go, that I like to work with you and that I consider that a certain work lies before me here, that I want to do. Then I outlined the plan to him that I gave you saying that it was not ripe to be formally submitted to him, but that I had that matter in mind and that, if it were to be carried out, it would be another thing that would hold me to N.Y. because I was heart and soul in for it.
>
> He has asked me to prepare a statement on the North Pacific Coast Expedition (do you consider that a good title?)[77]

Shortly afterward Boas asked Putnam to try to get an invitation to deliver the prestigious Lowell lectures in Boston for him. He wrote:

> Would not this be a good time for broaching the subject of the Lowell Lectures? You know I want to talk on the Indians of the North Pacific Coast. Please, do what you can to get a course there for me.[78]

Putnam wrote to Lowell, apparently unsuccessfully, but the matter did not end there. In 1910, thirteen years later, Boas again asked Putnam if he could get the Lowell lectures for him, and this time Putnam was successful. The lectures became Boas's book *The Mind of Primitive Man*.[79]

Since 1886 Boas had been doing field work on the northwest Coast, most of it under the sponsorship of the British Association for the Advancement of Science.[80] Now with Jesup's support he was able to direct a major expedition. Eventually Berthold Laufer, Gerard Fowke, Livingston Farrand, Harlan Smith, Roland Dixon, A.F. Chamberlain, Waldemar Bogoras, Waldemar Jochelson, John Swanton, and A.L. Kroeber were among those involved. The goal was to learn more of the prehistoric and historic relations of the native peoples on both sides of the Pacific, and investigators were sent along the littorals of the Pacific from the Columbia to the Amur Rivers and into the interiors of northwestern America and northeastern Asia. The expedition produced a considerable amount of ethnological material but no evidence for the great antiquity of man.[81] Putnam's role in the planning and carrying out of the Jesup Expedition was distinctly peripheral, and he was reduced to giving grandfatherly advice. In the summer of 1897 he wrote to Boas, who was in British Columbia:

> I wonder if you and [Harlan I.] Smith will catch the gold fever, and the next we shall hear of you will be in the Klondike region. I think it would pay to take a look at the sands of every little creek you pass over, for no one knows where the yellow metal will turn up in the northwest.[82]

Late in 1897 Boas visited the Peabody Museum in Cambridge and in a rare reference to Putnam's work wrote in a letter that he was "simply stunned" at the new material Putnam had brought together in the previous four years. The Turner Group material and the Hopewell material showed a peculiarly differentiated culture, Boas wrote, adding:

> You have it in your hand to open our eyes to an entirely new appreciation of the relation of the Ohio culture to southern cultures; . . . Your important discovery makes it a duty to you to bring the subject before the public at the earliest possible time. I wish I could find words to express strongly enough my feelings on this point. It is in your power to advance our knowledge of Amer. Anthropology immensely and I think you ought to find a way to spare time enough to do so. And it is just as much in the interest of Science, as it is your own interest and that of your co-workers to do so. . . .[83]

Putnam's reply, at the end of a letter on administrative matters for the American Museum, was as follows:

> Thanks for your kindly appreciation of the Peabody Museum and for your desire that I should work up the Turner Mound. Yes I wish to do this and have made a dozen starts, but what can I do? I've not time to

look at a specimen with all my administrative duties. This going to
N. Y. destroys my chance for work, as when I get back here after every
trip there are more things to be attended to. Than I can look after before I have to leave for N. Y. again and Oh this eternal grind and bread
winning![84]

Putnam's letter makes it clear that at least part of the reason for his
feverish activity was the need to augment his salary from the Peabody
Museum. The Peabody was his first love and had first claim on his loyalty.
Neither Jesup of the American Museum of Natural History nor President
Cleveland, who invited Putnam to become his commissioner of Indian affairs, could persuade him to leave it. "My Museum at Cambridge is my baby
and I must care for it," he told Cleveland.[85] Yet his combined salaries from
the museum curatorship and the Peabody professorship were about $2300.
The position was considered to be half-time so Putnam was free, but also essentially forced, to have part-time work elsewhere.

Suddenly events in California drew everyone's attention from New York to
the other side of the country. Putnam had interested Mrs. Phoebe A.
Hearst, who was a friend of his proteges Alice Fletcher and Zelia Nuttall, in
his search in California for evidence of early man. In 1901 Mrs. Hearst became interested in encouraging anthropological work at the University of
California and in establishing a museum to house her rapidly growing collections. Word of this traveled fast in anthropological circles, and in May of
1901 Zelia Nuttall inquired discreetly of Franz Boas, whom she knew
through professional meetings, if he might be available to go to California
and organize the "great task."[86]

Boas responded with a long letter in which he outlined his own plans for
establishing a comprehensive school of anthropology in New York and beyond this for directing all of the ethnological work done "on our continent."[87] He thought that there was no one at the moment capable of taking
charge of California ethnology but that in five years either Dixon, a student
of Putnam's, or Kroeber, a student of Boas's might be able to do so. He
suggested that Mrs. Hearst establish four five-year fellowships in ethnology
at Columbia and two in archaeology at Harvard. When the fellows were suf-
ficiently trained to do independent field work, they could be transferred
to the University of California. Boas asked for the opportunity to direct

this program which he felt would in five years give California a strong department.

Boas's plan did not prevail. Mrs. Hearst wanted to establish anthropology in California, not at Columbia or Harvard. She gathered together at her hacienda on September 7, 1901 Benjamin Ide Wheeler, president of the University of California, Mrs. Zelia Nuttall, Miss Alice Fletcher, and F.W. Putnam. They laid the plans for a department of anthropology at the University of California which the board of regents accepted three days later. Mrs. Hearst's gift provided for ethnological research in linguistics and mythology among the California Indians, to be done by A.L. Kroeber, who had just finished his Ph.D. under Boas at Columbia, and P.E. Goddard, a graduate student at the University of California. Mrs. Hearst also provided an additional gift:

> for the thorough geological and paleontological research of the gravel
> formations of California with special reference to the determination,
> if possible, of the geological time when man first appeared in
> California. [88]

This work was to be done under Putnam and J.C. Merriam, assistant professor of palaeontology. A temporary fireproof building was to be built immediately on the grounds of the university to house Mrs. Hearst's collections from Greece, Peru, Egypt, and California. There was to be no teaching in the department as yet, but there would be a series of lectures, the first of which would be given by F.W. Putnam, the chairman of the advisory committee. The advisory committee consisted of the five founders with the additions of Boas and J.C. Merriam. Boas continued to make suggestions, but his interest in research conflicted with the desire of the California members of the committee (Wheeler, Hearst, Nuttall, and Merriam) to concentrate on work at the department of the university.

Boas was left feeling that he had been wronged. Against his will a rival department of anthropology had been established on the other side of the continent and its work was being directed by the man who Boas thought already had more than his share of power and influence, a man who tended to put too much emphasis on archaeology and who lacked a comprehensive plan for the future of anthropology in America. Putnam, for his part, felt that his young friend and colleague was trying to oust him from positions and opportunities for work. Putnam took these to be his by right of all those qualifications he had earlier listed for Boas when the two of them were trying to have more influence at the American Museum of Natural History: his general scientific training, his long association with museums and expeditions, and his wide acquaintance with scientific men. [89]

The tension between them grew. In April of 1902 Boas drafted a letter to Putnam which he rewrote but did not mail. Two days later he sent Putnam a greatly toned-down version. In his original letter Boas complained of "many sleepless nights" and wanted "to regain our old harmonious relations" and "the old confidence."[90] The essential difficulty, he thought, was Putnam's absences from the museum which made it seem as if their work was at cross-purposes and as if Boas was withholding his plans from Putnam. Boas also mentioned "the California matter":

I confess that your action last summer hurt me to the quick, because it upset all that I had tried to build up for years, and I cannot convince myself that you were right in it. This matter has rankled in my mind for weeks, but you must have noticed that I got over it, and that I look at it simply as a point in regard to which our judgment was at variance.

In the later version, the one mailed to Putnam, Boas only said that lately he had the feeling "that things are not going in your Department, as they should, and that you feel irritated by many things that I may do or leave undone."[91] Boas suggested that each time Putnam came to New York he call a meeting of the whole department and have each man, "beginning with the lowest," report on work he had been doing. Boas felt this would help to create a feeling of unity and common understanding.

Putnam replied only:

My dear Boas

Thanks for your note duly received. . . .[92]

and went on to other matters. He knew and Boas must have known that calling the men in the department together to report on their work in hierarchical order was not the way Putnam liked to proceed. They both knew too that this was not the root of the difficulty.

Then discontent in California began to make itself felt in Cambridge and New York.

Mrs. Hearst was not pleased with the way the work was going. She did not like Kroeber "who flies into a rage when asked to do something unpleasant for him."[93] She thought the advisory committee plan unsatisfactory. She wanted to have someone present and in charge at California, someone who could command respect both inside and outside the department, and she suggested William T. Brigham, the director of the museum in Honolulu.[94]

Putnam telegraphed his disapproval and then wrote to Mrs. Hearst from New York. He was very harassed, he told her, doing in three months the work of eighteen. He was carrying on the museum work and preparing for the coming meeting of the International Congress of Americanists, all without the help of Dr. Boas, "my chief collaborator here," who was seriously ill.[95]

Putnam objected to the possible appointment of Brigham and expressed astonishment that there was any feeling that Kroeber was not satisfactory. "Dr. Boas regards him as a man of extraordinary ability," he wrote, particularly for linguistic investigations. Putnam was willing to reduce the advisory committee, as suggested, simply to President Wheeler, Mrs. Hearst, and himself. Then, aware that the California opportunity might slip from his hands, Putnam moved gradually to free himself from New York.

A new flareup from Boas undoubtedly spurred him on. The letter which Boas wrote on February 4, 1903 is not extant, but Boas must have used the occasion of Marshall Saville's appointment to the newly established Loubat Professorship of Archaeology at Columbia to express his dissatisfaction with the arrangements at the American Museum where he and Saville were still under Putnam's supervision. Putnam's long reply to Boas in a letter marked "Strictly *Personal* and *Confidential*" is in the Boas papers. Putnam wrote that he was "very much surprised and pained" that Boas had written the letter and suggested that on second thought Boas would be inclined to recall it. He could not tell Boas ahead of time about Saville's coming appointment. He went on:

I had to hold similar confidences at the time I was working for your appointment and still hold them. . . . as for either of you feeling that you cannot serve under my general advisory curatorship simply because you are professors of Columbia is certainly rather a personal slap at me to say the least. I am sure Boas that when you stop and think how I have always done all in my power to help you, how I have carefully held my own personality in the background and have let you go ahead and have aided you in every way; that it is owing to the Department of Anth. that both you and Saville got your Professorships; that we have cooperated in the work of making the Dept. what it is, and think of the many other things during our long association, you will realize what an unkind thing your letter is. I am sorry you wrote it and I earnestly hope you will recall it and send this one back to me, that the unpleasant matter may be wiped out of existence—I have no copy of this and regret that I have to write it. My efforts have been faithful ones for the Department, and I have done my best regardless of any personal effect to me. And I am hurt and disappointed at the unfortunate position you have taken. I trust it will prove but a flash, for your sake as well as for my own, and for the Dept. of anthropology which I faithfully serve.

Your friend,
FW Putnam[96]

This incident convinced Putnam that he should leave the American Museum completely. He could not do so, however, without moving to another position. On February 9, 1903 he wrote from Cambridge to Mrs. Hearst, remarking on how strange it was that they had happened to meet in New York. "I suddenly had the impulse, that evening, to call on your son; not knowing that you were there," Putnam wrote.[97] He told Mrs. Hearst that Jesup wanted him to give all his time to the American Museum, but he had refused. He was giving up his administrative work there, and his new role was to be that of "advising father."

With regard to California, Putnam wrote:

I am in constant touch with Dr. Kroeber—who writes me a weekly letter— . . . I think no mistake has been made in putting him in temporary charge of the executive work.

Putnam's maneuvers were successful. On March 26, 1903 he wrote of his perplexities and new possibilities to Zelia Nuttall. He had decided to direct only the archaeological work in New York, and "I shall withdraw entirely before long."[98] The Harvard faculty had made an offer to him to remain in Cambridge, giving up everything else, and three days earlier he had received a definite call from the University of California.

The decision could not have been very difficult. Putnam saw the possibility of getting money from Mrs. Hearst, far beyond any amount that would ever be available in Cambridge, for building a center for anthropological instruction and research "equal to any in the country," as he later expressed it.[99]

Putnam spent the summer months of 1903 in California as head of the Department of Anthropology. His official connection with the American Museum ceased at the end of that year. In 1904 he took a three-month leave of absence from the Peabody Museum for the California work and went again for the summer months, but he was saddened by a sudden cutback from Mrs. Hearst who was having financial reverses. In May, 1904 he wrote to President Wheeler:

It is a sad blow to me to have this curtailment and I know it is to you. We were making a splendid start for a great center of anthropological research and a great museum on the Pacific coast similar to those here in Cambridge, in New York, and in Chicago. I had the ambition to be instrumental in making this new center as I have been in the others named, and I do not intend to give up the trial. It is evident however that we must get others to aid in the work.[100]

The field expeditions, including Max Uhle's to Peru, and the archaeological and ethnological surveys of California were cut back. Putnam tried to find other sources of support with some success: the Archaeological Institute of America paid the cost of continuing cave explorations in California, and he persuaded the University of California to make Kroeber and Goddard assistant professors and pay their salaries. By 1908, however, Putnam was begging Mrs. Hearst for money just to keep the museum going.[101]

Meanwhile in 1904 Franz Boas was asked to summarize the history of anthropology for an international conference. He gave, not an account of anthropological work done,[102] but a history of anthropological theory in a way that greatly underplayed the American contribution. He mentioned only one American anthropologist, Daniel G. Brinton, whom he called "an extremist" in his support of independent invention of myths. Anthropology owed its very existence, he claimed, to the generalizing schemes of Herbert Spencer and E.B. Tylor. But these simple, brilliant theories must be followed by steady empirical work. What was needed was "detailed historical investigations" and then "psychological researches into the conditions of transmission, adaptation, and invention."[103] He mentioned with approval the quantitative methods of Francis Galton and Karl Pearson and the folk psychology of Steinthal, Wundt, Baldwin, Tarde, and Stoll. True, a great deal had been achieved by the "modest collector of facts," and Boas felt that the number of well-trained and truly scientific observers had increased during the last twenty years, but he singled out no individuals.

This paper spelled out the Boas program for anthropology, and it dropped a whole generation of American anthropologists from the historical record. There was no mention of Lewis Henry Morgan, no mention of John Wesley Powell, William Henry Holmes, Frank Hamilton Cushing, Alice C. Fletcher, and others whose work at the Bureau of American Ethnology and elsewhere was arousing the admiration of European scholars, and no mention of the man to whom Boas owed so much, F.W. Putnam. Subsequent generations of students were led to believe that Franz Boas developed his historical method in opposition to the evolutionary speculations of the nineteenth-century anthropologists. They did not know that it had also been Putnam's historical method. And they scarcely knew that alongside the evolutionary speculations in the nineteenth century there had been an empirical tradition derived from natural history, biology, and geology which had laid the foundations of the new science.

Having written his version of the history of anthropology, Franz Boas next changed his point of view on museums. Boas left the American Museum of Natural History in 1905, disgruntled with the lack of support there for his linguistic studies and other research. He was succeeded by his former student, Clark Wissler, who became curator of anthropology. In 1907 George Dorsey wrote an article in *Science* deploring the changed policy of the anthropology department in that museum. Dorsey had high praise for the work begun there ten to twelve years earlier under Putnam, when one felt in the halls "the spirit of investigation" and everywhere there was evidence of intelligent direction. The collections showed the actual conditions under which people lived and the influence of geography and of the culture of one tribe upon another. But recently, Dorsey wrote, much material has been put in storage and the rest organized into idealized area cultures in which the details are sometimes wrong and diversity is not shown. Popularization seemed to have become more important than research and study.[104]

Boas replied to Dorsey in *Science*. Although he might have been expected to agree that the first concern of museums was scientific investigation, instead he subtly relegated museums to public entertainment and instruction and the storage of materials. He even suggested that the American Museum of Natural History might do well to use some of its annual appropriations from the city to set up twenty small museums like branches of a public library. Public entertainment was needed, he wrote, to counteract "the influence of the saloon and the race-track."[105]

Then his real argument became apparent. The objects in a museum can give an "exceedingly fragmentary presentation of the true life of a people." They cannot show the psychological relations of cultures. They are only incidental expressions of those mental processes which are the real subject of anthropological inquiry. The specimen had such trifling importance in anthropology as compared with natural history that the exhibits ought to be kept entirely distinct. A visitor on his way to the anthropology halls ought not to have to come into contact with the natural history collections. Then, contradicting his earlier position, Boas declared that since there was so much disagreement among the best anthropologists over how to present anthropological data, no museum ought to presume to dictate by its arrangement what the science of anthropology shall be.

So Boas turned his back on his years of work in museums and on Putnam's methods of museum arrangements, not as wrong, but as unimportant. He did it carefully, praising Putnam in his article for having been the first to recognize that museums must not just collect specimens but must attack scientific problems. Putnam read the proofs of the article, made a few notes in the margin, and tried to respond positively to Boas about it. He commented in particular that it was important to give visitors to a museum accurate information even though they may be more interested in what is sensational.[106]

The correspondence between Putnam and Boas continued through these years of their somewhat wary relationship. In 1906 their varying ideas on the needs of the profession came into conflict. Both men had been involved in the founding of the American Anthropological Association in 1902, and Putnam was elected president of the AAA in 1905 and reelected in 1906, at a time when the question of the AAA's relations with Section H, Anthropology, of the AAAS was troublesome. Boas suggested in 1906 that there were too many scientific meetings. Attendance was poor and so was the quality of some of the papers. He wanted to turn the AAA into a publishing society. If the AAA did continue to meet, Boas thought they might have discussions on the teaching of anthropology in universities and on improving reviews in the journals.[107] Putnam, however, was a great believer in congresses and meetings. He replied gently but firmly to Boas that a committee could decide what discussions were advisable and that he thought it would be "very harmful to anthropological studies in this country" if the annual meeting of the AAA were to be given up.[108]

In 1907 the two men worked on a proposal to the newly established Carnegie Institution in Washington for work in anthropology in South America. Putnam liked Boas's statement of the ethnological side of the problem; but he wanted something added on a search for the first traces of man in South America and on the possibility of transatlantic migration in ancient times, long an interest of his. Boas wrote an accommodating reply.[109] The following year the two men struggled with plans for an archaeological school as proposed by Alice Fletcher and E.L. Hewett to be sponsored by the Archaeological Institute of America.

Any remaining tension between Boas and Putnam ended abruptly with the latter's seventieth birthday in April, 1909, for which Boas organized a dinner and a testimonial volume of papers. Three years earlier Berthold Laufer, the young China scholar whom Boas had found for the Jesup expedition, had edited a volume of papers in honor of Boas on the twenty-fifth anniversary of his doctoral degree. Boas recognized that it was inappropriate that he be honored ahead of his mentor, and he made amends with the party for Putnam, who was touched and grateful. Immediately afterward Putnam wrote to Boas:

I can never thank you enough for all you have done and for the beautiful and loving words you spoke at the dinner, and for the charming and hearty words you have given to the preface of the beautiful and valuable volume. . . . To know that through my long life of work I have reached the age of seventy surrounded with friends and without an enemy is indeed a happiness that I can heartily wish may come to all who have so honored me. . . . How I should like to be here a score of years hence to say of you what you have said of me. When that day comes my dear friend please recall these words.[110]

So Putnam was honored, and the estrangement which he had very much regretted was healed. In 1909 Putnam retired from California and became honorary curator and honorary director of the Peabody Museum and professor emeritus. He participated in the ground breaking for the third addition to the Peabody Museum in 1913. Two years later he died.

The relations between F.W. Putnam and Franz Boas reflect not only their personal characteristics but also an important transition in American intellectual life as incoming European scholars began to make their presence felt in the New World. Franz Boas had arrived in America with the prestige of a German Ph.D. and a list of published articles and reviews that by 1897 had more than one hundred entries. Putnam respected these qualifications. He addressed his letters to "Dr. Boas" except on those rare occasions when in a particular mood or in haste he would write "My dear Boas" or "Dear Boas." Putnam's own qualifications, by contrast, seemed modest. His only earned degree was an S.B. awarded by Harvard in 1898 "as of" the class of 1862. His published bibliography listed more than four hundred items, but the vast bulk of those are annual reports of his work for museums or notices of remarks made at scientific meetings.[111] Putnam wrote no long major work. Yet beneath the seeming casualness of Putnam's work was a scientific rigor not always apparent at first glance. One example of this was Putnam's approach to graduate education in anthropology.

Because Franz Boas produced the first Ph.D. in anthropology in the United States (A.F. Chamberlain at Clark University in 1892 with a dissertation in linguistics) and subsequently taught at Columbia many people who were to become well known in anthropology, it has been generally believed that it was Boas who professionalized anthropology in the United States. He brought, it has been assumed, Germanic rigor into what had been a field full of amateurs. In fact, however, between Chamberlain and A.L. Kroeber, who in 1901 was Boas's first Ph.D. at Columbia, doctoral degrees were received by four of Putnam's students—George A. Dorsey, Frank Russell, Roland B. Dixon, and John Swanton. Three more followed soon after in 1903 and 1904: William Curtis Farabee, George Byron Gordon, and Alfred M. Tozzer.[112] Putnam not only produced more "professional anthropologists" in the first years of the new science than did Boas; he also gave them more rigorous training. In 1896 Putnam suggested that advanced students in his department should study

> geology, physical geography including climatology, botany and zoology, human anatomy, psychology, linguistics, archaeology, ethnology including all phases of man's life—early religions, myths, folk-lore, institutions, and the development of arts and culture; ethnography including the distribution of man over the earth, characters of the different races and their modifications by migration and contact; etc.—to get general knowledge of man from his primitive state to his present condition in all parts of the world.[113]

Putnam meant what he said, setting up such a demanding program for Sylvanus G. Morley in general anthropology and in the "kindred sciences" of zoology, botany, and geology that Morley never finished it.[114] Putnam's students generally spent four years in graduate work, including time spent in the field and in some cases at Columbia studying methods in linguistics with Franz Boas, while for Boas's students including Kroeber, A.F. Chamberlain, H.K. Haeberlin, and Ruth Benedict, the norm was more nearly two years and a short dissertation. What Boas was interested in, Kroeber wrote later, was that students have an uncompromising adherence to his own values. They could learn what they needed to know later.[115] Putnam, on the other hand, wanted to be sure that his students worked out of a solid foundation in the natural sciences.

This difference between their doctoral programs is a reflection of the difference between German and American academic customs in the late nineteenth century. A.B. Meyer, the director of the Anthropological Museum at Dresden, Germany, commented in 1899 that an American Ph.D. took three or four years of study after the B.A. and represented "a stage of scientific maturity far above the level of the average German doctor."[116] He deemed it more equivalent to the German examination for the office of academic teacher or "privat-docent." His observations were confirmed by Hugo Münsterberg, a professor of psychology at Harvard University and a man well acquainted with German and American universities.

Putnam made a Ph.D. degree difficult, but he did not draw a line between professionals and nonprofessionals in anthropology. He welcomed amateurs into the field and started on their scholarly careers many people who were not interested in degrees, including Alice Fletcher and Zelia Nuttall. In part, the tension between Putnam and Boas was due to a difference in scientific styles, the difference between the hierarchical authoritarian German university tradition from which Boas had come and the freewheeling, open-ended, and sometimes chaotic American way of doing things. Boas can hardly be blamed for wanting to bring order into what he saw as a empirical and theoretical morass. Yet this led him to underestimate the quality of the American work and to underrate his colleagues.

F.W. Putnam was primarily an organizer and a builder of institutions, not a theorist. O.T. Mason of the National Museum in Washington, D.C. wrote to Putnam in 1889:

> I was reminded of you a thousand times in Paris, by Dr. Hamy, who looks like you, talks like you, trots around like you, is general secretary of everything, and an indispensable man-of-affairs to the Paris Anthropologists.—In all our meetings, nothing could go on until Dr. Hamy arrived; and to keep up the comparison, once in a while he came in a *little late.* [117]

After his twenty-five years as permanent secretary of the American Association for the Advancement of Science, Putnam was elected president in 1898. He was also a member of the National Academy of Sciences. He edited innumerable publications for others, for the Essex Institute and the Peabody Academy of Science in Salem, for the AAAS, the Wheeler survey, the Peabody Museum in Cambridge, the American Museum of Natural History, and the Department of Anthropology at the University of California, and he did it superbly. Bandelier wrote him, "between us and the historic gatepost—it is a vast difference between having a MSS in Your hands and in the hands of SOMEBODY ELSE—."[118] But he wrote little himself. The vast amount of archaeological work that he did (in more than thirty-seven states as well as in Central America and Mexico[119]) was largely empirical, the gathering of objects and data for future syntheses. Putnam did work out a theory of aesthetic development in art, showing how realistic representations of animate and inanimate forms are gradually conventionalized,[120] but he left most theory building to others.

There was one theory, however, which Putnam clung to stubbornly. He was convinced from his early days with Jeffries Wyman that man had been in America for at least ten thousand years, and he consistently supported attempts throughout the country to find tools or bones of ancient or palaeolithic man. For more than thirty years he kept work going at the river gravels in Trenton, New Jersey, where in 1875 some crude stone implements believed to be palaeolithic had been found. His evidence was attacked beginning in 1892 by William Henry Holmes and later Aleš Hrdlička, and Putnam's position came to be considered foolish as Holmes and Hrdlička built up a scientific orthodoxy which said that man could not have been in America for more than four thousand years.[121] Yet Putnam would not give up, and twelve years after his death, the discovery in Folsom, New Mexico, of a flaked point lodged between the ribs of an extinct mammal pushed the date for early man in America back beyond ten thousand years ago and proved that Putnam's hunch, if not his specific examples, had been correct. As Pliny E. Goddard summed up the situation in 1927, "in reality all these years the scepticism should have been in the other direction," toward the very recent peopling of America.[122]

F.W. Putnam stands at the end of the natural history tradition in nineteenth century American anthropology, at the turning point between nineteenth-century archaeology and natural history and the twentieth-century sciences of man. He did not quite make this transition personally. Putnam insisted that the discipline which he called anthropology was the science of man, including everything from psychology to classical studies. He argued against a proposal to change the name of Section H in the American Association for the Advancement of Science to "Anthropology and Psychology" and caused considerable controversy at the University of California when he insisted that George Reiser's publications on Egypt should come out under the imprint of the Department of Anthropology.[123] Yet in practice Putnam tended to think of anthropology as being primarily concerned with the early history of mankind. He did not make the transition in his own work, as Lewis Henry Morgan, John Wesley Powell, Frank Hamilton Cushing, and others did, from anthropology as natural history of the Indians to anthropology as a science of man which might throw light on the problems of every society, their own included.

Frederic Ward Putnam hoped to be remembered as the man who established anthropology in the universities of Harvard, Columbia, and California and as a builder of museums in New York, Cambridge, Chicago, and California. These are remarkable achievements, but Putnam's fate has been that the building of institutions and the enabling of others to do their work are contributions too seldom recognized as the important ones they are.

Notes and References

1. Edward S. Morse, "Frederick Ward Putnam, 1839–1915. An Appreciation," *Historical Collections of the Essex Institute,* LII (1916), 3.

2. Alfred M. Tozzer, "Frederic Ward Putnam, 1839–1915," *National Academy of Sciences Biographical Memoirs,* XVI (1935), 125.

3. Frederic Ward Putnam, "Henry Wheatland," *Proceedings of the American Academy of Arts and Sciences,* XXXI (1896), 364.

4. Ralph W. Dexter, "Some Herpetological Notes and Correspondence of Frederic Ward Putnam," *Journal of the Ohio Herpetological Society,* V (1966), 110.

5. Alfred L. Kroeber, "Frederic Ward Putnam," *American Anthropologist,* XVII (1915), 713.

6. Jules Marcou, *Life, Letters, and Works of Louis Agassiz,* 2 vols. (New York, Macmillan, 1896), I, 88.

7. F.W. Putnam, *Twenty-fifth Annual Report,* Peabody Museum of American Archaeology and Ethnology (1891), 2.

8. Edward Lurie, *Louis Agassiz: A Life in Science* (Chicago, University of Chicago Press, 1960), 256–264; Ralph W. Dexter, "The 'Salem Secession' of Agassiz Zoologists," *Essex Institute Historical Collections,* CI (1965), 27–39.

9. A.B. Meyer, "Studies of museums and kindred institutions of New York City, Albany, Buffalo, and Chicago, with notes on some European institutions," *Smithsonian Institution Annual Report,* 1903 (1905), 534.

10. Geoffrey Hellman, *Bankers, Bones and Beetles: The First Century of the American Museum of Natural History* (New York, The Natural History Press, 1969).

11. This "gift for science in Essex County" of $140,000 was the one uncontemplated gift George Peabody made in the United States on his visit there after the Civil War, a tes-

timony to the persuasive powers of young
F.W. Putnam, for Peabody received hundreds of requests. George Peabody had the
general outline of his other benevolences
($150,000 each to Harvard and Yale for
museums of science, $2,000,000 for a Fund
for Southern Education, and $2,500,000 for
model housing in London slums) well in mind
before he left London. (Franklin Parker,
George Peabody: A Biography, Nashville,
Vanderbilt University Press, 1971, 165).

12. F.W. Putnam, *First Annual Report* of
the Trustees of the Peabody Academy of Science (1869), 51–52.

13. European museums of ethnography
were begun about the same time, i.e., the
third quarter of the nineteenth century. For a
brief summary of the development of
ethnological museums in Europe and a bibliography see the first chapter of Robert
Goldwater, *Primitivism in Modern Art* (New
York, Vintage Press, 1938, rev. ed., 1966,
1967).

14. Jules Marcou, *op. cit.*, 142.

15. J.O. Brew, "Introduction," *One
Hundred Years of Anthropology* (Cambridge,
Harvard University Press, 1968), 12.

16. F.W. Putnam, "The Peabody Museum
of American Archaeology and Ethnology in
Cambridge," *Proceedings of the American
Antiquarian Society*, VI (1889), 182.

17. A. Irving Hallowell, "The Beginnings of Anthropology in America," in F. de
Laguna, ed., *Selected Papers from the American Anthropologist, 1888–1920* (Evanston,
Illinois, Row, Peterson and Co., 1960), 88.

18. Jeffries Wyman, "An account of some
kjoekken moeddings, or shell-heaps in
Maine and Massachusetts," *American Naturalist*, I (1868), 561–584.

19. Jeffries Wyman, "Primitive Man,"
American Naturalist, X (1876), 279.

20. F.W. Putnam, "Jeffries Wyman,"

*Proceedings of the American Academy of Arts
and Sciences*, II (1875), 496–505.

21. Alfred L. Kroeber, "Frederic Ward
Putnam," *American Anthropologist*, XVII
(1915), 714.

22. *Proceedings of the American Association for the Advancement of Science*, XXII
(1873).

23. Joseph Henry wrote, "To gratify men of
literature as well as advance an important
branch of knowledge, from the first much attention has been given [by the Smithsonian
Institution] to anthropology, including linguistics, antiquities, and everything which
tends to reconstruct the history of man in the
past; this being a common ground on which
the man of letters and of science could meet
in harmonious collaboration." (*Annual Report of the Smithsonian Institution for 1872*,
1873, 18).

24. Joseph Henry, *Annual Report of
the Smithsonian Institution* (1877), 22. In
Europe at this time "anthropology" generally
meant physical anthropology, as it had in the
United States before the Civil War. The
term had been used in something like its
present broader sense however by the short-
lived Societé des observateurs de l'homme,
founded in Paris in 1800 [Aleš Hrdlička,
Physical Anthropology (Philadelphia, The
Wistar Institute of Anatomy and Biology,
1919), 10] and was gradually so used after
1871 by the Royal Anthropological Institute
in Britain [George W. Stocking, Jr., "What's
In a Name? The Origins of the Royal Anthropological Institute (1837–71)," *Man*,
n.s. VI (1971), 369–391].

Putnam's interest in establishing "anthropology" as the general designation of the
new science is evident as early as 1870. In
that year he became co-editor with A.S.
Packard of the *American Naturalist*, and immediately a new category of topics appears

in the magazine, that of "anthropology," including entries in archaeology, physical anthropology, and linguistics. See the *American Naturalist*, IV (1870).

25. Putnam, "The Peabody Museum of American Archaeology and Ethnology in Cambridge," 185.

26. F.W. Putnam, "On Methods of Archaeological Research in America," *Johns Hopkins University Circulars*, No. 49, (1886), V:89.

27. *Twenty-fifth Annual Report*, Peabody Museum (1891), 2.

28. *Report upon United States Geographical and Geological Explorations and Surveys West of the 100th Meridian*, in charge of First Lieut. George M. Wheeler, Vol. VII. Archaeology (Washington, D.C., 1879).

29. *Eleventh Annual Report*, Peabody Museum (1878), 203.

30. Carl Resek, *Lewis Henry Morgan: American Scholar* (Chicago, University of Chicago Press, 1960), 22–23, 27, 40.

31. Lewis Henry Morgan, "Report to the Regents of the University, upon the articles furnished to the Indian Collection," *Third Annual Report of the Regents of the University on the condition of the State Cabinet of Natural History and the Historical and Antiquarian Collection*, rev. ed. (Albany, 1850).

32. John Wesley Powell, "Sketch of Lewis Henry Morgan," *Popular Science Monthly*, XVIII (1880), 114; Lewis Henry Morgan, *League of the Ho-de-no-sau-nee, or Iroquois* (Rochester, Sage and Bros., 1851).

33. Morgan wrote ruefully at the end of his study of the American beaver, "My unrestrained curiosity has cost me a good deal of time and labor." [*The American Beaver and His Works* (Philadelphia, J.B. Lippincott, 1868), ix]. Tragedy stalked him too, for it was on a trip up the Upper Missouri to gather information about kinship systems and beavers that he failed to yield to his wife's urgent message to return home at once. When Morgan next had word from his family, his two daughters were dead from scarlet fever. Morgan brought his traveling adventures to an abrupt end and did not go exploring again until near the end of his life when he made a six weeks trip to New Mexico.

34. F.W. Putnam, "Sketch of Hon. Lewis H. Morgan," *Proceedings of the American Academy of Arts and Sciences*, XVII (1882), 430.

35. Lewis H. Morgan, *The American Beaver and His Works*, iv-vi.

36. "There is, perhaps, nothing in the whole range of man's absolute necessities so little liable to mutation as his system of relationship," Morgan said in 1859 at the AAAS meeting. Leslie A. White quotes from a MS Morgan read, "System of Consanguinity of the Red Race and Its Relation to Ethnology," in Lewis Henry Morgan, *The Indian Journals, 1859–62*. ed. and with introduction by Leslie A. White (Ann Arbor, University of Michigan, 1959), 7.

37. Lewis Henry Morgan, "Systems of Consanguinity and Affinity of the Human Family," *Smithsonian Contributions to Knowledge*, XVII (1870).

38. Resek (*op. cit.*, 94–95) credited Morgan's friend, the clergyman Joshua McIlvaine, with suggesting the developmental possibility to Morgan. Morgan first tried it out in "A Conjectural Solution of the Origin of the Classificatory System of Relationship," *Proceedings of the American Academy of Arts and Sciences*, VII (1868), 436–477.

39. Lewis Henry Morgan, *Ancient Society, or Researches in the Lines of Human Progress from Savagery through Barbarism to Civilization* (New York, Holt, 1877). Morgan did make one reference to "the principles of natural selection," but this was in the context of

one particular biological change in human beings, an increased intellectual capacity due to the elimination of brother-sister incest in the "punaluan" form of marriage. See Marvin Harris, *The Rise of Anthropological Theory* (New York, Thomas Y. Crowell, 1968), 182–183. Harris also gives (184–188) an analysis of the contemporary status of various parts of Morgan's theory.

40. Lewis Henry Morgan, "Montezuma's Dinner," *North American Review*, CXXII (1876), 265–308; Morgan to Putnam, Jan. 29, 1876, Putnam Papers, Harvard University Archives.

41. Putnam to Morgan, Aug. 5, 1876, Lewis Henry Morgan Papers, University of Rochester Library.

42. Putnam to Morgan, June 8, 1876, Aug. 5, 1876, Morgan Papers.

43. Putnam to Morgan, Jan. 9, 1880, Morgan Papers.

44. Morgan to Putnam, May 17, 1875, Peabody Museum Archives.

45. Morgan to Putnam, Jan. 29, 1876, Morgan Papers.

46. Adolph Bandelier, "On the Art of War and Mode of Warfare of the Ancient Mexicans," *Tenth Annual Report*, Peabody Museum (1877), 95–116; "On the Distribution and Tenure of Land," *Eleventh Annual Report*, Peabody Museum (1878), 385–448; "On the Social Organization and Mode of Government of the Ancient Mexicans," *Twelfth Annual Report*, Peabody Museum (1879), 557–699.

47. Morgan to Putnam, Dec. 21, 1876, Peabody Museum Archives.

48. Morgan to Putnam, Feb. 7, 1877, Peabody Museum Archives.

49. Putnam to Morgan, Jan. 31, 1880, Morgan Papers. Charles Eliot Norton's first published writing was on American archaeology—a long unsigned review-discussion of Squier and Davis's work in

"Ancient Monuments in America," *North American Review*, LXVIII (1849), 466–496.

50. *Second Annual Report of the AIA* (1881), 34–36; *Tenth Annual Report of the AIA* (1889), 47.

51. Morgan to Putnam, Jan. 13, 1880, Peabody Museum Papers, Harvard University Archives.

52. Morgan to Putnam, Jan. 30, 1880, Peabody Museum Papers.

53. Putnam to Morgan, Jan. 31, 1880, Morgan Papers.

54. Leslie A. White, ed., *Pioneers in American Anthropology: The Bandelier-Morgan Letters, 1873–1883*, 2 vols. (Albuquerque, University of New Mexico Press, 1940), II, 203.

55. Bernhard Stern, *Lewis Henry Morgan: Social Evolutionist* (Chicago, University of Chicago Press, 1931), 195.

56. *Eleventh Annual Report*, Peabody Museum (1878), 193.

57. F.W. Putnam, "Sketch of Hon. Lewis H. Morgan," 432.

58. W.H. Holmes, "Lewis Henry Morgan, 1818–1881," *Biographical Memoirs of the National Academy of Sciences*, VI (1909).

59. F.W. Putnam, "The Serpent Mound of Ohio," *Century Magazine* (April, 1890), 871–888. Putnam wrote to his wife, "It is a splendid thing darling—this preservation of this wonderful old monument and I feel it to be the grandest act of my life that I have been instrumental in bringing it about. I am so elated over it." (Putnam to his wife, May 30, 1887, Putnam Papers).

60. F.W. Putnam, "Letter" in Berthold Laufer, ed., *Boas Anniversary Volume* (New York, G.E. Stechert, 1906).

61. George W. Stocking, Jr., "From Physics to Ethnology," in *Race, Culture, and Evolution* (New York, The Free Press, 1968), 142, 150. See also George W. Stocking, Jr., "Anthropology as Kulturkampf: Sci-

ence and Politics in the Career of Franz Boas," in Walter Goldschmidt, ed., *The Uses of Anthropology*, Special Publication of the American Anthropological Association (1979).

62. Franz Boas, "The occurrence of similar inventions in areas widely apart," *Science*, IX (1887), 485. George Stocking touches on this controversy in "From Physics to Ethnology," and it is the basis for John Buettner-Janusch, "Boas and Mason: Particularization vs. Generalization," *American Anthropologist*, LIX (1957), 318–324.

63. O.T. Mason, "The occurrence of similar inventions in areas widely apart," *Science*, IX (1887), 534.

64. Franz Boas, "Museums of ethnology and their classification," *Science*, IX (1887), 588.

65. John Wesley Powell, "Museums of ethnology and their classification," *Science*, IX (1887), 614.

66. Franz Boas, "Museums of ethnology and their classification," *Science*, IX (1887), 614.

67. George A. Dorsey, "The Development of Anthropology of the Field Columbian Museum—A Review of Six Years," *American Anthropologist*, II (1900), 247–265; Ralph W. Dexter, "Putnam's Problems Popularizing Anthropology," *American Scientist*, LIV (1966), 315–332; Ralph W. Dexter, "Frederic Ward Putnam and the Development of Museums of Natural History and Anthropology in the United States," *Curator*, IX (1966), 150–155; Ralph W. Dexter, "The Role of F.W. Putnam in founding the Field Museum," *Curator*, XIII (1970), 21–26.

68. F. Boas to Putnam, Jan. 4, 1894, Putnam Papers.

69. Putnam to Boas, April 30, 1894, Franz Boas Papers, American Philosophical Society Library.

70. Boas to Putnam, May 7, 1894, Putnam

Papers. In a subsequent letter Boas explained to Putnam what he thought had happened at Chicago. T.C. Chamberlin, a prominent geologist in Chicago, knew that J.W. Powell was in political trouble with the Geological Survey and wanted to resign from it, while retaining his position as head of the Bureau of Ethnology. The Bureau could not pay his salary, however, unless someone left, so Chamberlin obliged Powell by getting a place for Holmes in Chicago. (Boas to Putnam, May 21, 1894, Putnam Papers). Apart from these political considerations however, Holmes on his own merit deserved and perhaps got the job. He had just done some excellent work at the Bureau and was at this time one of the outstanding anthropologists in the country.

71. A good description of this period in Boas's life is Curtis M. Hinsley, Jr. and Bill Holm, "A Cannibal in the National Museum: The Early Career of Franz Boas in America," *American Anthropologist*, 78 (1976), 306–316.

72. Putnam to Boas, Oct. 4, 1895, Boas Papers.

73. Boas to Putnam, Dec. 5, 1895, Dec. 9, 1895, Putnam Papers.

74. Boas to Putnam, Dec. 18, 1895, Putnam Papers.

75. Boas to Putnam, Oct. 16, 1896, Oct. 19, 1896, Boas Papers.

76. Putnam to Boas, Oct. 19, 1896, Boas Papers.

77. Boas to Putnam, March 9, 1897, March 10, 1897, Putnam Papers.

78. Boas to Putnam, March 19, 1897, Putnam Papers. A pencilled note on this letter says "wrote to Lowell, Mar. 20."

79. Boas to Putnam, May 3, 1910, Nov. 14, 1910, Putnam Papers.

80. See Jacob Gruber, "Horatio Hale and the development of American anthropology," *Proceedings of the American*

Philosophical Society, 3 (1967), 5–37 and *The Ethnography of Franz Boas: Letters and Diaries of Franz Boas Written on the Northwest Coast from 1886 to 1931*, compiled and edited by Ronald P. Rohner (Chicago, University of Chicago Press, 1969).

81. Franz Boas, "The work of the Jesup North Pacific Expedition," *Science*, XVI (1902), 893; Edwin N. Wilmsen, "An Outline of Early Man Studies in the United States," *American Antiquity*, XXXI (1965), 178.

82. Putnam to Boas, July 28, 1897, Boas Papers.

83. Boas to Putnam, Dec. 5, 1897, Putnam Papers.

84. Putnam to Boas, Dec. 9, 1897, Boas Papers.

85. anon. "Frederick Ward Putnam," *American Indian Magazine*, III (1915), 225.

86. Ross Parmenter, "Glimpses of a Friendship," in June Helm, ed., *Pioneers of American Anthropology* (Seattle, University of Washington, 1966), 96–97. Parmenter's article is an excellent and detailed study of the correspondence between Zelia Nuttall and Franz Boas. Nuttall, who worked in Mexican anthropology, called Putnam "my dear Godfather in science." (Nuttall to Putnam, Feb. 5, 1908, Putnam Papers).

87. *Ibid.*, 100.

88. Minutes of the Meeting of Sept. 7, 1901, Putnam Papers.

89. Putnam to Boas, May 14, 1899, Boas Papers.

90. Boas to Putnam, April 4, 1902, Boas Papers.

91. Boas to Putnam, April 6, 1902, Boas Papers.

92. Putnam to Boas, April 14, 1902, Boas Papers.

93. George H. Pepper to Putnam, Sept. 15, 1902, Putnam Papers.

94. Alice C. Fletcher to Putnam, Sept.

9, 1902, Benjamin Wheeler to Putnam, Aug. 25, 1902, both in Putnam Papers.

95. Putnam to P.A. Hearst, Sept. 17, 1902, Putnam Papers.

96. Putnam to Boas, Feb. 6, 1903, Boas Papers.

97. Putnam to Mrs. Hearst, Feb. 9, 1903, Putnam Papers.

98. Putnam to Zelia Nuttall, March 26, 1903, Putnam Papers.

99. Putnam to Archer M. Huntington, New York City, March 27, 1905, Putnam Papers. A comparison of amounts of money, although incomplete, is instructive. The Peabody Museum at Cambridge and the Professorship were based on an original endowment of $150,000, yielding an annual income of approximately $7,500. An early proposal for the Jesup expedition at the American Museum suggested a budget of $5,000 a year for six years. (Boas to Jesup, Jan. 19, 1897, Putnam Papers). Mrs. Hearst gave more than $300,000 for anthropology in California during the first five years of the department there. (Putnam to Archer M. Huntington, March 27, 1905, Putnam Papers).

100. Putnam to Wheeler, May 30, 1894, Putnam Papers.

101. Putnam to Huntington, March 27, 1905, Putnam to Wheeler, Feb. 22, 1906, Putnam to P.A. Hearst, June 23, 1908, Putnam Papers.

102. For this approach to the history of a discipline, see Frederick Starr, "Anthropological Work in America," *The Popular Science Monthly*, XLI (1892), 289–307.

103. Franz Boas, "The History of Anthropology," *Science*, XX (1904), 520.

104. George A. Dorsey, "The Anthropological Exhibits at the American Museum of Natural History," *Science*, XXV (1907), 584–587.

105. Franz Boas, "Some Principles of

Museum Administration," *Science*, XXV (1907), 921–933.

106. Putnam to Boas, May 28, 1907, Boas Papers.

107. Boas to Putnam, Jan. 3, 1906, Boas Papers.

108. Putnam to Boas, Jan. 25, 1906, Boas Papers.

109. Putnam to Boas, Feb. 16, 1907, Aug. 29, 1907; Boas to Putnam, Aug. 28, 1907, Aug. 31, 1907, Boas Papers.

110. Putnam to Boas, April 23, 1909, Boas Papers. A long excerpt from the speech which Boas gave at the dinner is printed in Alfred M. Tozzer, "Frederic Ward Putnam, 1839–1915," *National Academy of Sciences Biographical Memoirs*, XVI (1935), 125–151.

111. Frances H. Mead, "Bibliography of Frederic Ward Putnam," in *Putnam Anniversary Volume* (New York, 1909), 601–629.

112. Regna Darnell, "The Development of American Anthropology 1879–1920: From the Bureau of American Ethnology to Franz Boas," unpub. Ph.D. dissertation, University of Pennsylvania, 1969. Appendix III is a useful chart on early Ph.D.s in American anthropology. Swanton is an ambiguous case, for although his doctoral degree was from Harvard he was more interested in linguistics than archaeology and so had been sent by Putnam to study with Boas in New York.

113. *Thirtieth Annual Report*, Peabody Museum (1896), 9.

114. Putnam to S.G. Morley, June 27, 1910, Peabody Museum Papers. Putnam told Morley he needed to work harder. "I want you to pass with credit and do credit to us all," he wrote. See also George A. Dorsey, "History of the Study of Anthropology at Harvard," *The Denison Quarterly*, IV (no date but 1896?), 77–97.

115. A.L. Kroeber, "Franz Boas: The Man," in Walter Goldschmidt, ed., *The Anthropology of Franz Boas*, Memoir 89, American Anthropological Association, LXI (1959), 14.

116. A.B. Meyer, "Studies of museums and kindred institutions of New York City, Albany, Buffalo, and Chicago, with notes on some European institutions," *Smithsonian Institution, Annual Report*, 1903 (1905), 311–608, 362, translation revised by the author from *Abhandlungen und Berichte des Königlichen Zoologischen und Anthropologische-Ethnographischen Museums in Dresden*, Band IX (1900–1901) and Band X (1902–1903).

117. O.T. Mason to Putnam, Oct. 21, 1889, Peabody Museum Papers.

118. A. Bandelier to Putnam, Sept. 30, 1897, Putnam Papers.

119. Alfred M. Tozzer, "Memoir of Frederic W. Putnam," *Proceedings of the Massachusetts Historical Society*, (June, 1916), 484.

120. F.W. Putnam, "Conventionalism in Ancient American Art," *Bulletin of the Essex Institute*, XVIII (1886), 155–167.

121. W.H. Holmes, "Are There Traces of Man in the Trenton Gravels," *The Journal of Geology*, I (1893), 15–37; W.H. Holmes, "The Antiquity Phantom in American Archaeology," *Science*, LXII (1925), 256–258; Aleš Hrdlička, "Skeletal Remains Suggesting or Attributed to Early Man in North America," *Thirty-Third Bulletin of the Bureau of American Ethnology* (1907).

122. Pliny Earle Goddard, "Facts and theories concerning Pleistocene Man in America," *American Anthropologist*, XXIX (1927), 266.

123. Putnam to Boas, Jan. 25, 1906, Boas Papers; Kroeber-Putnam letters in Putnam Papers.

Chapter Three
Alice C. Fletcher
(1838–1923)

The best description of Alice Fletcher is still that written just after her death by Charles F. Lummis, newspaperman and flamboyant Californian. She was a "Quiet Force," he wrote, equalled only by the 2500 horsepower Corliss engine before which he had stood in awe at the Philadelphia Centennial Exposition when he was seventeen years old. "A plain, gentle, modest little woman," one might enter a meeting room and not even notice her at first but gradually her opponents would find themselves stranded as the "quiet, deep river" drifted along. "She didn't fight—any more than the snowflake and the sunbeam fight. Like them, she Just Kept On."[1]

Of course Lummis was on her side, struggling with her to get the Archaeological Institute of America, which was mainly interested in Greece, to recognize the importance of American archaeology. Opponents of Alice Fletcher's programs saw her as a "dreadfully opinionated woman."[2] One of her great strengths, however, was that she always had more than opinions. She never pretended to know something she did not know. Instead she set out immediately to learn about it. As Lummis wrote, "Alice Fletcher knew to the roots whatsoever she attempted to write or talk about." It was this thorough preparation along with her general indifference to self and self-interest that made her the "Quiet Force" she was.

Alice Fletcher was forty years old when she began her long career in anthropology. This relatively late start calls to mind another of the most famous of women anthropologists in America, Ruth Benedict, who discovered anthropology at the age of thirty-three after a childless marriage and numerous attempts to "find herself" in other areas.[3] But Alice Fletcher was not a twentieth-century woman searching for a way to find meaning in her life. She was a nineteenth-century woman searching for ways "to do good," a distinction that is more than semantics. Alice Fletcher was confident that her values, a composite result of education, high-mindedness, and thorough study, were the right ones, and she did not hesitate, as did Ruth

Benedict, to urge them on others. The turning to anthropology was for her only one small step in the series of small steps that made up her life, each guided by the quiet determination that was apparent to anyone who met her clear-eyed gaze.

Alice Cunningham Fletcher was born in 1838 in Havana, Cuba of New England parents. Her mother, Lydia Adeline Jenks, was "a highly educated and accomplished lady of Boston."[4] Her father, Thomas Gilman Fletcher, was a graduate of Dartmouth College and a prospering lawyer in New York City until the attack of consumption which took them to Cuba in a vain attempt to restore his health. He died the following year when Alice was twenty-one months old, and Mrs. Fletcher eventually married again. Alice Fletcher grew up in a morally earnest household presided over by her straitlaced stepfather where the only fiction she was allowed to read was that by Charles Dickens.[5] She was educated in the best schools in New York, and in one of them, a boarding school in Brooklyn, she as "Little Alice," the youngest pupil in the school was befriended by an older girl, Miss E. Jane Gay. They happened to meet again at a lecture in New York City in the 1870s, and Miss Gay was thereafter her close friend and frequent traveling companion.[6]

After graduation Alice Fletcher traveled in Europe, returning to teach in private schools in New York. She was active in Sorosis, a pioneer women's club, and helped to found the Association for the Advancement of Women in 1873. In addition to these feminist activities, she worked for the temperance and anti-tobacco movements. Her earnestness, in combination with thoroughness and a ready sense of humor, made her a natural for the lecture platform. Speaking to large groups in support of one cause or another was an activity that continued through her entire life. The topics she took up ranged from the passion play at Oberammergau, feminism, and temperance in her early years to archaeology, anthropology, and Indian welfare. The first record of her public presentations in anthropology is a series of eleven "Lectures on Ancient America". Illustrating them with watercolor drawings, she gave the lectures in November 1879 under the sponsorship of the struggling young Minnesota Academy of Sciences. She discussed the mound builders, the people of the pueblos, earliest traces of man, antiquities of the coast, comparative archaic art from Egypt, Assyria, India, and Greece, and the value of anthropological study.[7] She must have been a success for, although there is no direct mention of her in bulletins published by the academy, the officers noted that some of their public lectures had drawn large audiences and that no department of modern investigation had awakened so much interest as had anthropology.[8] To F. W. Putnam, the curator of the Peabody Museum of American Archaeology and Ethnology at Harvard, she wrote that she was "trying to do her small share to strengthen the hands of scholars by awakening a public response."[9]

The expertise for these lectures came from wide reading and some excavating she had done in shell heaps in Maine and Massachusetts under the tutelage of F. W. Putnam. There is no record of when Alice Fletcher first met Putnam or how she came to study informally with him, but by 1879 she had caught his enthusiasm for the young and perennially underfunded field of anthropology in general and his own Peabody Museum in particular. Alice Fletcher enlisted in the cause and at first took her own task to be that of building public support and finding resources for projects Putnam wanted to accomplish. Soon, however, she became an independent scholar in her own right, a transition which Putnam supported and helped make possible. He encouraged her to present papers at the annual meetings of the American Association for the Advancement of Science. When the Archaeological Institute of America was founded in 1879, he helped her join.

The first annual report of the Archaeological Institute of America included a long paper by Lewis Henry Morgan, "A Study of the Houses of the American Aborigines," which ended with Morgan's proposals for work in American archaeology.[10] Alice Fletcher clipped out a newspaper review of the report and sent it to Putnam, along with her own comments:

> Mr. Morgan's paper, in common with much that he writes is suggestive, but one can not help wishing that he would not walk over the entire continent in such seven-league boot style with his favorite theory.[11]

She also wondered why Morgan wanted the AIA to take charge of the study of American antiquities. Would not a scientific institution be a better leader for such an enterprise than a group of laymen? In this she echoed what Putnam himself was thinking.

Alice C. Fletcher at her writing desk

Alice C. Fletcher with James Stuart and Chief Joseph

But Alice Fletcher's attention was soon diverted from archaeology and the AIA, as a chance came to experience Indian life at first hand.

In 1880 Alice Fletcher met Susette (Bright Eyes) La Flesche and Francis La Flesche, two young Omaha Indians who were traveling through the East with the journalist Thomas H. Tibbles and the Ponca Chief, Standing Bear, to arouse people against the removal of the Poncas from their tribal lands. Within a year she had made plans to travel west with Bright Eyes and Mr. Tibbles (who were by then husband and wife) and then push on farther alone. She wanted to study the life of Indian women, hoping to add to "the historical solution of 'the woman question' in our midst," and she wanted also to make a contribution to ethnology.[12] She sought advice from Putnam and from John Wesley Powell at the Bureau of Ethnology and set out in 1881 on the long trip to Nebraska.

For the next twenty years Alice Fletcher's concerns were mainly the life and problems of contemporary Indians. She lived and traveled with the Omahas for weeks at a time, learning their customs and listening to their fears that their land allotments dating from 1867 were not secure. She went herself to Washington, D.C. to urge the passage of the special Severalty Act for the Omahas in 1882, an act which was intended to make the land secure to the Omahas by giving them individual titles. Then at the request of the United States Indian Commissioner she went back to the reservation in 1883–1884 to make the land allotments to the Omahas. She knew that parcels of land alone would not solve the Indians' problems. Simultaneously she encouraged communal grazing schemes, helped young Indians to go away to the Carlisle Indian School in Pennsylvania or to the Hampton Institute in Virginia, and initiated a system of loans to help them build new homes when they returned to the reservation. She made public speeches, on behalf of the latter projects in particular. Her efforts, along with those of others, aroused so much public pressure for Indian education that in 1885 the United States Senate asked the secretary of the interior for a report on the progress of "Indian education and civilization," a report that she in turn was asked to prepare. She spent much of the next two years on it, traveling even to Alaska for a firsthand look at conditions there. The final report, nearly seven hundred pages long, was a massive survey of the Indian reservations and a history of the various government bureaus concerned with Indian affairs and of the treaties made with each tribe. N.H.R. Dawson, the commissioner of education, commended her "zeal, industry, and judgment."[13]

Inevitably she was drawn into the Lake Mohonk Conferences of the Friends of the Indian, a liberal and reformist group which met every fall from 1882 on at a Quaker resort on a lake in New York state. When she could not be present in person, she sent letters from the field which were read to the assembly.[14] Although small, the group, which included college presidents, judges, and clergymen, was a powerful political force. Their goal was citizenship for the Indians and the dividing up of Indian reservations as rapidly as possible. Due in large part to their efforts, the Dawes Act of 1887 extended the breaking up of reservations and the alloting of land in severalty to other Indian tribes at the discretion of the president.[15]

Again Alice Fletcher was asked to do some of the parceling out of the allotments. She worked among the Winnebagos from 1887 to 1889 and among the Nez Perces from 1890 to 1893, (see Plate IV) accompanied in the latter case by her friend E. Jane Gay, who learned photography in the hope that she would be named an official member of the party. In her letters from the field, E. Jane Gay left a graphic account of the hardships the two middle-aged women endured in the Nez Perce country in Idaho: mud, snow, wild pigs, bears, wild horses, reluctant Indians, and greedy white cattlemen.[16]

Alongside this political and official activity, Alice Fletcher kept up a steady undercurrent of ethnographic study, a study which was furthered by her close relations with the La Flesche family and by a sudden illness. In 1883 while she was making the Omaha allotments, she became very ill with inflammatory rheumatism. Francis La Flesche put her into his wagon and drove her sixty miles to the nearest mission station and throughout her convalescence continued to show concern for her. The warm bonds thus forged between them continued through the rest of her life. In 1891 when she was fifty-three she informally adopted Francis La Flesche, then age thirty-five, as her son, and thereafter she, Francis La Flesche, and E. Jane Gay made up a lively and much-frequented household at 214 First Street, S.E. in Washington, D.C.[17]

Another consequence of the illness was a permanent lameness; she had fallen while she was still weak and injured one leg, thereafter bent in a ninety-degree angle at the knee. This caused her to limp, but it did not stop her activity or burden her spirit. One young friend recalled that Alice

Fletcher could have her hearers convulsed with laughter as she told how she had once gotten into the sunken bath at Mrs. Hearst's hacienda and then could not get out again and had to call for help.[18]

To help her pass the long hours of her convalescence, the Omahas sang songs to her; and a whole new world, that of Indian music, opened up to her. She began to transcribe the songs, eventually with the aid of a graphophone and the assistance of Francis La Flesche. Together they built up the largest collection of Indian music then in existence. She also studied tribal ceremonies. The Omahas felt that she had helped them keep their land, and in gratitude they performed their secret calumet ceremony especially for her and gave her permission to study it and any other tribal rite she wished. Later they sent their Sacred Pole and articles from the sacred tent of war via her to the Peabody Museum for safekeeping.[19] In the early 1880s she presented papers to the AAAS on "The Sun Dance of the Ogallala Sioux," "Observations on the Laws and Privileges of the Gens in Indian Society," and "Symbolic Earth Formations of the Winnebagos." In 1884 the Peabody Museum published her descriptions of five different ceremonies among the Hunkpapa, Oglala, and Santee Sioux.[20] One particularly valuable aspect of Alice Fletcher's ethnography is that she almost always gave a detailed account of the circumstances in which she gathered the information, a practice which she began in these first reports. In 1886 Putnam appointed her officially an assistant at the Peabody Museum. There was some tension built into this appointment, however, because Putnam did not approve of the allotment work to which she was giving first priority. He kept his distance from the Lake Mohonk reformers.

Lewis Henry Morgan had by 1878 moved beyond conventional wisdom to declare that "Indian arts for the maintenance of life are far more persistent and effective than we are disposed to credit."[21] He suggested in *Nation* that instead of trying to turn them into farmers, the Plains Indians might be fit into the national economy by herding cattle in place of buffalo. They could perhaps supply meat for the whole eastern market. Another possibility was factory systems for Indian reservations.

F. W. Putnam wrote immediately to him:

> I believe so thoroughly that some such plan as you propose is the only hope for the Indians that I shall be glad to do all I can in working with you to bring it about.[22]

Morgan's illness and death and the success of the Lake Mohonk group put an end to such plans, but Putnam continued, however modestly, to support the Indians in their own way of doing things. He spoke out against abuses on the reservations and the forcible "civilizing" on the Indians in 1892 (for which Alice Fletcher chided him[23]). At the end of his life he supported an early pan-Indian group, the Society of American Indians, one of whose members was his friend and former student Arthur C. Parker, a Seneca.[24]

It was perhaps her disagreement with F. W. Putnam on Indian policy that led Alice Fletcher to make a rigid distinction between her work "for science" and her efforts in public policy. They were two separate aspects of her life, one which she discussed with Putnam and one which she did not. In the 1880s she read her ethnological papers to Section H of the AAAS and gave an account of her allotment work among the Omahas to Section I: Economic Science.[25] After a visit with Putnam and his wife in 1885 she wrote to them:

> Oh: how refreshing to get away from the seething interests of the "live Indian" and to contemplate Archaeological and historical problems. The heartache is gone out of them. . . .[26]

Often she expressed to Putnam her feelings of guilt at having to lay aside her scientific work for practical affairs. She assured him that it worked out for the best since, because the government paid her expenses, she could go places that would otherwise be impossible. But it was not easy to find time for scientific work. For a time on the Nez Perce reservation she tried to rise before dawn in order to work on ethnology before the regular work of the day began.

In a poignant letter to Putnam from Ft. Lapwai, Idaho in 1891, she described the dilemma. It was November, and she was living in a tent in the midst of storm and frost. She wrote:

> I have had the worst struggle of my life. I never met such greed. such a determination to rob a people, as I have found here in Idaho. One would think these Indians had hardly a right to live, and not a right to possess their land. . . . I wanted to complete my Century articles, to gather legends, to make measurements, all of which I could have done

but for the disturbances a lot of unprincipled men have been able to make. I have been distressed beyond words at all this. And mainly because I felt I was disappointing you.[27]

The Century articles were popular accounts she was writing for *Century Magazine* about life among the Omahas.[28] The measurements were physical measurements of the Nez Perces she was supposed to be getting for the physical anthropology exhibits that Putnam's assistant, Franz Boas, was putting together for the World's Columbian Exposition. But she kept at the Nez Perce allotments until they were finally finished in 1893.

The general failure of the allotment program has caused Alice Fletcher to be much criticized. It resulted in subsistence farming, if that, and massive legal complications, and by 1933 two-thirds of the land given out in allotments was in white hands.[29] How could a sensitive ethnographer be so blind to the seemingly inevitable results of forcing such drastic cultural change on unwilling and unprepared peoples? How could someone with her keen appreciation of Indian life turn into the martinet she became on the Nez Perce reservation, where they did not take kindly to her policies?[30]

The answer seems to be threefold. First of all, Alice Fletcher had adopted the point of view of the first Indians she met, the La Flesche family, whose views in fact were not shared even by a majority of the Omahas.[31] Joseph La Flesche, the half French, half Indian leader of the Omahas and the father of Susette and Francis La Flesche, saw allotment as a way of preventing "removal," the callous and brutal moving of whole groups of peoples away from their homes to barren lands to the south. A threat which constantly hung over them. But Joseph La Flesche also thought that the Indian way of life was a thing of the past. He encouraged his children to learn English and to go away to school. He worked to abolish his own office of chief because he believed the tribal system was an obstacle to the advancement of his people.[32] Ever afterward Alice Fletcher believed that forward-looking Indians held these same views.

The second factor is that Alice Fletcher worked out in the field where she felt the political heat of the white man's desire for Indian land. She knew that it was hardly a question of preserving the reservations. They were falling away before the intense pressures exerted by cattlemen, railroad men, and nearby settlers. The question was whether the Indians would get allotments of land or no land at all. Alice Fletcher worked doggedly to see not only that they got land but that it was the best land. She went herself to examine the sites, and she would not be bought off by white agents and settlers who hovered around wherever the land holdings were changing.

Finally, Alice Fletcher went west much influenced by the latest scientific thinking in anthropology, the ideas of Lewis Henry Morgan. If the American Indians were truly at the stages of Upper Savagery and Lower and Middle Barbarism, as Morgan had suggested, then the solution to their current troubles was for them to move as rapidly as possible up the ladder to Civilization. Instead of fighting off white society, the Indians ought to embrace it; they should prepare to compete with the white man on his own terms.

Fletcher seldom expressed her social evolutionist thinking, perhaps in deference to Putnam, who objected to such theorizing and insisted on straightforward, factual reports. Nevertheless, she dropped occasional hints. "I have taken such a 'header into barbarism', as a friend of mine puts it," she wrote to Putnam soon after she had arrived in Nebraska, "as I would not advise any lady to attempt."[33] She was most explicit in an early popular article for *Century Magazine*, "On Indian Education and Self-support," in which she wrote of the very different "sociologic status" of the Indian and of the "archaic form" of their society, which was perhaps comparable to the social condition that "preceded our present advancement."[34] Although Fletcher appreciated many aspects of Indian life (she noted that Indian women thought American laws with respect to the property rights of married women most unfortunate), in general she was convinced that "civilization" was higher, better, and above all, inevitable, in both practical and theoretical terms.

She was well aware of the plight the Indians found themselves in. From the Winnebago Reservation in Nebraska in 1887 she wrote a letter to her Lake Mohonk friends pleading with them not to desert the Indians, not to think that since the Dawes Act had passed their work was done.[35] Many difficulties still lay ahead. But the more difficulties she recognized and the more the Indians resisted allotment—the Nez Perces in particular would not cooperate—the more convinced she became that it was not only a way to secure the Indians' land but a positive good in its own right, for it would spur the Indians on to assimilation. Reformers thought her a noble woman, for unlike certain unnamed anthropologists who wanted "to preserve the Indian in order to study him,"[36] she was more concerned to help them. This she did even when "helping them" meant encouraging them to abandon their Indian customs as rapidly as possible.

By 1890 Alice Fletcher was a famous woman, honored for both her philanthropic and her scientific work. A wealthy Pittsburgh woman, Mrs. Mary Copley Thaw, gave a fellowship to Harvard University specifically to support her for the rest of her life. In honor of the Thaw Fellowship, friends gave a reception for her in Washington, D.C. in February of 1891, and eight hundred people came to shake her hand. Characteristically her comment to F.W. Putnam was:

> I felt glad of all this for your sake—for the honor was not to me but to the work which we have at heart.[37]

The fellowship strengthened her ties to the Peabody Museum, but she continued to live in Washington, moving about this time to the house on First Street purchased for her by Mrs. Thaw and other friends.

She was still very much under Putnam's tutelage. After a visit to the Columbian Exposition at Chicago in 1893, she wrote to him:

> I have learned much, and this, like so much else that has made my life worth anything, I owe to you. I can never forget your kindness, and the pains you have taken to open new fields of study to me. I only wish I could render you some return.[38]

The following year from the safe distance of Germany where she had gone on a trip financed by Mrs. Thaw, she dared to admit that sometimes she wished she were a man: "I am aware that being a woman I am debarred from helping you as I otherwise could."[39] But at the same time she was becoming a confident scholar in her own right, and her anthropology took on new depth as she went beyond the mere reporting of rituals and observed customs to serious theoretical analysis. Three examples of this in the years before 1900 are her account of the "Ghost Dance," her study with Francis La Flesche of Indian music, and her paper on totemism.

The infamous massacre of Sioux Indians at Wounded Knee, South Dakota, in December of 1890 was an outgrowth in part of the soldiers' reponse to Ghost Dance phenomena. Exactly one month before the massacre took place, Alice Fletcher read a paper on the Ghost Dance to the American Folk-Lore Society, a paper that ought to have had wider dissemination for in it she showed a profound understanding of what was happening. The spread of the Ghost Dance she saw as the result of a crisis situation where the Indians had been crowded off coveted lands onto tracts of barren soil. Their livelihood—the buffalo and other game—had been killed off, and their children were being educated in a new language with new ideas. Many Indians could find hope only in supernatural expectations, and they acted in accord with their belief that the "Indian Messiah" would come to their aid. Her sensitivity to social causation was not generally shared at the meeting. Franz Boas commented during the discussion that he thought that crazes like this should not be attributed to any great extent to politics but were probably nervous diseases.[40]

Franz Boas and Alice Fletcher could disagree however and still be friends. She thought highly enough of him to write to Putnam in 1896:

I wish that Dr. Boas was available [for an office in the AAAS], for he is one of our strongest, if not the best ethnologist we have. He has both brains and culture, he does not go off at half-cock.[41]

Two years later she found that she and Boas had converged on a similar interpretation of totemism. Independently they had each discovered that the totem, at least among the Omahas and the Northwest Coast tribes, was an individual's mascot become hereditary. The tribes did not believe, as J.G. Frazer and other European scholars had argued, that they were actually descended from the totem animal.[42] She hurried an article into print in order that Boas alone not be given credit for what was really an instance of simultaneous discovery.

Meanwhile she and Francis La Flesche worked on their collection of several hundred Omaha Indian songs. Their monograph "A Study of Omaha Indian Music" was published by the Peabody Museum in 1893. In addition she wrote a short book, *Indian Song and Story*, numerous articles on Indian music, and later the excellent entry on "Music and Musical Instruments" in the *Handbook of American Indians* published by the Bureau of American Ethnology. [43]

In 1898 Alice Fletcher began work on Pawnee rituals with two men from the Pawnee tribe, James R. Murie and Tahirŭssawichi. Their account of a long ceremony which she called "The Hako" was published by the Bureau of American Ethnology in 1904. [44] When that was finished, she and Francis La Flesche began to pull together the Omaha material into what became their most important work, *The Omaha Tribe*, a long monograph published in 1911. *The Omaha Tribe* was later described as "one of the most sought after studies ever published by the BAE." [45]

A new chapter in Alice Fletcher's life began in 1899 when she began to take an active part in the national affairs of the Archaeological Institute of America, an organization which was trying once again after a lapse of fifteen years to take on significant projects in American archaeology. Alice Fletcher took the problem to heart, and within ten years she had succeeded in establishing a school for American archaeology in Sante Fe, later the School of American Research. The project was not without its cost, however, for it meant estrangement from her friend and mentor, F.W. Putnam.

The AIA had started out in 1879 as a Boston organization, but the need for money and the fear that competing societies might be organized in other cities soon led the Bostonians to widen their base. They founded new societies in New York and Baltimore and joined the three together in 1884 in a reorganized AIA which thereafter consisted of affiliated local societies held together by a Council in which each society was represented. F.W. Putnam, who had fought in vain for an emphasis on American archaeology in the organization, dropped his membership at this time, but Alice Fletcher continued hers. She became a member of the New York Society but transferred to the Boston Society in 1889 when she became Thaw Fellow at the Peabody Museum. Two years later she dropped out completely, reappearing in 1895 as vice-president of the new Washington Society and moving to the Baltimore Society in 1899 when the Washington Society collapsed.

The AIA had undertaken one project in American archaeology. At the suggestion of Lewis Henry Morgan they had sponsored the work of Adolph Bandelier in the American Southwest from June of 1880 through 1884, and thereafter they continued to appeal for money to finance the printing of his long and expensive reports.[46] The failure of the organization to carry on American work after 1884 was deplored by some of its members. In 1888 an anonymous correspondent to the editors of the *American Journal of Archaeology*, the official organ of the Institute, complained that "American" in the title of the journal was misleading for one of the grandest fields of archaeology, that here at home, was being contemptuously and almost absolutely neglected. To this charge the editors, Charles Eliot Norton and the J.L. Frothinghams, Sr. and Jr., wrote a spirited reply. In America, they wrote, there was only prehistoric archaeology and then the American Indians, a race which lacked the "latent energy" to rise to civilization and so could not illuminate "the dim recesses of our own natures."[47] American archaeology deserved some space surely, but certainly not half the space in the journal as the correspondent had suggested.

This classicist view, that educated men partook in some way of the inherent genius that had given rise to the great civilizations of Greece and Rome but that was lacking in other societies, continued to dominate the AIA. In the same volume the editors printed an account of F.W. Putnam's archaeological work in the Ohio Valley and urged readers to give it substantial support, but tangible Institute support went elsewhere, in particular to the American School of Classical Studies in Athens, founded in 1882, and to a similar school established in Rome in 1895. Four vigorous local societies of the AIA had been launched in the Midwest by 1890, in Chicago, Detroit, Minneapolis, and Madison, but most of the funds other than membership dues continued to come from New England.[48]

It was a troubling drop in national membership between 1891 and 1896 that again brought up the question of American archaeology in the Council of the Institute. The drop coincided with a national financial depression, but the Council wondered if some American explorations might not stimulate interest in the AIA.[49] John Williams White from Cornell had succeeded Charles Eliot Norton and Seth Low from Columbia University as president of the AIA, and in 1897 he appointed a committee to look into the matter.

The committee's report a year later was discouraging, at least from the standpoint of the AIA. So much archaeological work was going on in the United States, supported by both the federal government and by private organizations and individuals, that there was hardly a place for the Institute with its limited resources.[50] The committee recommended, however, that a Council member be elected who would distinctly represent the interests of American archaeology. The Council agreed, and Charles P. Bowditch, a Boston businessman who had become interested in Mayan antiquities while on a pleasure trip to Yucatan in 1888, was chosen. Bowditch was the major benefactor of the Peabody Museum at Harvard, planning and largely supporting the annual expeditions of that museum to Central America. Beginning in 1898 Bowditch became the prime force in the AIA behind American projects, urging, in particular, although by no means exclusively, Central American projects.[51]

Bowditch brought F.W. Putnam back into the AIA in time for the twentieth anniversary meeting held at Yale in 1899. Charles Eliot Norton gave the major address, and half of the papers presented at the meeting were by people connected with the School at Athens, but Bowditch presided over one session on American archaeology in which F.W. Putnam and Alice Fletcher participated. Alice Fletcher felt that her invitation was due to Mrs. Sara Y. Stevenson of the American Exploration Society of Philadelphia.[52] In the light of later events it is interesting to note that she moved to prominence in the AIA, not through her associates at the Peabody Museum, but through a wealthy woman friend and patron.

Franz Boas joined the group in 1901 when the annual meeting was held in New York City. Boas gave a paper on "Some Problems in North American Archaeology,"[53] and subsequently he, Bowditch, and Putnam were formed into a committee for American Archaeology in the AIA. In 1901 they recommended Alfred Tozzer, a student of Putnam's, for the fellowship in American archaeology which had just been established by Bowditch, and Tozzer set off for Mexico to study the Maya and Lacandon Indians.

The AIA seemed to be settling in behind work in Central America, until suddenly it found itself being pulled across the country to the American southwest, almost through no fault of its own. Requests came in from California and Colorado for help in organizing local societies. Western men and women wanted to affiliate themselves with a prestigious national organization in order to call attention to the destruction of archaeological monuments which was going on all around them, destruction caused by careless travelers, local plunderers, and even by the military. Soldiers in the army of the United States, it was reported, "have been known to push an ancient building over a cliff into the canyon below 'just to see how it would sound.' "[54]

The two people in the AIA who had experience in preserving ancient monuments in the United States were F.W. Putnam and Alice Fletcher. She had helped him raise money among "the ladies of Boston" to purchase and preserve the Serpent Mound in Ohio, after which the Ohio legislature passed the first law in the country for the preservation of ancient monuments.[55] Subsequently she had urged the American Association for the Advancement of Science to try to get Congress to act on the matter, and in 1888 she and Matilda Stevenson were appointed a committee to see what they could do.[56] Nothing much came of their efforts, and Alice Fletcher realized that one of the problems was that there was no western scientific institution which could add its weight to pressure being brought to bear on Congress.[57]

Now in 1903 and 1904 there existed what was lacking before: western pressure. The AIA created an elaborate committee on the preservation of American antiquities which included Fletcher, Putnam, Boas, Bowditch, and many others, and they met with a similar committee from the American Anthropological Association to plan their lobbying strategy.[58] While these plans were being made, two of the most energetic of the western men, Charles Lummis and Edgar L. Hewett, took matters into their own hands. Lummis had gone to Harvard with Theodore Roosevelt, and calling up that old association, he and Hewett along with W.H. Holmes of the Bureau of American Ethnology and James Garfield, the Secretary of the Interior, called on Roosevelt at the White House and persuaded him to back their cause. In 1906 Congress passed a general bill for the preservation of American antiquities, the Lacey Act, and also a special bill for the preservation of the cliff dwellings in the Mesa Verde region of Colorado, a special project of Hewett's. Hewett and Lummis nominated the scientific institutions to be given permits for excavation, and that became the offical list.[59] Among the committee members, Boas and Putnam in particular were somewhat disgruntled, not wanting the granting of permission to fall into the hands of a single government official, but there was nothing they could do.[60]

Charles F. Lummis was the founder of the Society of the Southwest, a local society of the AIA and soon the marvel of the entire organization.

Lummis was a journalist, the editor of *Out West*, and the originator of the
slogan "See America First."[61] He had early won fame by walking to
California. Later he had accompanied Adolph Bandelier on some of the latter's explorations. Lummis founded the Society of the Southwest in Los
Angeles in 1903, and under his guidance the Society established the
Southwest Museum, sent out two archaeological expeditions, collected
hundreds of folksongs in Spanish and twenty-four Indian languages, and
gathered up photographs of southern California and books and paintings
from the Franciscan missions. The Southwest Society soon had more than
three hundred members, or one-fifth of the total membership in the AIA,
the result, Lummis explained happily, of applying modern business principles to the service of scholarship. They spent twice as much as any other
local society of the AIA on printer's ink and postage stamps, but also "an
important reason for the success of the Southwest Society is that it is *doing
things*."[62]

Charles F. Lummis represented not so much a coming together of business principles and scholarship, for that was fully developed in Charles P.
Bowditch, but a new energetic way of doing both. There was a sudden injec-
tion into the staid AIA of western energy, drive, and need for action. New
citizens of California, New Mexico, Colorado, and Utah, often with growing
fortunes, wanted to build local institutions and preserve local history. They
were carving out a future for themselves and their children, and they
wanted to adopt or create for themselves a worthy past. Lummis wrote to
Charles Eliot Norton in 1906:

> Our public is intensely conscious locally and intensely patriotic. . . .
> we are incredibly strained to be not only good citizens of our own gen-
> eration, but to be our own fathers, grandfathers, and great-
> grandfathers, none of whom were here to provide us with the things
> that as thoughtful Americans we desire to have.[63]

Lummis and others did not really feel they needed help in what they were
doing, but they wanted national recognition, and they were not averse to
adding the prestige of an eastern organization to their projects.

The AIA was eager to cooperate. They were now truly a national organization, and the activities of the western societies allowed them, almost

painlessly, to carry out one of their stated purposes and silence their critics. In general the annual expenses of the organization had been covered by membership dues. With the sudden jump in membership, the AIA found itself for the first time with extra money. It seemed only fair to spend it on American projects. The committee on American archaeology, Putnam, Bowditch, and Boas, was enlared in 1905 to include J. Walter Fewkes of the Bureau of American Ethnology, Francis W. Kelsey from the University of Michigan, Alice Fletcher, and Charles Lummis, and they were given increased appropriations to spend. They published Tozzer's final report on his four years as Fellow in American Archaeology, paid Putnam $500 for explorations in California caves, and gave some money directly to the Southwest Society.[64]

In 1906 Edgar L. Hewett applied for and received the American fellowship. Hewett was a professional educator and an active member of the Colorado Society of the AIA. He had decided in 1903 at the age of 38 to give up the presidency of New Mexico Normal University in Las Vegas in order to devote full time to anthropology. He had inquired about the possibility of studying under Putnam in California, for his wife's health would not permit their moving to Cambridge,[65] but ended up enrolled for a Ph.D. at Geneva, Switzerland. The work Hewett proposed to do in 1906, a broad survey of the Southwest and Mexico suggested to him by Fewkes, was very different from the specific project which Tozzer had done under the direction of the committee, but they decided to let him go ahead.[66] So in 1906 besides his lobbying activity in Washington, D.C. for the Lacey Bill, Hewett did surveys in Colorado and Utah, assisted in explorations sponsored by the Southwest Society, and traveled down through Mexico to Mexico City.[67]

In Mexico Hewett looked up Alice Fletcher who was visiting Zelia Nuttall at the latter's home, Casa Alvarado at Coyoacan, D.F. Alice Fletcher accompanied him on field expeditions in the valley of Mexico and at Puebla and Cholula and down to Oaxaca, Monte Alban, and to Mitla, observing his field methods and talking over the work with him. Together they began to make plans for work in American archaeology that would soon throw the American committee of the AIA into turmoil.

From Mexico Alice Fletcher wrote to F.W. Putnam, praising Hewett's work. She was eager to talk with Putnam and Bowditch and have them meet with Hewett. Of the AIA she wrote:

I have held on from the foundation of this Organization thro. all these years waiting for the dawn of the day that now seems to be coming— and I want to tell you and Mr. Bowditch frankly what I have observed and lay certain matters before you. [68]

Without comment Putnam passed the letter along to Bowditch to read.

Then Alice Fletcher heard of the growing restlessness of the Southwest Society, and her plans took on new urgency. She rightly sensed that they were "at an important juncture of affairs"[69] in American archaeology. Eight years earlier it had seemed that there was so much archaeological activity in the United States that there was hardly room for the AIA, but that situation had been changed by the death in 1902 of John Wesley Powell.

John Wesley Powell had created the Bureau of Ethnology in 1879, the same year in which Charles Eliot Norton founded the AIA. For the next twenty years Powell thought of himself as the hub or work in archaeology and anthropology within the United States. But under Powell's quiet and more modest successor, W.H. Holmes, the Bureau had declined in activity, appropriations, and aspirations. At the same time the museums and university departments of anthropology which F.W. Putnam had built up with private philanthropy began to look farther afield than the Americas. Mrs. Hearst's collections which were the nucleus of the department at the University of California included materials from around the world. The Jesup expedition under Boas and Putnam at the American Museum of Natural History had gone into Siberia, and Boas was trying to extend work to China. Even had they been willing to limit their work to the confines of the United States, university departments and museums could not take the Bureau's place as a coordinating agency for there was rivalry between them, and none had the inherent power of a government agency.

The decline of the Bureau of American Ethnology left a void, and it was Alice Fletcher who sensed this and set about to fill it. The western societies of the AIA needed to be convinced that the national organization could continue to be of value to them. What better way could there be to solve these two problems than to bring them together? The AIA could become the new coordinating agency for work in American archaeology. It would need to have a center in the Southwest near the western societies and in the heart of the most important archaeological area in the country.

Alice Fletcher presented her plan to the Committee on American Ar- chaeology in December of 1906. She proposed that the AIA undertake "the preparation of a map of the culture-areas of the American continent, as a contribution to the world-study of the human race,"[70] that a Director of American Archaeology be appointed to coordinate the work of the local societies in accordance with the basic plan, and that a school of American archaeology be established to give instruction in field research. The Com- mittee accepted her plan as a general long range program, hoping it would inspire the western societies to full cooperation, and as a first step ap- pointed Hewett Director of American Archaeology in the AIA.

In response to a notice tacked up by Tozzer at Harvard, A.V. Kidder, Sylvanus G. Morley, and J.G. Fletcher went to Colorado in the summer of 1907 to learn field archaeology under Hewett. Jesse Nusbaum began his work as a photographer at Mesa Verde in 1907, and the Utah Society spon- sored an expedition led by Byron Cummings which included Neil Judd among the student workers. It was a golden summer, for these men were among the leaders in Southwest archaeology during the next several decades.

Events were moving too fast for Bowditch, who resigned as chairman of the American committee in October of 1907, suggesting Alice Fletcher to take his place. There was great interest in the proposed School of American Archaeology. Santa Fe wanted it, and four other cities made informal over- tures. "The Western people are alive and willing—more so than the East at present realizes," Alice Fletcher wrote to Putnam.[71] In December she pushed the proposed School through the annual meeting of the AIA, and it became an established fact.

Putnam cautioned her to go slow, but more serious opposition began to come from Franz Boas. Boas had been working with the German ar- chaeologist Edouard Seler and with Nicholas Murray Butler, president of Columbia University, on plans for an International Archaeological School in Mexico City, to be sponsored jointly by Mexico, Germany, France, Swe- den, the AIA, the Hispanic Society of America, Harvard, and Columbia. The project was about to be launched after delays owing to political compli- cations, and Boas wondered if Hewett's plan which included work in Mexico might not jeopardize it. He thought too that an American School ought to include more than archaeology, and he wondered about Hewett's qualifications.[72]

Hewett traveled in the western states in 1908 seeking support for the School from state universities and from legislatures and then, on a five month leave of absence, went to the University of Geneva to complete his doctorate, visited the AIA schools at Athens, Rome, and Jerusalem, and studied excavations in Egypt, Syria, and Greece. There was extensive correspondence between him and Alice Fletcher through these months as they both braced themselves for the coming struggle with Franz Boas. Boas had told Hewett in New York that he thought students should spend a year studying linguistics with him at Columbia before going out into the field, and they had also argued about the best way to train students:

> He [Boas] holds that the student, even in an observational science must read, read, read, before going into the field, so that he will know what he is looking for and how to interpret what he sees; taking occasion to criticise Prof. Putnam's methods in rather uncomplimentary terms. I pointed out the fact that in the matter of method Prof. Putnam stands exactly with Agassiz and practically all teachers of science of our time. He holds, however, that they carry it to great extremes. Well, our discussion probably resulted in a "draw". . . .[73]

The confrontation came in November of 1908 when the committee on American archaeology met in Cambridge. Alice Fletcher presided, Putnam was elected secretary, and Boas, Bowditch, and Hewett were also present. Four of the nine committee members were absent: the President and Secretary of the AIA, Francis W. Kelsey and Mitchell Carroll, Mrs. John Hays Hammond, and Charles Lummis. Unexpectedly it was Bowditch who took the floor and for three hours argued against turning the American committee into an American school. His point of view carried, for Putnam and Boas voted with him. The controversy was only beginning, however, for Alice Fletcher and Hewett undid the results of the meeting by sending mail ballots to the absent members of the committee, all of whom voted with them.[74] Alice Fletcher also ordered Sylvanus G. Morley, who had just been appointed Fellow in American Archaeology, to go to Washington to help Hewett with work there. She did it on her own authority and without consulting other members of the committee.

It was too much for Bowditch who was now wrathful. He sent a strongly worded protest to Alice Fletcher and also, backed by Putnam, to the council of the AIA. It was then Alice Fletcher's turn to express her sorrow, regret, and astonishment that Putnam had thus joined in calling into question her actions. "Dr. Tozzer tells me that you and Mr. Bowditch do not wish to have the American School take its place beside the other schools of the Institute," she wrote.[75] But, she protested, the American School already exists. It was established a year ago. There must be a school, for no one will endow a committee.

Alice Fletcher and Hewett had their way. The Committee on American Archaeology vanished, and in its place appeared the Managing Committee of the School of American Archaeology. Through the spring of 1909 Putnam, Boas, and Bowditch deliberated as to what form their opposition should take, Putnam still hoping that everything could be arranged harmoniously.[76] Finally, however, when a meeting of the American Committee promised for June was suddenly cancelled and when the Bowditch-Bixby Fund for Central American work was put in the general treasury and Bowditch was almost deliberately insulted, Putnam, Boas, and Bowditch sent in their resignations from the American committee and withdrew from the AIA.[77]

Alice Fletcher was clearly hurt, not by the actions of Boas and Bowditch from whom she had learned to expect opposition, but by Putnam's abandoning what she believed they had both been working for. Her concern to organize research in American archaeology, to encourage local projects, to establish new centers which could appeal to new and growing sources of support—these projects were in the Putnam tradition. He too had sensed the potential in the Far West, and, although his plans for California had not gone as he had hoped, he would have liked to have tried again. But a long friendship with Bowditch and a renewed friendship with Boas, who had just arranged the grand celebration for his seventieth birthday, deterred him. He chose to resign from the committee, limply giving as his reason the pressure of his own work.[78]

Alice Fletcher persevered. She studied Spanish architecture to prepare herself for decisions in the repairing of the Old Palace in Sante Fe which the Territory of New Mexico gave to be used jointly by the School and the Museum for New Mexico. She visited the summer field camps and presided over the annual meetings of the Board of Regents of the School of American Archaeology until 1912 when she turned the chairmanship over to W.H. Holmes.

Alice Fletcher made a triumphant trip to England in 1910, recognized as one of America's most famous anthropologists. She spoke to the British Association for the Advancement of Science, was elected a vice-president, and even invited to preside, although she declined. She gave an address at Cambridge, visited Oxford, and met the leading British anthropologists. The Englishmen found the amount of anthropological activity going on in America astounding, she reported to Miss Mead, Putnam's faithful secretary, and she tried "to give our dear Professor all credit and also the Peabody Museum."[79]

Alice Fletcher wrote frequently to Miss Mead in these years, and it is as if it were a way of writing to Putnam without actually doing so. She sent him messages, wanting him to know that she was still working for the science they had at heart.[80]

The School of American Archaeology began well. Adolph Bandelier, Byron Cummings, Kenneth M. Chapman, S.G. Morley, John P. Harrington, and Jesse L. Nusbaum were all on the staff. Hewett brought Earl Morris into archaeology,[81] and Morris worked at Aztec, New Mexico under the auspices of the St. Louis Society of the AIA, while A.V. Kidder began work at Pecos. Morley's lifelong study of the ancient Maya began while he was connected with the School of American Archaeology. The Carnegie Institution of Washington did not take on his work until mid-1914.

A transition in the School took place in 1916 as Santa Fe found itself the center of a growing art colony. Robert Henri, Marsden Hartley, and John Sloan were among the painters who gathered there, and writers came too, including D.H. Lawrence who went to Taos in the early 1920s. Hewett was partly responsible for making Santa Fe an art colony, for he described it and the Indian culture in the Southwest so glowingly to Robert Henri, whom he had met in San Diego in 1916, that Henri came to spend the summers of 1916, 1917, and 1922 in Santa Fe. His presence and his enthusiasm attracted many other painters.

Hewett seized on this new possibility with his usual energy. He found studio space for the painters and arranged to have art shows at the Old Palace. In the pages of *Art and Archaeology*, a popular monthly journal published by the AIA, he began to publicize the native and modern art of the Southwest.[82] Late in 1916 he changed the name of the School of American Archaeology to the School of American Research, a change that would indicate, he hoped, the new broadening of its interests. He wrote:

No reason is recognized for limiting research to scientific subjects. The artists who are painting here are just as truly researchers as are the scientists. . . . In truth, anthropologists, with a few conspicuous exceptions, have done scant justice to the Indian culture. . . . It is through the artists and poets and scientists combined that this remarkable race is at last being truthfully represented.[83]

Once again Hewett was taking on new projects and spreading his resources thinner then ever, but he was not seriously challenged. William Henry Holmes did not even visit Santa Fe after 1918, but he stayed on as chairman of the managing committee of the school until 1922 when he was replaced by Frank Springer, a Las Vegas attorney, who was the School's most generous benefactor and the donor of the new Art Museum.

One of the continuing problems of the School was that the massive funding Hewett and Alice Fletcher had envisioned did not materialize. The Southwest Society loosened its connections with the AIA even while the School was being planned in 1907. Potential donors in Colorado lost interest when the School was located in Sante Fe, and New Mexico proved to be a small financial base from which to draw. It was a noble idea—to find regional support for a great scientific institution in the Southwest, but it was difficult to bring about. It was finally one of the new national philanthropic foundations which came to the aid of the anthropologists in Santa Fe.

The founding in 1927 of the Laboratory of Anthropology was a vindication of Alice Fletcher's conviction that there should be a center for anthropology in the American Southwest. John D. Rockefeller, Jr. gave the money for the Laboratory, and the incorporators were many of the most prominent American anthropologists including Roland Dixon of Harvard, F.W. Hodge of the Museum of the American Indian, Clark Wissler of the American Museum of Natural History, Neil Judd, A.V. Kidder, S.G. Morley, and Earl Morris. Kidder became the chairman of a large board of trustees which included both Franz Boas and Edgar L. Hewett.[84] The latter remained director of the School of American Research for nearly twenty more years, until his death in 1946.

Although Hewett's critics and detractors were many,[85] he made fundamental contributions. He brought many of the leading American archaeologists of the next generation into the field. His field schools and camp sessions were precursors of the Pueblo Bonito conferences arranged by Neil Judd and A.E. Douglass in 1922, 1923, and 1925 and of the Pecos Conferences Kidder called together beginning in 1927.[86] In promoting the arts and cultures of the American Southwest, he helped to write a whole chapter in the cultural history of the United States in the twentieth century. Most important of all, he led the campaign to preserve archaeological monuments in the Southwest, including Mesa Verde, Chaco Canyon, Frijoles Canyon (Bandelier National Monument), and the ruins at Jemez, Pecos, Quivira, and Quarai. W.H. Holmes wrote in 1916:

> it is the School of American Archaeology, under the direction of Dr. Edgar L. Hewett, that has probably done more than all other agencies combined to explore, expose, protect, and make available to the public and to science these truly marvelous achievements of prehistoric American genius.[87]

This was his—and Alice Fletcher's—most lasting legacy.

Alice Fletcher died in Washington, D.C. in 1923 at the age of eighty-five. Francis La Flesche tended her devotedly through her long final illness.[88] She left an institution, the School of American Research, a classic ethnography based on twenty-nine years of close association with the Omahas, *The Omaha Tribe,* and pioneering studies of Indian music. She had started a movement to preserve archaeological monuments. She had tried to help Indian peoples keep their land. Looking back over her life near its end, she said:

> There is no story in my life. It has always been just one step at a time—one thing which I have tried to do as well as I could and which has led on to something else. It has all been in the day's work.[89]

Elsewhere however Alice Fletcher explained herself in a deeper and truer, albeit more sentimental, fashion. There is a bronze tablet in her honor on the south wall of the patio of the Art Museum in Santa Fe. On it are these words of hers:

Living with my Indian friends I found I was a stranger in my native land. As time went on, the outward aspect of nature remained the same, but a change was wrought in me. I learned to hear the echoes of a time when every living thing even the sky had a voice. That voice devoutly heard by the ancient people of America I desired to make audible to others.[90]

At one level this was clearly her goal: to help Americans appreciate Indian life and the "high-mindedness" of which Indian peoples were capable.[91] But she here also gave expression to something scarcely allowed out of her own subconscious because of her respect and affection for F.W. Putnam, a conviction that anthropology must move out from the East Coast establishment to where land and sky reassert themselves and where most Indian peoples live. This was at least one of the meanings for her of the School of American Research in Santa Fe.

Notes and References

1. Charles F. Lummis, "In Memoriam. Alice C. Fletcher," *Art and Archaeology*, XVI (1923), 75–76.

2. Nancy O. Lurie, "Women in Early American Anthropology," in June Helm, ed., *Pioneers of American Anthropology* (Seattle, University of Washington Press, 1966), 45. Lurie quotes Paul Radin in personal conversation.

3. Margaret Mead, *An Anthropologist at Work: Writings of Ruth Benedict* (Boston, Houghton Mifflin, 1959), 3–5.

4. "Brief Biographical Account of Alice C. Fletcher," MS., Alice Fletcher Papers, National Anthropological Archives, Smithsonian Institution.

5. Thurman Wilkins, "Alice Cunningham Fletcher," in Edward T. and Janet James, eds., *Notable American Women, 1607–1950* (Cambridge, The Belknap Press

of Harvard, 1971), 630–633; "Biographical sketch of Alice Fletcher," 3 pp. MS., Peabody Museum Archives.

6. Jane Gay Dodge, "Brief Biography of E. Jane Gay," typewritten MS., Schlesinger Library, Radcliffe College.

7. Program for lectures, Nov., 1879, sponsored by the Minnesota Academy of Sciences, Alice Fletcher Papers.

8. N.H. Winchell, "Address by the President," *Bulletin of the Minnesota Academy of Sciences*, I (1880), 390; P.L. Harch, "Address by the President," *Bulletin of the Minnesota Academy of Sciences*, II (1881), 11.

9. A.C. Fletcher to F.W. Putnam, Jan. 3, 1880, Peabody Museum Papers, Harvard University Archives.

10. Lewis Henry Morgan, "A Study of the Houses of the American Aborigines," *First*

Annual Report, Archaeological Institute of America, 1879–1880 (1880), 27–77.

11. Fletcher to Putnam, July 15, 1880, Peabody Museum Papers.

12. Fletcher to Lucien Carr, Aug. 3, 1881; Fletcher to Putnam, Aug. 10, 1881, both in Peabody Museum Papers. The alacrity with which Alice Fletcher seized this opportunity suggests that it was not a new idea to her. An early popular account of her life states that once in her reading she came upon the story of the scholar who left Oxford to follow the wandering gypsies and learn their wisdom, and that she then had the idea of going someday to do likewise in her own country among the Indians. (Mary R. Parkman, *Heroines of Service,* New York, The Century Company, 1918, 215).

13. Alice C. Fletcher, *Indian Education and Civilization.* A Report Prepared in Answer to Senate Resolution of February 23, 1885, under the Direction of the Commissioner of Education, Washington, D.C. (1888), 10.

14. *Proceedings of the Fifth Annual Meeting of the Lake Mohonk Conference of the Friends of the Indian* (1887), 12–13, 63–69.

15. Francis Paul Prucha, ed., *Americanizing the American Indians: Writings by the "Friends of the Indian", 1880–1900* (Cambridge, Harvard University Press, 1973), 103. Also on the Dawes Act see Frederick E. Hoxie, "Beyond Savagery: The Campaign to Assimilate the American Indian, 1880–1920," Ph.D. dissertation, Brandeis, 1977 and Wilcomb E. Washburn, *The Assault on Indian Tribalism: the General Allotment Law (Dawes Act) of 1887* (Philadelphia, 1975).

16. *Choup-Nit-Ki: Letters of Jane Gay from Idaho* (London, 1905), 2 vols., in the Schlesinger Library, Radcliffe College. See also Allen C. and Eleanor D. Morrill, "The Measuring Woman and the Cook," *Idaho*

Yesterdays, 7 (1963), 2–15, A.C. and E.D. Morrill, "Talmaks," *Idaho Yesterdays,* 8 (1964), 2–15, and A.C. and E.D. Morrill, *Out of the Blanket: The Story of Sue and Kate McBeth, Missionaries to the Nez Perces* (Moscow, The University Press of Idaho, 1978).

17. Margot Liberty has written perceptively on La Flesche's contributions to anthropology in "Native American 'Informants': The Contribution of Francis La Flesche," John V. Murra, ed., *American Anthropology: The Early Years,* 1974 Proceedings of the American Ethnological Society (St. Paul, West Pub. Co., 1976), 99–110 and "Francis La Flesche, Omaha, 1857–1932," in Margot Liberty, ed., *American Indian Intellectuals,* 1976 Proceedings of the American Ethnological Society (St. Paul, West Pub. Co., 1978), 44–59. Carobeth Laird describes a dinner with Fletcher and La Flesche in Washington in 1918 in *Encounter with an Angry God: Reflections of My Life with John Peabody Harrington* (Morongo Indian Reservation, Banning, California, Malki Museum Press, 1975), 82–83.

18. Jane Gay Dodge, "Brief Biography of E. Jane Gay," typewritten MS., Schlesinger Library, Radcliffe College.

19. Francis La Flesche, "Alice C. Fletcher," *Science,* LVII (1923), 116; Alice C. Fletcher, "The sacred pole of the Omaha Tribe," *Proc., AAAS,* XLIV, 44 (1895), 270–280.

20. See *Proc. AAAS,* XXXI (1883), 580–584, XXXII (1884), 395–397, XXXIII (1885), 615–617, 654–665; *Sixteenth Annual Report of the Peabody Museum,* III (1884), 260–333.

21. Lewis Henry Morgan, "The Indian Question," *Nation,* 27 (1878), 332. See also L.H. Morgan, "The Hue and Cry Against the Indians," *Nation,* 23 (1876), 40–41 and

L.H. Morgan, "Factory Systems on Indian Reservations," *Nation*, 23 (1876), 58–59. In the last work he wrote before his death Morgan expressed the hope that no national administration would ever adopt the late Secretary of the Interior Carl Schurz's allotment plan for dividing up reservations, for he had personally observed the disastrous effects of that policy among the Shawnee tribe in Kansas. (Lewis Henry Morgan, "Houses and House-Life of the American Aborigines," in *Contributions to North American Ethnology*, IV, U.S. Geographical and Geological Survey of the Rocky Mountain Region, (1881, 80–81). See also Fred Eggan, "Lewis H. Morgan and the Future of the American Indian," *Proceedings of the American Philosophical Society*, 109 (1965), 272–276.

22. Putnam to Morgan, Nov. 30, 1878, Lewis Henry Morgan Papers.

23. Fletcher to Putnam, Oct. 18, 1892, Putnam Papers. Alice Fletcher told Putnam that the facts he had were incorrect and also that as an important official at the Chicago Exposition, he should be above politics. Commissioner Thomas Morgan's policies at this time however included a system of fines, withholding of rations, and prison terms for Indians who participated in the sun dance, scalp dances, or war dances, who consulted medicine men or kept their children out of school. See Francis Paul Prucha, ed., *Americanizing the American Indians: Writings by the "Friends of the Indian," 1880–1900* (Cambridge, Harvard University Press, 1973), 302.

24. Hazel W. Hertzberg, *The Search for an American Indian Identity: Modern Pan-Indian Movements* (Syracuse University Press, 1971), 111. On Parker see Hazel W. Hertzberg, "Arthur C. Parker, Seneca, 1881–1955," in Margot Liberty, ed., *American Indian Intellectuals*, 128–138 and Hazel

W. Hertzberg, "Nationality, Anthropology and Pan-Indianism in the Life of Arthur C. Parker (Seneca)," *Proceedings of the American Philosophical Society*, 123 (1979), 47–72.

25. Alice C. Fletcher, "Lands in Severalty to Indians; Illustrated by Experiences with the Omaha Tribe," *Proc. AAAS*, XXXIII (1885), 654–665.

26. Fletcher to Putnam, July 18, 1885, Peabody Museum Papers.

27. Fletcher to Putnam, Nov. 11, 1891, Peabody Museum Papers. See also Fletcher to Putnam, Sept. 20, 1889, Aug. 6, 1891, Peabody Museum Papers.

28. Alice C. Fletcher, "Politics and 'Pipe-Dancing'," *Century Magazine*, 45 (1893), 441–455; "Indian Songs: Personal Studies of Indian Life," *Century Magazine*, 47 (1894), 421–431; "Hunting Customs of the Omahas," *Century Magazine*, 47 (1895), 691–702; "Tribal Life Among the Omahas," *Century Magazine*, 51 (1896), 450–461.

29. Nancy O. Lurie, "Women in Early American Anthropology," in June Helm, ed., *Pioneers of American Anthropology*, 51 refers to Harold C. Fey and D'Arcy McNickle, *Indians and Other Americans* (New York, 1959) on the results of the Dawes Severalty Act.

30. She and Jane Gay telegraphed the U.S. Indian Commissioner to stop the "heathen celebrations" which the local agent was allowing, and as a result the tribe split. See A.C. and E.D. Morrill, "Talmaks," *Idaho Yesterdays*, 8 (1964), 10.

31. D.S. Otis, *The Dawes Act and the Allotment of Indian Lands*, ed. and with introduction by Francis Paul Prucha (Norman, University of Oklahoma Press, 1973), 42. Otis's excellent study was originally published in 1934 in Readjustment of Indian affairs (hearings on H.R. 7902 before the

House of Representatives' Committee on Indian Affairs), pt. 9, 428–489 under the title "History of the allotment policy."

32. Norma Kidd Green, *Iron Eye's Family: The Children of Joseph La Flesche* (Lincoln, Nebraska, Johnsen Publishing Co., 1969), 47.

33. Fletcher to Putnam, Nov. 7, 1881, Peabody Museum Papers.

34. *Century Magazine*, IV (1883), 312–315.

35. "Letter from A.C. Fletcher from Winnebago Agency, Nebraska, Sept. 23, 1887," in *Proceedings of the Fifth Annual Mohonk Conference of the Friends of the Indian* (Philadelphia, 1887), 14–17.

36. Prucha, *Americanizing the American Indians*, 10. Richard H. Pratt, the head of the Carlisle Indian School, made this charge against the Bureau of American Ethnology. (Elaine Goodale Eastman, *Pratt, the Red Man's Moses*, Norman, University of Oklahoma Press, 1935, 188–194)

37. Fletcher to Putnam, Feb. 8, 1891, Putnam Papers.

38. Fletcher to Putnam, Nov. 7, 1893, Putnam Papers.

39. Fletcher to Putnam, Oct. 19, 1894, Peabody Museum Papers.

40. Alice C. Fletcher, "The Indian Messiah," *Journal of American Folklore*, IV (1891), 57–60. Boas's comments are in the same vol., 5–6. Fletcher's social insights were borne out by James Mooney's classic study, although Mooney also compared the visionary aspects of the Ghost Dance with other religious phenomena related to trances, visions, and seizures. See James Mooney, *The Ghost-Dance Religion and the Sioux Outbreak of 1890*. Fourteenth Annual Report of the Bureau of Ethnology (1896).

41. Fletcher to Putnam, June 22, 1896, Peabody Museum Papers.

42. Fletcher to Franz Boas, Oct. 11, 1897 and Jan. 10, 1898, Franz Boas Papers, American Philosophical Society Library. Alice C. Fletcher, "The Import of the Totem," *Science*, n.s. 7 (1898), 296–304; Franz Boas, "The Origin of Totemism," in *Race, Language, and Culture* (New York, The Free Press, 1940), 316–323, an expansion of earlier statements written in 1896, 1897, 1898, and 1916. In 1940 Boas dissociated himself from the "American theory" of totemism, writing that no single psychic process produced the wide variety of phenomena lumped together as "totemism." But Alice Fletcher had never made that wide a claim. She was concerned to show that J.G. Frazer's theory was based on erroneous data (he had used a quotation from J. Owens Dorsey which was a misrepresentation of the Omaha saying), and she made explicit the fact that she was discussing totemism only as it existed among the Omahas.

43. Alice C. Fletcher aided by Francis La Flesche and J.C. Fillmore, "A Study of Omaha Indian Music," *Archaeological and Ethnological Papers*, Peabody Museum of American Archaeology and Ethnology, I (1893), 237–287; A.C. Fletcher, "Love Songs among the Omaha Indians," *Memoirs*, International Congress of Anthropologists, ed. by C. Staniland Wake (Chicago, The Schulte Publishing Co., 1894), 153–157; "Music and Musical Instruments," *Handbook of the American Indians North of Mexico*, Bureau of American Ethnology, Bulletin 30 (1907, 1910), 958–961; "Music as Found in Certain North American Indian Tribes," *The Music Review* (1893), 534–538; A.C. Fletcher, "Indian Songs," *Century Magazine*, XLVII (1894), 421–431; John C. Fillmore, "A Study of Indian Music," *Century Magazine*, XLVII (1894), 616–623; A.C. Fletcher, "Indian Songs and Music,"

Proc. AAAS, XLIV (1896), 281–284; "Indian Songs and Music," *Journal of American Folk-lore*, XI (1898), 85–104; *Indian Story and Song from North America* (Boston, 1900).

44. Alice C. Fletcher and James Murie, *The Hako: A Pawnee Ceremony*, Twenty-Second Report of the Bureau of American Ethnology (1904); A.C. Fletcher, "A Pawnee Ritual Used When Changing a Man's Name," *American Anthropologist*, I (1899), 82–97; A. Fletcher, "Tribal Structure: A Study of the Omaha and Cognate Tribes," *Putnam Anniversary Volume* (1909), 254–267.

45. Alice C. Fletcher and Francis La Flesche, *The Omaha Tribe*, Twenty-Seventh Report of the Bureau of American Ethnology (1911); Neil M. Judd, *The Bureau of American Ethnology: A Partial History* (Norman, University of Oklahoma Press, 1967), 52.

46. Adolph F. Bandelier, "Historical Introduction to Studies among the Sedentary Indians of New Mexico," *Papers of the Archaeological Institute of America*, I (1881), 1–33; "A Visit to the Aboriginal Ruins in the Valley of the Rio Pecos," *Papers of the Archaeological Institute of America*, I (1881), 34–133; "Report of an Archaeological Tour into Mexico in the Year 1881," *Papers of the Archaeological Institute of America*, II (1884); "Final Report of Investigations among the Indians of the Southwestern United States, carried on mainly in the years from 1880–1885," Parts I and II, *Papers of the Archaeological Institute of America*, American Series, III, IV (1890–1892).

47. *American Journal of Archaeology*, IV (1888), 260.

48. *Eleventh Annual Report of the Archaeological Institute of America* (1890), 53.

49. "Eighteenth Annual Report of the Archaeological Institute of America," in *American Journal of Archaeology*, 2nd ser., I (1897), 82.

50. "Nineteenth Annual Report of the Archaeological Institute of America," in *American Journal of Archaeology*, 2nd ser., II (1898).

51. Alfred M. Tozzer, "Charles Pickering Bowditch," *American Anthropologist*, XXIII (1921), 354; "Twentieth Annual Report of the Archaeological Institute of America," *American Journal of Archaeology*, 2nd ser., III (1899), 665. Bowditch's suggestions ranged from major projects such as following the migrations of ancient tribes of Mexico or investigating thoroughly a particular locality to such things as sponsoring lecturers on American archaeology, giving prizes for the best original work in American archaeology, and undertaking facsimile publications of some of the Mexican codices.

52. Fletcher to Putnam, Oct. 10, 1899, Putnam Papers.

53. Franz Boas, "Some Problems in North American Archaeology," *American Journal of Archaeology*, 2nd ser., VI (1902), 1–6.

54. "Twenty-Fourth Annual Report of the Archaeological Institute of America," in *American Journal of Archaeology*, 2nd ser., VII (1903), Supplement, 6.

55. Fletcher to Putnam, July 3 (no year—1886?), Putnam Papers.

56. Alice C. Fletcher, "On the Preservation of Archaeologic Monuments," *Proc. AAAS*, XXXVI (1888), 317; A.C. Fletcher and T.C. Stevenson, "Report of the Committee on the Preservation of Archaeologic Remains on the Public Lands," *Proc. AAAS*, XXXVII (1889), 35–37.

57. Fletcher to Putnam, Aug. 5, 1887, Putnam Papers. An act passed in 1890 for the preservation of Casa Grande was due largely to the efforts of Mrs. Mary Hemenway. (F.W. Putnam, "The Serpent Mound of

Ohio," *Century Magazine*, April, 1890, 873).

58. Twenty-fifth and Twenty-sixth Annual Reports of the Archaeological Institute of America in Supplements to the *American Journal of Archaeology*, VIII (1904), 5 and IX (1905), 5. Charles Lummis and Edgar L. Hewett were also members of the Archaeological Institute of America committee.

59. Dudley C. Gordon, "Lummis and the Lacey Act," *The Masterkey*, 42 (1968), 17–19.

60. Franz Boas to Putnam, Feb. 26, 1904, March 7, 1904; Putnam to Boas, April 6, 1904, Franz Boas Papers, American Philosophical Society Library.

61. Hope Gilbert, "He Discovered the Southwest for Americans," *The Desert Magazine* (Sept., 1944), 13–16.

62. "Twenty-sixth Annual Report of the Archaeological Institute of America," in *American Journal of Archaeology*, IX (1905), Supplement, 4. See also *Eighth Bulletin*, The Southwest Society of the Archaeological Institute of America, including Seventh Annual Report (Los Angeles, Calif., 1911).

63. C.F. Lummis to Charles Eliot Norton, Dec. 9, 1906. Norton sent Bowditch a copy of the letter which is in the C.P. Bowditch Papers, Archives of the Peabody Museum, Harvard.

64. Charles P. Bowditch, "First Report of the Committee on American Archaeology," *American Journal of Archaeology*, IX (1905), 41–44. Almost immediately however, Norton and Bowditch among others began to fear that if the Institute grew too rapidly Eastern academics would lose control of it. (Norton letters to Bowditch, 1907, Charles P. Bowditch Papers) Two groups, the scholars and the popularizers, subsequently struggled for many years for control of the AIA.

65. Hewett to Putnam, Aug. 1, 1903, Peabody Museum Papers.

66. Franz Boas to Putnam, Feb. 7, 1906, Franz Boas Papers.

67. Charles P. Bowditch, "Report of the Committee on American Archaeology," *American Journal of Archaeology*, X (1906), 5.

68. Fletcher to Putnam, Oct. 30, 1906; also Fletcher to Putnam, Aug. 29, 1906, both in F.W. Putnam Papers.

69. Fletcher to Putnam, Nov. 4, 1906, Putnam Papers.

70. Charles P. Bowditch, "The Work of the Institute in American Archaeology," *American Journal of Archaeology*, XI (1907), 47, quoting from her report.

71. Fletcher to Putnam, Oct. 10, 1907, Putnam Papers.

72. F. Boas to Putnam, Jan. 8, 1908, Franz Boas Papers. For the work of the International School in Mexico see Franz Boas, "Summary of the Work of the International School of American Archaeology and Ethnology in Mexico, 1910–1914," *American Anthropologist*, XVII (1915), 384–391, A.M. Tozzer, "Report of the Director for 1913–1914," *American Anthropologist*, XVII (1915), 391–395, and Ricardo Godoy, "Franz Boas and His Plans for an International School of American Archaeology and Ethnology in Mexico," *Journal of the History of the Behavioral Sciences*, 13 (1977), 228–242.

73. Hewett to A.C. Fletcher, March 14, 1908, A.C. Fletcher Papers, National Anthropological Archives.

74. Minutes of the Committee on American Archaeology, AIA, meeting of November 14, 1908, Boas Papers (in Boas-Putnam correspondence); Fletcher to members of the Committee on American Archaeology, Dec. 19, 1908, Boas Papers.

75. Fletcher to Putnam, Dec. 30, 1908, Putnam Papers.

76. Putnam to Boas, March 4, 1909; Boas to Putnam, March 8, 1909, Boas Papers.

77. F. Boas to C.P. Bowditch, Nov. 19, 1909; Putnam to Bowditch, Dec. 20, 1909; text of Bowditch's remarks at the AIA meeting, Dec. 1909; memoranda: "My Reasons for Distrusting Dr. Edgar L. Hewett" and "My Reasons for No Longer Trusting Miss Alice C. Fletcher," by C.P. Bowditch, and *Correspondence between Edgar L. Hewett and Franz Boas* (privately printed, 1910), all in C.P. Bowditch Papers, Peabody Museum Archives.

78. Fletcher to Putnam, July 30, 1909, Putnam Papers.

79. Fletcher to Miss Frances H. Mead, July 12, 1910; also Dec. 22, 1910, Peabody Museum Papers.

80. In a letter to Miss Mead on Sept. 17, 1910, Alice Fletcher actually addressed herself in one paragraph to Putnam and then, realizing her mistake, went back over it correcting the pronouns (Peabody Museum Papers). Fletcher and Putnam did exchange a few letters directly in these years.

81. Florence C. Lister and Robert H. Lister, *Earl Morris and Southwestern Archaeology* (Albuquerque, University of New Mexico Press, 1968), 10.

82. Two issues of *Art and Archaeology*, IX (1920) were devoted to American Indians, with emphasis on the Southwest. There were articles by Hewett, Fletcher, La Flesche, Holmes, and Frances Densmore, and the painter Marsden Hartley called for the development of an "American esthetics" based on Indian ceremonies. Later that year D.H. Lawrence wrote, "America, Listen to Your Own," in *The New Republic*, 25 (Dec. 15, 1920), 68–70. See also William Innes Homer, *Robert Henri and His Circle* (Ithaca,

Cornell University Press, 1969), 202, 205, and Paul A. F. Walter, "The Santa Fe-Taos Art Movement," *Art and Archaeology*, IV (1916), 330–338.

83. Edgar L. Hewett, "Report of the Director of American Archaeology," *Bulletin of the AIA*. IX (1918), 33.

84. "Museum and Laboratory for the Study of Indian Life," *Science*, 71 (Jan., 1930), 61–62. The Laboratory was an outgrowth of the Indian Arts Fund which the Rockefellers had also supported.

85. Some of the charges against Hewett were that he was tight-fisted and authoritarian and a hard man to work for, and more generally, that he spread himself too thin, did only superficial work, and wrote only popular books. See fn. 77 and 86.

86. Neil M. Judd, *Men Met Along the Trail* (Norman, University of Oklahoma Press, 1968), 129. See also Alfred V. Kidder, "Reminiscences in southwest archaeology, I.," *The Kiva*, 25, No. 4 (1960), 1–32.

87. W.H. Holmes, "Masterpieces of Aboriginal American Art: V. The Great Dragon of Quirigua," *Art and Archaeology*, IV (1916), 269. See Paul A. F. Walter, Sr., "A Half Century of Achievement," in Donald D. Brand and Fred E. Harvey, eds., *So Live the Works of Men*. 70th Anniversary Volume honoring Edgar Lee Hewett (Albuquerque, University of New Mexico Press, 1939), 46. J.J. Brody in *Indian Painters and White Patrons* (Albuquerque, University of New Mexico Press, 1971), 85 writes that besides bringing Anglo artists to Sante Fe, Hewett did more than any other single person to encourage modern Indian painting.

88. Francis La Flesche to Miss Emma Jane Gay, April 20, 1923, E. Jane Gay Papers, Schlesinger Library, Radcliffe College. There are several facts, however, which hint at an ambivalence that Francis La Flesche

felt about the course of his own life. In his later years as a recognized anthropologist he was active in pan-Indian movements, whose goals were counter to the assimilation of Indians for which Alice Fletcher had worked, and in 1918 he testified in Congressional hearings in favor of the peyote religion. It was, he said:

responsible for the moral regeneration of the Omaha, following a period after allotment when drunkenness and lawlessness prevailed on the reservation and when the Indian Bureau, the Indian Rights Association, and the missionaries did "absolutely nothing!" (Hazel W. Hertzberg, *The Search for an American Indian Identity: Modern Pan-Indian Movements*, Syracuse University Press, 1971, 266).

There is also the matter of his two wills. Alice Fletcher left the income from her estate to Francis La Flesche, with the provision that after his death it should go to the School of American Research. When Francis La Flesche wrote a will in 1928, he left money to the School of American Research, to Rosa his third wife with whom he had lived only briefly, and to a nurse-caretaker. Then he went back to Nebraska where he died in 1932 after writing a second will in which, with no mention of the first will, he gave everything to his brother. As Norma Kidd Green noted in *Iron Eye's Family: The Children of Joseph La Flesche*, 204–205, the two wills spoke of two separate sides of his life, never completely reconciled. The second will was contested by Hewett, Rosa, and the nurse, and the case was settled out of court. Susette La Flesche was similarly troubled at the end of her life. See Dorothy Clarke Wilson, *Bright Eyes: The Story of Susette La Flesche, an Omaha Indian* (McGraw-Hill, 1974).

89. Mary R. Parkman, *Heroines of Service* (New York, The Century Company, 1918), 230.

90. Santa Fe tablet.

91. It is in this context that a comment of Franz Boas's about her ought to be interpreted. Boas wrote that Alice Fletcher did not like Kroeber's collection of Arapaho traditions for some of the stories were extremely gross, and she "wanted to know only the ideal Indian, and hated what she called the 'stable boy' manners of an inferior social group." (Franz Boas, "History and Science in Anthropology: A Reply," *American Anthropologist*, XXXVIII 1936, 137–141), reprinted in F. Boas, *Race, Language and Culture*, (New York, The Free Press, 1940, 1966), 306.

Chapter Four
Frank Hamilton Cushing
(1857–1900)

There is no stranger figure in the history of American anthropology than Frank Hamilton Cushing. Brilliant, quixotic, he was called a genius by his friends, and among American anthropologists he may have first claim to that label. He was the first to do field work of the sort that has become the foundation of twentieth century anthropology, and he fumbled his way to the modern concept of "culture" or better, "cultures," with implications of wholeness, plurality, and relativism. These are only two among a host of structures for work in anthropology that Cushing pulled out of his own short and tumultuous life.

Cushing's scientific work was intensely personal. His was a full-blown anticipation of the confessional styles of Malinowski and Lévi-Strauss. But with Cushing it was more than style. It was also method and content. Cushing acted first and then thought about what he had done. He threw himself along the path of his own intuition and afterward stepped back to reflect disarmingly upon what had happened. The results were sometimes triumphs, sometimes disasters, and as Cushing threaded his way along, he could scarcely see which was which. Subsequent generations of anthropologists have been equally puzzled as to the meaning and value of his work.

Frank Hamilton Cushing was born on July 22, 1857, in a little village in Erie County, Pennsylvania. At birth he weighed one and a half pounds, and for the next eighteen months he was kept on a pillow.[1] His father, a physician, moved the family to Barre Center in western New York when Frank was three years old. Dr. Thomas Cushing was a free-thinking and rather eccentric man. He did not insist that his son attend school regularly, and Frank spent much time wandering alone in the woods. The area was rich in Indian remains, and the collection of these and of geological specimens became young Cushing's greatest interest. His keen eyes learned to recognize abandoned Indian camp sites simply from changes in the ground cover. Although Cushing had several siblings, he seems not to have played much with them or with other children, perhaps because of his frailness. He spent hours poring over the family dictionary and often went into the woods carrying it on his head. a practice which may have contributed both to his erect carriage and to his subsequent elegant literary style. He liked to tinker and showed marked mechanical ability. He made himself a ship mounted on wheels and, at another time, wings with which he jumped out of a barn loft, serenely confident that he would be able to fly.

In 1870 the family moved to the town of Medina, New York, and Frank built himself a hut in which he often lived for several days at a time. It was there that he made the astonishing discovery that a bone—it was a piece of an old toothbrush—could be used to take flakes off a flint-like substance. Cushing made an arrowhead and then another and another until his hands were cut and bruised.[2] It was the first instance of his uncanny ability to re-produce items of Indian technology. Eventually he invented techniques of basket weaving, pottery forming and firing, skin tanning, and copper embossing, all of which enabled him to make objects almost identical with the Indian originals.

A neighbor who was interested in what Cushing was discovering urged him to write to Joseph Henry and Spencer F. Baird, the officers of the Smithsonian Institution, and in its Annual Report for 1874 the Smithsonian Institution published the seventeen year old boy's paper on "Antiquities of Orleans County, New York." Cushing enrolled briefly at Cornell University in 1875 intending to study geology, but he left after a few months to become an assistant in ethnology at the Smithsonian. There he helped prepare the exhibits which the National Museum was putting together for the Philadelphia Centennial Exposition, and at the Exposition he astonished visiting archaeologists with his knowledge of native handicraft and his demonstration of arrowhead making. The following year at the age of nineteen he was named Curator of the Department of Ethnology at the National Museum.

Cushing's arrowhead discovery was exciting partly because of the importance that was beginning to be given to crude arrowheads and stone tools. After 1865, when Sir John Lubbock coined the terms "palaeolithic" and "neolithic," crude stone tools were often labelled "paleoliths" and were taken to be evidence that tool-making man had lived in America since before the last ice age. In 1869 while John Wesley Powell was on his famous trip down the Colorado River, he saw Shoshoni Indians making arrowheads that resembled paleoliths. This turned Powell against the idea that Paleolithic man had inhabited the New World, and his Bureau of Ethnology became an active center of opposition to that theory.[3] Cushing had now shown that the technique was so non-esoteric that a young boy could discover it. But the fact that some "paleoliths" were not old did not mean that none were. The whole question of when a "paleolith" is truly paleolithic was not settled until William Henry Holmes made a definitive study of the problem in the 1890s.

In Washington Cushing soon entered into John Wesley Powell's orbit, and Powell supported him thereafter with a steadfastness that was remarkable, through extended leaves of absence for illness or better offers and even through professional scandal. Cushing moved first to a study of the Zuni Indians, next to Southwestern archaeology with the Hemenway expedition, then to manual investigations of Indian technology, and after that to archaeological exploration in the muck along the Florida Keys. When he died at the age of forty-three, he had just begun a new shell heap project in Maine. Powell watched with a kind of helpless fascination as Cushing immersed himself in a project, threw out after much pressure a few brilliant but unfinished pieces, and then with masses of unpublished material in his head and his notes, moved on to a new interest. Of them all it is the first, his Zuni study, which makes him the important figure that he is.

Cushing's identification with the Zunis began in the summer of 1879 when Spencer Baird, then Secretary of the Smithsonian, asked him if he would like to accompany a collecting expedition to the Hopi and Zuni villages in the Southwest. Collecting meant acquiring objects of native manufacture for the National Museum in exchange for a few trinkets. Cushing was delighted to leave the confines of the museum, and he hoped to be able to collect, not material objects, but data on life in the pueblos. He got instructions from Powell, who was the immediate supervisor of the expedition, and then set out with Colonel and Mrs. James Stevenson and J.K. Hillers, the photographer who had accompanied Powell into the Grand Canyon. He expected to be gone about three months.

Cushing and the others arrived at Zuni in late September. The party camped on the plain north of the pueblo, and visits were made back and forth. Gradually the work of the expedition was begun. The Stevensons did

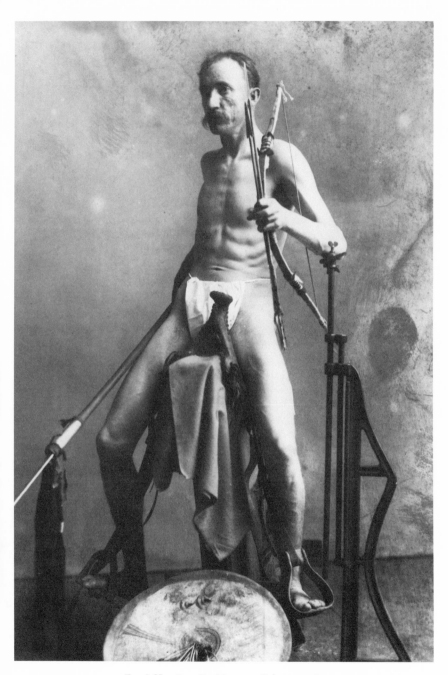

Frank Hamilton Cushing as a Dakota warrior

the trading,[4] Hillers took photographs, and Cushing wandered about the pueblo, taking notes and making sketches. He made friends with the children, but the older people showed increasing hostility toward his recording activities. Finally, seeking an ally in the pueblo, he moved uninvited into a room in the home of the governor of the pueblo. There he stayed when, after some weeks, the rest of the Stevenson party moved on to the Hopi.

Cushing's acceptance into Zuni society came slowly and by stages. First he was watched constantly, and the governor, Palowahtiwa, and others urged him repeatedly to stop his sketching activity. Tension built to a crisis point, a religious ceremony during which Cushing was threatened and might perhaps have been killed, had he not responded by brandishing his own knife and boldly exhibiting (rather than hiding) his sketchbook. This show of bravery won the respect of Palowahtiwa who henceforth took charge of him. When the Stevensons on their way back to Washington brought Cushing official permission to remain longer in the pueblo, Palowahtiwa decided to make the best of it. Cushing was given a Zuni costume, and his own clothing and hammock disappeared. "Here," said Palowahtiwa:

> take these two blankets,—they are all you can have. If you get cold, take off all your clothes and sleep next to the sheepskins, and *think* you are warm, as the Zuni does. You must sleep in the cold and on a hard bed; that will harden your meat. And you must never go to Dust-eye's house [the Mission], or to Black-beard's [the trader's] to eat; for I want to make a Zuni of you. How can I do that if you eat American food?[5]

"With this," Cushing wrote, "he left me for the night." Later Cushing had his ears pierced in a special ceremony, and he was given the name Té-na-tsa-li or Medicine Flower, in recognition of the effectiveness of some of the simple remedies he had brought with him.

Cushing described his introduction into Zuni life in a three part series, "My Adventures in Zuni," which was published in *Century Magazine* in 1882–1883. Like the other few things that Cushing brought to completion, "My Adventures in Zuni" was more than it appeared at first to be. On the surface a simple account of his adventures, it was actually a careful description of the cycles of Zuni life interwoven with the story of his own slow penetration into it. He took the reader through the seasons of the year in

Zuni and through the cycle of human life, from his own "birth" into Zuni
society to, at the end, the death and burial of an aged Zuni who had been his
friend. Already Cushing's wry stance, now inside, now outside the society,
the intricacies of his mind, and his impressive synthesizing abilities were
apparent.

Cushing stayed at Zuni on the first trip for two and a half years, leaving
only to visit Fort Wingate or to explore mines and archaeological remains in
the area or to visit nearby Indians including the Hopi and the Havasupai.
He kept in touch with Spencer Baird and John Wesley Powell, who discussed his activities in the annual reports they wrote for, respectively, the
Smithsonian Institution and the Bureau of Ethnology. To Baird and Powell
and other friends in the East, Cushing complained of the food and the physical conditions under which he lived and of his health. His work was interrupted frequently by his serious illnesses, pulmonary difficulties, and
stomach troubles. His wants were continuous: would they give him more
time, more money, more supplies? At Zuni Cushing set a pattern that continued through the rest of his life, of spending more than he had, borrowing,
and being constantly in debt.

Baird and Powell repeatedly urged Cushing to return to Washington, but
he resisted. In an attempt to placate them, he added collecting to his other
activities. He urged Spencer Baird to send him, not trinkets, which the
Zunis disdained, nor military goods, which could scarcely be given away,
but ocean shells, raw cotton, and imitation turquoise and blue and green
stones.[6] For Baird personally, who was an ornithologist, Cushing gathered
eggs of various species of woodpeckers, eagles, hawks, falcons, and owls.[7]

In October of 1881 after Cushing had been at Zuni for two years, he was
initiated into the lowest rank of the sacred order of Priests of the Bow. The
initiation marks the point at which Cushing's status changed from that of an
outsider to that of an insider in Zuni life. As whole new realms of knowledge
were opened to him, he realized that his work had just begun. There were
twelve other degrees in the society of the Priesthood of the Bow and ten different medicine orders in the tribe. Although Cushing had hoped to leave
Zuni for good at the beginning of 1882, now he could not. He wrote to
Spencer Baird asking for permission to stay in Zuni for one or two more
years. He had however a different plan for the immediate future. He wanted
to bring a party of Zuni elders to Boston and Washington on a three month
tour.

Cushing wanted to return to the East for several reasons. He hoped, in company with his Zuni friends, to attract attention and to find financial support for his work. He also hoped to get married. The Zunis had been pressing him to take a Zuni bride, but he had other intentions. Cushing and Emily Tennison Magill, the daughter of a Washington banker, were married in Washington, D.C. in July, 1882 in the middle of the Zuni trip.[8] But aside from personal matters and his obvious enjoyment of all the publicity surrounding the trip, Cushing was after something else. He had a debt to the Zuni people which he wanted to repay.

Cushing was pioneering in a new method of ethnological investigation. Sylvester Baxter, the Boston journalist who became one of Cushing's major publicists, thought Cushing's method consisted simply in making himself one with the people he was studying.[9] But in Cushing's own mind it was more complex than that, for although he might "become a Zuni," he was still always something else, a member of a different society which he had no desire to turn his back on. Cushing preferred to describe his method as "the reciprocal method."[10] Folklore and myths were not collected but rather exchanged. He liked to note for the Zunis similarities between their method of ritual response and that of the Church of England, or similarities between their epic and the *Iliad*. In storytelling rounds at night in the pueblo of Zuni, he took his turn by telling European folktales. The trip to Washington, D.C. and Boston with Naiiutchi and Kiasi, senior and junior priests of the Order of the Bow, Palowahtiwa, the governor, Pedro Pino, the aged governor, and Nanahe, an adopted Hopi,[11] was Cushing's way of returning their hospitality, his way of showing them his society as they had shown him theirs.

It was difficult, however, to explain all of this to Spencer F. Baird, who resisted even Cushing's hint that, as a result of the trip, he might be able to get a series of the Zuni sacred dancing costumes for the National Museum.[12] Cushing's kind of ethnography was costing more than Baird had anticipated and seemed more clearly related to the work of the Bureau of Ethnology than to that of the National Museum. In January of 1882 Baird accepted an offer from John Wesley Powell, who even agreed to pay Cushing's debts, and Cushing was transferred officially to the Bureau of Ethnology.[13]

The trip East, despite its occasional carnival quality, was for Cushing and the Zunis a serious affair. The party of six took a train to Chicago where they admired elephants, witnessed a dance at the Palmer House, and went to a play at the Grand Opera House. In Washington, D.C. they were greeted by President Chester A. Arthur. Pedro Pino stayed with James and Matilda Stevenson in Washington, while the rest of the party went on to Boston, where Cushing hoped to find financial backing. The response in Boston, immediately, and in the long run (the Hemenway expedition), surely exceeded Cushing's fondest hopes. The mayor took them to a minstrel show, three receptions were given for them in the Old South Meeting House, and before an overflowing audience in the Hemenway Gymnasium at Harvard, Cushing harangued the crowd and then led his friends in a ceremonial dance.[14] F.W. Putnam guided them through the Peabody Museum in Cambridge and held a reception for them in his home.[15] Journalists waited on the shore of the Boston harbor while, in boats provided by the mayor, the Zunis were carried out to Deer Island. There they performed a ritual ceremony and replenished one of their sacred possessions, a quantity of sea water.[16]

From Boston, Cushing and the Zunis returned to Washington, D.C. where Cushing lectured and introduced his friends to the National Academy of Sciences and to the Anthropological Society of Washington. On one of these occasions, when Cushing appeared, as he often did, in his Zuni outfit, John Wesley Powell growled at him to "go home and get dressed."[17] Powell was trying to get some of Cushing's work into print, and Cushing did during the trip produce "Zuni Fetishes" for the Second Annual Report of the Bureau of Ethnology. One evening in Washington, Cushing and one of the Zunis called on Alice Fletcher and Francis La Flesche. With her customary thoroughness, Alice Fletcher made detailed notes afterward on the Zuni's dress and manners and the comparisons they had made between Zuni and Omaha customs.[18]

Late in the summer of 1882, Cushing took his new bride and two Zuni companions, Palowahtiwa and Naiiutchi, to visit his old home in New York State.[19] En route they stopped at the Seneca Iroquois reservation of Tonawanda, the same reservation where in 1846 Lewis Henry Morgan and two friends had been adopted into the Seneca tribe.[20] Here Cushing was astonished to discover what he called "the tenacity of Indian customs."[21]

The Seneca Iroquois had been in close contact with whites for three generations. Some of them remembered Cushing who as a young boy had purchased bows and baskets from them. When he came dressed as a Zuni however, he was received as such. The party was warmly welcomed and was adopted into the Seneca tribe. After guarded inquiry about Zuni songs, sacred dances, and medicine practices, the Seneca performed their own sacred dances, which were different from any Cushing or his father had ever seen at local fairs. Cushing found that the Seneca still spoke their native language and had kept intact their government institutions, folklore, and myths, notwithstanding the modern appearance of the reservation with its churches, schoolhouses, steam thrashing machines, and automatic binder reapers. In a letter to Sylvester Baxter which Baxter immediately published, Cushing announced his discovery. The lesson he drew from it immediately was that young would-be investigators did not have to travel as far as Zuni to do the kind of work he was doing. The larger lesson, the staying power of "customs," he continued to mull over in his mind.

The need for money to help finance the trip East drove Cushing to try his own hand at popular journalism. Besides "My Adventures in Zuni," he wrote an account of his journey to visit the Havasupai for the *Atlantic Monthly* in 1882. Cushing's popular articles, along with those of Alice Fletcher and John Wesley Powell were the beginning of a new phase in American literature on the Indians, coming after the confusions and inaccuracies in James Fenimore Cooper's *Leatherstocking Tales* and Longfellow's *Hiawatha*.[22] Cushing's description of the Havasupai, "The Nation of Willows," was later substantiated with only minor exceptions by Leslie Spier's *Havasupai Ethnography*.[23]

By October of 1882 Cushing was back at Zuni, this time accompanied by his wife, her sister, and a cook. He now had his own household, but his work was constantly interrupted by his illnesses and by various political controversies. He angered the Navahos by shooting at their horses, which he claimed were on Zuni land, and he helped the Zunis fight off a land grabbing scheme in which a powerful United States Senator, John A. Logan of Illinois, was involved.[24] It was probably both political considerations and the increasing concern of Cushing's friends for his health which caused John Wesley Powell to recall him to Washington in 1884.[25]

Upon his return Cushing wrote one report for the Bureau of Ethnology. "A Study of Pueblo Pottery as Illustrative of Zuni Culture Growth" showed his facility in the Zuni language and contained his famous analysis of the change in Zuni pottery after the Spanish conquest. The Spanish brought horses and sheep, and after their arrival the Zunis made fewer baskets but more pottery, although the quality of the pottery deteriorated. Cushing's explanation was that horses increased trade with nomadic tribes from whom the Zunis got baskets so they made fewer of their own. Sheep dung was a handy source of fuel for firing pots, but it was not as good as brush wood or coal so the pots which were made were inferior.[26] Such were the complicated and far-reaching effects of culture contact.

To make money, Cushing sent nineteen installments on "Zuni Breadstuff" to an Indianapolis grain trade journal, the *Millstone*, which published them in 1884–1885. Later republished in book form, *Zuni Breadstuff* is a tour de force of what can be learned of a society from a study of its food habits.[27] Cushing described the many things Zunis make from corn, ranging from breads and sweets to fermented drinks and survival packs for long journeys. He discussed other foods and the folklore, philosophy, ritual ceremonies, and social customs connected with each of them. He described agricultural practices, including irrigation and earth banking, and hinted that his readers might learn something from the Zuni way of farming. It was a brilliant series of articles and his most comprehensive account of Zuni life.

But Powell wanted more formal reports. Each year in the annual report of the Bureau of Ethnology he wrote hopefully of the work Cushing was doing. Meanwhile Cushing fell ill repeatedly and took extended vacations.

A way out of the stalemate into which Cushing had settled came in mid-1886, when the elderly Boston philanthropist, Mrs. Mary Hemenway, invited Cushing and his wife to visit her. Cushing took a leave of absence from the Bureau, and they moved into a cottage on the Hemenway estate at Manchester-by-the-sea. Palowahtiwa, Waihusiwa, and Heluta came from Zuni to help Cushing with his linguistic work and stayed for several weeks. Out of their joint efforts came a superb collection of Zuni folktales, which was published in a beautiful volume after Cushing's death with photographs taken at Zuni by J.K. Hillers and A.C. Vroman.[28] It was *Zuni Folk Tales* which led Edmund Wilson to claim that Cushing ought to have been recognized not only as a classic anthropologist but also as an artist.[29] Also included in this volume is what was probably one of the first folklore experiments in the field.[30] At Manchester-by-the sea, Cushing had told the Italian tale of "The Cock and the Mouse." Nearly a year later he happened to hear Waihusiwa retell the story at Zuni, and, recognizing the importance of this for comparative studies on modes of thought and methods of making folktales, he carefully recorded Waihusiwa's version.

Over afternoon tea Cushing explained and interpreted the folktales to Mrs. Hemenway, and he found himself persuading her to finance an archaeological expedition to the Southwest. Cushing hoped to find ancient Zuni cities which might prove to be a link between the great pre-Columbian civilizations in Mexico and South America and contemporary tribes in New Mexico. He hoped also to find evidence for his hypothesis that the sevenfold division of space he believed characteristic of Zuni thinking had been common to all sedentary tribes in western America. This was presumably the great vision he set before Mrs. Hemenway, after which, as Cushing wrote later, "Mrs. Hemenway honored me with greater confidence in my ability to carry on such a work than I possessed of myself."[31]

The Hemenway Southwestern Archaeological expedition, as it came to be called, was the first major expedition to go to the American Southwest. Besides Cushing, who was in charge and who intended to do the ethnology and supervise the archaeology, Dr. Herman F.C. ten Kate was invited as a physical anthropologist, and Adolph Bandelier was hired as historian. Charles A. Garlick, a topographical engineer, became field manager for the expedition, and John Wesley Powell had a hand in two appointments: his brother-in-law, Professor Almon H. Thompson, as geographer-business manager and Frederick Webb Hodge from the Bureau of Ethnology as Cushing's secretary and personal assistant. Mrs. Cushing and her sister, Miss Margaret Magill, were also in the group.[32] Cushing, not yet thirty years old, set out in December of 1886 with generous financial backing, a superb staff, and the enthusiastic approval of his superiors in Washington, D.C.

Immediately however the expedition was plagued by Cushing's penchant for publicity and soon also by his ill health. He delayed the departure for the field in order to entertain Mrs. Hemenway and her party who were passing through Albuquerque on their way to California.[33] Then hardly had he surveyed the field when he announced to the local press an unfortunately

erroneous conclusion: that the Zunis were descendants of the Toltec race
who had once lived in the area. Through intense summer heat in the Salt
River Valley and despite severe stomach pains Cushing tried to keep going,
but by August he was spending most of his time on the cot in his tent. Back
in Massachusetts Sylvester Baxter and Captain John Bourke recommended
to Mrs. Hemenway that Dr. Washington Matthews, an Army surgeon who
was studying the Navahos, take over Cushing's responsibilities.

Ten Kate had not yet arrived to join the expedition, and Matthews was
disturbed to find that the human bones which were unearthed at Los Muertos were being neglected. He had an anatomist, Dr. Jacob L. Wortman,
sent out from the Army Medical College with preservation materials, and
meanwhile he persuaded Cushing to try to regain his health in the more
favorable climate of California.[34]

In California away from the expedition, Cushing did begin to feel better.
Soon he was travelling around the state answering the questions of reporters
and giving lectures before large audiences on Zuni life and his recent discoveries in the Salt River Valley.

In January of 1888 he was back at work. The Los Muertos area had proved
to be rich in ruins, and the staff of the expedition traced some one hundred
and fifty miles of prehistoric irrigation canals. Sylvester Baxter spent several months at the camp, gathering material for the extensive publicity he
was soon to give the expedition in *The Boston Herald* and in *The American
Architect and Building News*.[35] He and Cushing made a special trip to see
Casa Grande, the famous prehistoric ruin which had just been declared a
national monument partly through the efforts of Mrs. Hemenway.

Sylvester Baxter returned to the East in April, and shortly thereafter
Cushing fell ill again. He moved the excavations to new sites up the Salt
River Valley, but in October he returned to Washington, leaving the work in
the care of Hodge. The following summer Mrs. Hemenway sent Dr. Jesse
Walter Fewkes to Arizona first to report on the state of the expedition and
then to take it over and reorganize it. Under Fewkes it continued at intervals
until Mrs. Hemenway's death in 1894.[36]

The Hemenway expedition is usually considered a failure. Emil Haury,
who worked on the Hemenway materials for his doctoral dissertation, was
hard on Cushing, as was Frederick Webb Hodge, who wrote in an introduction to Haury's book of Cushing's "uncanny insight" but also of his "over-
wrought imagination" and of the "woefully small body of descriptive

data."[37] On the other hand, Cushing's attempt to investigate the ancient and modern sedentary cultures of western America has been called the beginning of the problem-centered archaeology of the next century.[38] Cushing described what is now known as the Hohokam culture, and he studied the ruins of an extensive irrigation system in southern Arizona. A final contribution to have come from the Hemenway expedition has scarcely yet been recognized. This is the modern anthropological concept of culture.

In 1871 the English anthropologist E.B. Tylor published a two volume work, *Primitive Culture*, in which he defined "culture or civilization" as

> that complex whole which includes knowledge, belief, art, morals, law, custom, and any other capabilities and habits acquired by man as a member of society.[39]

With Tylor, the term "culture" entered anthropology. What Tylor meant by culture however was not what a contemporary anthropologist means, that is, the unique social heritage or way of life of a particular society. Culture, for Tylor, was the level of civilization of a society, its place on the ladder of social evolution.[40] Tylor had little or no sense of cultural pluralism (except in the hierarchical sense), of cultural relativism, or of cultures as integrated, coherent units. Culture was singular, consisting of amount or degree of civilization, measured on a universal scale. What was required to get from Tylor's concept of culture to the modern anthropological understanding was a person unusually sensitive to the richness and integration of another society and singularly free of ethnocentric bias. Cushing was, perhaps uniquely among anthropologists in the late nineteenth century, just such a person. Yet even for him this new way of looking at human societies came only slowly, step by step.

Cushing had sensed when he first went to Zuni that their way of living in the world was different from but as complex as his own. He had grown up in a free-thinking household. He did not have sectarian religious training. His formal schooling was haphazard. All of this suggests that he may have grown up less committed than were many of his contemporaries to the major belief systems of his society, such things as patriotism, Christianity, progress, and civilization. At the same time he had lived in an area rich in enthusiasms: the same upstate New York which had produced Joseph Smith and the Mormons, and Shakers, and "burned over" areas of fervent evangelism. He himself ranged up and down the ladder of human emotions, being by turns ambitious, then playful, then full of excited plans, and then wrung with despair, but through it all ran the same cosmic seriousness that he knew in the society around him, the same need to make sense out of life. The "unconscious sympathy" which Alice Fletcher felt was Cushing's greatest trait[41] led him to recognize in Zuni life this same search for order and meaning. The key word here is "order," for what Franz Boas later thought to be a result of accumulated historical accidents (culture as a product of history) Cushing came to see as the result of an intellectual and social structuring of reality.

On the trip East in 1882 with the Zunis, Cushing had used E.B. Tylor's term "culture," speaking of the Zunis as remnants of a vast culture in the Southwest.[42] Sylvester Baxter, writing at the same time, referred to Zuni as the oldest of the pueblo families, "the father of their *Kultur,* as the Germans would say," indicating his awareness of the German origin and meaning of the term "culture" as Tylor and now Cushing were using it, that is, as customs in general, not refinement and cultivation.[43] In the same year Cushing recognized in New York the tenacity of Indian customs. Both Cushing and Baxter began to make pointed references to similarities between Zuni culture and that of the Western classical tradition. The Zunis too had an ancient or classical language as well as an everyday language. The Zunis too entrusted their history to a native Homer.

In *Zuni Breadstuff* (1884–1885) Cushing took pains to make things clear to his readers, who were, he said, "controlled by a culture totally at variance with that of the Zunis."[44] To Tylor's concept of culture as accumulated customs, Cushing was beginning to add notions of cultural relativism, of the plurality of cultures, and of cultural determinism.

Then in 1888 Cushing sent a paper called "Preliminary Notes on the Origin, Working Hypothesis, and Primary Researches of the Hemenway Southwestern Archaeological Expedition" to the International Congress of Americanists meeting in Madrid. In it Cushing suggested that a society is perhaps structured around what he called a guiding "Idea." He wrote that it seems:

> a people carry through all succeeding environments—relatively unmodified—the impress of the *Idea* of the earliest environment which affected their Culture.[45]

For any group of people, ethnologists ought to try to discover what Idea dominated or possessed them, how and through what influences the Idea originated and became fixed, and finally how ever after that Idea modified not only all lesser ideas but also the institutions characteristic of that culture.

The phrasing is awkward, but the concept is the same as that which would be formulated by H.K. Haeberlin in 1916 and by Ruth Benedict beginning about 1924. Cultures have themes, or patterns, as Benedict called them, organizing principles around which the society is structured.

Among the Zunis Cushing had found that the dominant idea was a search for the middle place and a corresponding tendency, based on their organization of space, to divide everything into seven parts. The six Zuni priests and one priestess were each related to a region of space: north, south, east, west, upper, lower, or the middle, which in part contained all the others. The pueblo of Zuni was divided into six parts with a seventh part representing the whole, and Cushing showed that this was the origin of Spanish traditions about the legendary seven cities of Cibola (Zuni). Zuni myths and their social organization reflected this same septenary system. Cushing thought its origin might have been an early Zuni settlement in the midst of great plains, where the Zunis could be near their fields and at the same time have a wide field of vision out in all directions as they watched for approaching enemies. From this geographical location in the middle of great plains surrounded on all sides by mountain ranges, they developed their spatial conceptions based on seven subdivisions, and this eventually permeated their culture. Cushing thought that the buried cities he had examined on the Hemenway expedition were destroyed by earthquakes, and he imagined that afterward the Zunis would have moved farther east, attempting again to reach the Middle Place, the stable center of the world. In his final wild hypothesis that perhaps all the sedentary cultures of western America were dominated by this penchant for septenary division, Cushing used "cultures" for the first time in the plural, a practice he was to continue.

Cushing's paper was not published until 1890, but from 1888 on the term "cultures" was used in print by his friend Sylvester Baxter. In "The Old New World, An illustrated letter from Camp Hemenway, Arizona" in the *Boston Sunday Herald* in 1888 and in a six part series on "Archaeological Camping in Arizona" in *The American Architect and Building News*, Baxter described Cushing's work and wrote of the study of "the aboriginal cultures of America" and of the spreading of "primitive cultures."[46] That Baxter was simply reflecting Cushing's ideas is apparent from a review he did at about the same time of Cyrus Thomas's work on the mound builders. In it Baxter wrote (with no sense of contradiction) of tribes on "the same stage in the scale of culture," and he referred to the "culture-status" and the "grade of culture" of different tribes.[47]

This difference between the way in which Cushing used the term "culture" and the way it was used by John Wesley Powell and Cyrus Thomas at the Bureau of Ethnology continued. In the Thirteenth Annual Report of the Bureau Cushing called the Zunis "heirs of two cultures."[48] His "Outline of the Zuni Creation Myths" was an analysis of how a dominating "Idea," or rather two dominating "Ideas," served to give structure to this particular culture. Powell meanwhile in his introduction to the volume was mainly concerned to spell out the difference between "primitive" and "civilized" ways of thinking. He wrote:

> All primitive philosophies are more or less mythic and unreal— indeed, the whole course of intellectual development among mankind has been one of constant elimination of unreality.[49]

This was Powell's scheme, of stages of culture from savagery, barbarism, and civilization to enlightenment.

Cushing did not argue the issue with his mentor, but he persisted in his views. In "The Arrow," his vice-presidential address to Section H of the American Association for the Advancement of Science in 1895, he spoke of "cultures."[50] By 1896 his use and meaning of the term had begun to be accepted by important parts of the professional anthropological community. Daniel G. Brinton and F. W. Putnam spoke of "cultures" after Cushing did at a meeting of the American Philosophical Society.[51] Franz Boas read a paper at the American Association for the Advancement of Science meeting in 1896 in which he repeatedly used "cultures" in the plural, as in "the cultures of various peoples."[52]

But after Cushing's death in 1900, Franz Boas changed his mind. When Boas wrote *The Mind of Primitive Man* (1911), he incorporated some paragraphs he had written in 1894, but he removed from them the troublesome word "culture," substituting for it "civilization" or "general progress."[53]

Boas could no longer use "culture" to mean degree of civilization, but with the new use of the term he was also uneasy, and so he avoided it altogether. What bothered Boas was the implication that cultures were wholes, that they were in some sense integrated, coherent units. What he wanted anthropologists to study was the transmission of cultural traits from group to group.

For twenty years Boas impressed this methodology on American anthropology. It was quite likely the result not only of his rigid empiricism and distaste for generalizations but also of the geographical area in which he worked and the nature of the work he did. Boas studied the Northwest Coast tribes who had long been in contact with Europeans. He did not stay in one place but moved from group to group in order to study trait diffusion. Even for the Kwakiutls, the people Boas knew best, he did not learn the language but relied on interpreters and a Chinook jargon.[54] Boas, in short, did not look for and was ill prepared to find cultural coherence. It was not until his students began to study the Zunis and other pueblo peoples that the concept of culture reemerged in American anthropology.

The pioneer was H.K. Haeberlin who died of diabetes in 1918 at the age of twenty-seven after a brilliant start in anthropology. Haeberlin suggested in 1916 that Pueblo culture was not a summation of diffused traits but was organized around the "idea of fertilization." He cited several of Cushing's papers but referred to Cushing only indirectly, noting that "the characteristic individuality of the Pueblo culture has always been tacitly recognized and has been ascribed in a vague way to environmental factors."[55] Franz Boas had great respect for Haeberlin,[56] whom he had brought from Germany, and within a few years three other of his students, Edward Sapir, Ruth Benedict, and Margaret Mead, began to speculate about types or dominant ideas in particular cultures.

In 1924 and 1925 Ruth Benedict did summer field work at Zuni. Simultaneously she was being influenced by Edward Sapir who was interested in Jung's concept of innate psychological types. Sapir began to make theoretical analogies between "psychological orientations" in individuals and in cultures, and in 1926 he labeled certain cultures "introverted" and others "extroverted."[57] The following year he wrote a paper on "The Unconscious Patterning of Behavior in Society."[58] Sapir discussed these ideas with Ruth Benedict and Margaret Mead, and when Benedict went to work with the

Pima in the summer of 1927 she had a way of accounting for what she called the "unbelievable" contrast between the Pimas and the Zunis.[59] Using Nietzsche's terms, she described Pueblo society as Apollonian with moderation the ideal, whereas all the surrounding cultures, including the Pima, were Dionysian.[60] Her famous book *Patterns of Culture* (1934) is essentially an elaboration of this idea, that cultures are integrated around certain psychological configurations. Franz Boas continued to think that there were great methodological difficulties inherent in the study of cultural wholes,[61] but he wrote an introduction for Benedict's book nevertheless. She was the student who was perhaps closer personally to him than any other.

There are clearly similarities between Ruth Benedict's depiction of the Zunis as moderation-loving and Cushing's description of the Zuni search for a safe place in the "Middle of the World." But Cushing would probably have been impatient with Benedict's concept of culture, with its lack of interest in origins, and with its psychological thrust, for he was interested in social structure and spatial orientation as related to the geographical environment and to myths and rituals.

Benedict had read Cushing's best known works, but Boas's attitude toward him did not encourage her to take him seriously. "He was an exceedingly able man. [pause] I'm afraid his work will have to be done all over again," is the way one student remembered Boas's evaluation of Cushing.[62]

What remains finally of interest is the impact which the pueblo peoples, and in particular the Zunis, have had on American anthropology. The pueblos were first visited by white men in 1540, when the Coronado expedition moved through the American southwest. They were colonized beginning in 1598 by the Spanish, who tried during the seventeenth century to eradicate native religious beliefs and practices. This ended with the Pueblo Revolt of 1680, and although the Spanish were back by 1692, their power was never again what it had been. When the United States acquired the Territory of New Mexico in 1848 as a result of the Mexican War, the pueblos were subjected to the interest and visits of military expeditions, traders, missionaries, the western surveys, government agents, and finally anthropologists. Through it all they kept a way of life so unique and coherent that three separate times, with Cushing, with Haeberlin, and with Benedict, it inspired the formulation of the modern anthropological concept of culture,[63] one of the most basic concepts in twentieth century social science.

Cushing, having produced "Preliminary Notes" on the Hemenway expedition, collapsed. It was the low point in his life. He was so ill and depressed in 1889 when his friend Captain John G. Bourke, a second lieutenant in the 3rd United States cavalry and an ethnologist, visited him in a Washington, D.C. hospital, that he asked Bourke to keep his memory alive:

> Make the reputation you are surely going to make when your books shall appear, but let the world know of my hard work and say that my method was the correct one in ethnological investigation.

Bourke responded:

> Cushing, old man, you're sick, nervous, and excitable: you are the first ethnologist in the world today and no one can remove you from your pinnacle.[64]

But he was ill and immobilized. It was nearly two years before Cushing recovered his former zest and (to some extent) his health. Then in the early 1890s he poured out a series of intricate and impressive theoretical papers.

He first returned to the Zuni materials and produced an "Outline of Zuni Creation Myths" for the Thirteenth Report of the Bureau. He began by arguing that despite the seeming acceptance of much of Roman Catholicism, the Zuni philosophy and religious system had survived intact. It was like a drop of oil in water, surrounded but not penetrated "by the flood of alien belief that descended upon it."[65] The Zunis had absorbed from the Spanish only such things as fit their way of life or were in accord with what they already believed. But Cushing showed that at one time in Zuni history acculturation had been a very important phenomenon. The Zunis were of one linguistic stock but of two distinct physical types and clearly the heirs of two cultures, as shown in their legends and burial customs. Cushing developed further his earlier structural analysis of Zuni society and the importance of the septenary division, but alongside this he found a dualism which he attributed to the merging of the two cultures. In this one brilliant paper he set out the structure or configuration of Zuni culture, discussed the conditions under which acculturation does or does not take place, and considered the effect of the environment on the culture.

Although he had promised more on the Zunis, Cushing turned next to a theoretical discussion of the evolutionary importance of human hands. He argued that by the use of his hands man had, in effect, domesticated himself and that the hands, aided by little more than hypnotic suggestions from the mind, could guide the modern investigator to a reconstruction of past human activity. Cushing thus fumbled his way toward a basic premise of materialist conceptions of history, that what men make or do is more fundamental than what they think. He distinguished between the growth of culture in a particular people and the culture-growth of the entire human race. Human hands were guides to both. He found the origin of art and of various number systems (as had Tylor before him) in the shape of the human body, especially the hands.[66]

Cushing continued to develop and celebrate his manual skill over the next several years. He found new ways of making arrows, worked at copper embossing, and made pottery by molding and baking clay in pits of sand.[67] Just as he had immersed himself in Zuni society and become a Zuni, so now he wanted to work his way back in time through past stages of human life and become a primitive man, experiencing his needs and satisfying them under his conditions. He gave the justification for this in his vice-presidential address to Section H of the American Association for the Advancement of Science in 1895 when he said:

> . . . let it be remembered that well-nigh all anthropology is personal history; that even the things of past men were personal, like as never they are to ourselves now. They must, therefore, be both treated and worked at, not solely according to ordinary methods of procedure or rules of logic, or to any given canons of learning, but in a profoundly personal mood and way. If I would study any old, lost art, let us say, I must make myself the artisan of it.[68]

A chance observation of a monkey led Cushing to think that the study of tools might even take him back to the antecedents of human society. He was sitting for his portrait in the studio of his friend, the Philadelphia artist Thomas Eakins. (see Plate I) For the portrait they turned part of the artist's studio into an imitation Zuni room, and Eakins painted Cushing in Zuni costume, pock-marked and thin, looking old and tired, in poignant contemplation of the fate of an ancient civilization.[69] Eakins had a pet monkey which Cushing watched during sittings for the portrait, and he noticed that the monkey used tools: that it opened nuts by banging them on hard objects and grabbed at a stick when it wanted to lunge at the cat.[70] Tool-making was not solely a human perogative.

Cushing's manual journeys back in time were interrupted when, stopping in at the University Museum in Philadelphia one afternoon in 1895 to visit his friend Stewart Culin, he learned of some unusual archaeological discoveries that had just been made on the Florida keys. He went with his personal physician Dr. William Pepper, who was also the head of the University Museum, to see the objects and within two weeks was on the scene in Florida.[71] Rope and wood had been found in the muck and peat deposits. Could there be remains here comparable to those of the Swiss lake dwellers? Cushing went back to Philadelphia, where Dr. Pepper joined Mrs. Phoebe A. Hearst to form the Pepper-Hearst expedition, with Cushing in charge. John Wesley Powell gave him another leave of absence from the Bureau of American Ethnology, and in late February of 1896 the expedition set out for Florida.

Cushing and several assistants worked side by side in the "water-soaked, foul-smelling muck and peat beds of Marco and neighboring keys."[72] The results were worth their discomforts, for they found wooden spear throwers, clubs, food vessels, toy canoes, war clubs, and parts of boxes. Most remarkable of all were fifteen wooden masks, carved and painted to represent animals, one of which was the head of a deer with moveable wooden ears. Along with the masks there were "maskoids" or as Cushing called them, "figureheads," whose animal shapes and marking helped him to identify the masks. It was a major and astonishing discovery, for such objects had not been found earlier in Florida and have not been found since.[73]

The expedition lasted for three months, and then Cushing, who was exhausted and ill, returned to Washington. With his wife, he moved into Mrs. Hearst's house to recuperate. Mrs. Hearst's bounty had, however, its negative side. William Randolph Hearst had just bought the *New York Journal*. He wanted to be the first to announce the results of the expedition financed by his mother, and he wanted the results to be spectacular. Obligingly Cushing claimed to have found a connection between his Florida work and the ancient Mayan civilizations, [74] but this was immediately challenged by the highly respected anthropologist W.H. Holmes. Two years earlier Holmes had pointed to traces of Mayan influence on the pottery of several of the southern states, but he found nothing in Cushing's discoveries to substantiate the claims the latter was making.

In the fall of 1896 a new storm broke. William Dinwiddie, a photographer at the Bureau of American Ethnology, claimed that Cushing had fabricated a painted shell supposedly discovered in Florida. Dinwiddie was discharged from the Bureau for "neglect of duty" after an investigation by John Wesley Powell, and when he tried to interest the *New York Herald* in the story with the hope of bringing about a Congressional investigation, Mrs. Hearst hired a lawyer to protect Cushing's and the Bureau's interests. [75] Meanwhile Frederick W. Hodge, the former Secretary of the Hemenway expedition, let it be known privately that Cushing had faked the famous turquoise shell toad found on the Hemenway expedition which had gone with the rest of the Hemenway materials to the Peabody Museum at Harvard. [76] "I wish that Mr. C. who has some excellent qualities as an investigator, could have the guidance of which you speak," Alice Fletcher moaned to Putnam. [77]

With these charges hovering over him, Cushing went to Philadelphia where he gave the members of the American Philosophical Society a long, excited, and somewhat fanciful account of his discoveries in Florida. Daniel Brinton and F.W. Putnam, who were both present, neatly separated the wheat from the chaff in his account, telling him gently that he had not found a new culture but rather had greatly extended knowledge of the culture previously known to have existed in Florida and Georgia. They were both impressed with the finds, and Putnam in particular liked Cushing's interpretation of the wooden masks, as a way of expressing an animal face on the human face, for that was what Franz Boas had found among the Indians of the Northwest Coast. [78]

Putnam's honest appreciation of Cushing's work did not keep him from insisting that a complete accounting had to be made of the circumstances surrounding the discovery of the shell toad, for he wanted to be able to exhibit the work at the Peabody Museum in good conscience. Finally, after delaying for many months, Cushing poured out the story to him. Cushing assured Putnam that the toad could be exhibited as authentic. It had been found in House Mound IV at Los Muertos. He admitted that he had done considerable restoration work with greasewood gum and glass fragments and that perhaps he had made a mistake in heating and buffing the toad until the restored portions were indistinguishable from the rest. But did he, Cushing asked, deserve the charges of liar, fraud, and drunkard that were thrown at him without pity by the same men who would undo Putnam too if they could? With this oblique reference to recent meetings of the American Association for the Advancement of Science and of the British Association for the Advancement of Science in Detroit and Toronto, where Putnam's evidence for paleolithic man in America had been roundly attacked, Cushing rested his case.[79]

Hodge told his side of the story more than thirty years later in a letter to Emil W. Haury. They had seen a genuine shell frog encrusted with turquoise mosaic in a private collection in Arizona, and Cushing was very eager to find something similar. One day at camp on the expedition Cushing sent two Zuni Indians out to gather mesquite gum and then went into retirement in a closed tent. Later he emerged holding in his hand a beautiful mosaic frog. The matter was treated casually until Edward S. Morse, a member of the Board of Advisors for the expedition, visited Camp Hemenway. Then, to Hodge's astonishment, Cushing told Morse that the frog had been found in the ruins. Morse took the frog back East with him for safekeeping and to show to Mrs. Hemenway, and it became part of the collections.[80]

Hodge was not a disinterested observer,[81] but his account suggests what may have happened. Cushing was eager to come up with spectacular finds. He prided himself on being able to reproduce items of Indian technology. He thought of himself as a Zuni and believed Los Muertos to be an ancient Zuni site. Conceivably he tried his hand at making something he wanted to find, and when Morse accepted it as authentic, the deed was done. Possibly a similar thing happened in Florida. Cushing could not resist trying to copy what he had found, and then gradually the line between what was found and what was made became unclear.

Cushing struggled through 1898 and 1899 to write the report on his Florida work. Again a diversion appeared, for while resting and working in Maine, he found some shell heaps which interested him. Major Powell, ever open to Cushing's uncanny instincts, came up to help him make preliminary explorations. On April 10, 1900 in the midst of this new project, Cushing, as he was eating dinner with his wife, choked on a fishbone and died before help could be summoned. He was forty-three years old.

A shocked anthropological community arranged for a memorial meeting in Washington, D.C. "I loved him," John Wesley Powell told the assembled group, "as a father loves his son."[82]

One of the recurring questions about Frank Hamilton Cushing is why he published so little of what he knew about Zuni life. Philip Phillips, in a recent and engaging memoir on Cushing, suggested that this was perhaps due to his reluctance to violate the confidences of the Zuni people.[83] Cushing's recurring illnesses might also be seen as a way of escape from this dilemma.

The evidence however suggests otherwise. It was not only his Zuni material that Cushing failed to publish. Almost every paper he wrote, even on topics such as copper-working and arrow-making, ended with the declaration that this was but the first part of a major study soon to follow, but the major studies never appeared. Cushing was a painstaking writer and could hold himself to the task only with difficulty. But reluctant he was not, for he shared with a host of late nineteenth century pre-Freudian venturers in the psychological realm the understanding that at bottom there are no secrets anyway.[84] Intuitively, with unconscious sympathy, human beings understand one another. Alongside this there are cultural systems, of which no single one is any more foolish than another, but neither need the inquirer be bound by its dictates, as of secrecy.

Cushing had few illusions about himself or anyone else. Life for him was a game with tragic dimensions, a game in which everyone wore masks and played various roles. Despite his deep respect for Indian life, he was willing to use threats and deceit to get what he wanted, whether it was secret information from the Zunis or material goods for purchase from the Hopis. This side of his character was particularly apparent during his five day visit to Oraibi in 1883. By his own account, Cushing taunted the Hopis, harangued them about the power of "Washington," and brandished his pistol until some of them agreed to trade with him.[85] He manipulated Pahlowatiwa and the other Zunis just as with bribery, flattery, and intimations he manipulated Mary Hemenway, Phoebe Hearst, William Pepper, Spencer Baird, and John Wesley Powell. Almost always, enough of the pessimistic visionary came through that they loved him the more for it.[86]

Thomas Eakins caught in the portrait of Cushing the fatalistic pessimism which ran through Cushing's thinking about the American Indians. Unlike Alice Fletcher, he did not have a program which if acted upon would make everything come out all right. He was not a part of the optimistic, progress- and civilization-celebrating current in late nineteenth century America. He saw little that the United States government could do for the Indian peoples. He rose from a sick bed in January of 1897 to speak to the Board of Indian Commissioners, where he gave a heartfelt testimony to the ability of the Indians to learn what they wanted to know, stressing also the interrelatedness of all aspects of Indian life. The government, he warned, should not tamper lightly with tribal customs. The Indians had been asked to give up the wearing of blankets, but, Cushing asked:

> What would you do, for example, if asked by an Indian to give up wearing the dress—coat for ceremonial occasions, even if he gave the reason he probably would give, that it made you resemble a swallow or a crow?[87]

Cushing urged the government to send its brightest and most sensitive men to the reservations to learn from the Indians before trying to teach them anything. That was the most he could hope for.

Cushing saw himself in the same way that Alice Fletcher saw herself, as an interpreter of Indian life to those outside it. A dramatic shift in tone and method took place between their kind of ethnographic work and that done by Franz Boas and his students. Cushing gloried in the cleverness of the Zuni people, and implicitly in his own cleverness, in being able to follow along and trace the interconnections in their culture. He was an insider telling the rest of the world something it did not know. For later anthropologists the approach was more often that of scientists telling one another things about a group of people which the people did not know about themselves.

The date for this change in attitude and scientific method can be set at 1913 from a review which Robert Lowie wrote in that year of *The Omaha Tribe* by Alice Fletcher and Francis La Flesche. Lowie had been one of Franz Boas's first students at Columbia and had also come under the influence of the German positivist, Ernst Mach.[88] Lowie chided Fletcher and La Flesche for classifying their wealth of material "according to the canons of aboriginal rather than scientific logic."[89] Under "Social Life" they had included, not only "such legitimate topics" as kinship terms, courtship and mating customs, and etiquette, but also cooking and foods, dressing and tanning skins, quill work, weaving, and personal adornment. They had also ignored the work of their predecessors, particularly the Reverend J. Owen Dorsey,[90] and they took too seriously the legends about the origin of the tribe.

Alice Fletcher commented on Lowie's review in a letter to F.W. Putnam's secretary. She wrote:

> [It] is to me droll reading. He has theories and notions which rule his views very strongly. The book could be better, but he is unfair to it. I did not want to attack Mr. Dorsey, because he is dead. He did not understand the Omaha language and made dreadful mistakes and he too, had theories which colored his views. I've let the Omaha tell their own story, rather than fill my pages with stories told about them. I can wait for truth to prevail.[91]

So the issue was joined. Did Cushing and Fletcher and La Flesche who were knowledgeable insiders have the "truth" about the Zunis and the Omahas, or did their knowledge need to be translated into rigorous methodological categories in order that scientific laws could be discovered? Boas and Lowie chose the latter route, and Cushing's reputation, in the United States in particular, has barely survived.

It has been otherwise in France. In 1903 Emile Durkheim and Marcel Mauss used Cushing's studies of "Zuni Fetishes" and "Zuni Creation Myths" as the basis of an analysis of primitive forms of classification which they published in *Année sociologique*.[92] It was their work and also his own study of North American mythology which led Claude Lévi-Strauss to Cushing. In 1952 Lévi-Strauss wrote:

> Frank Hamilton Cushing's insight and sociological imagination entitle him to a seat on [Lewis Henry] Morgan's right, as one of the great forerunners of social-structure studies. The gaps and inaccuracies in his descriptions, less serious than the indictment of having "overinterpreted" some of his material, will be viewed in their true proportions when it is realized that, albeit in an unconscious fashion,

Cushing was aiming less at giving an actual description of Zuni society than at elaborating a model (his famous sevenfold division) which would explain most of its processes and structure.[93]

Lévi-Strauss's praise is justified, his qualification less so, for Cushing was not unconscious of what he was doing. Cushing did not pretend to be giving an actual or objective description of Zuni society, somehow detached from himself as the observer. This is the difference between his scientific method and that of Boas and Lowie. Cushing was always there in the middle, a unique individual and a member of one society, experiencing and trying to make sense of another society. The method of field work which Cushing himself thought was his greatest achievement he called "the reciprocal method." He threw himself into Zuni life and tried to figure it out. Then he invited his Zuni friends to do the same in his society, and he took them to Chicago, Washington, D.C., and Boston to give them a chance to do so. From one society across to the other he and the Zunis tried to understand one another. They did not pretend there was neutral scientific ground somewhere outside themselves on which they could stand to make observations and write descriptions.

Frank Hamilton Cushing was the first to formulate and make use of the anthropological concept of culture. He was, in Lévi-Strauss's words, "one of the great forerunners of social-structure studies." He was the first professional anthropologist to go and live with the people whom he wanted to study. He tossed out hints about the importance of hands and of manual skills in anthropology which have not yet been pursued. Perhaps it was luck which led him to spectacular archaeological discoveries in Florida and to prehistoric irrigation canals in the Southwest, but even here the creative intelligence which constantly ferreted out new possibilities was apparent. He was, as one of his contemporaries wrote, in a class by himself.[94]

Notes and References

1. William Henry Holmes, "Frank Hamilton Cushing, 1857–1900," *American Anthropologist*, II (1900), 354–380, 356. Other biographical information is in A.F. Chamberlain, "In Memoriam," *Journal of American Folklore*, 13 (1900), 129–134; John Wesley Powell, "Necrology: Frank Hamilton Cushing," *Twenty-first Annual Report*,

Bureau of American Ethnology, 1899–1900 (Washington, D.C., 1903), xxxv–xxxviii; Walter Hough, "Frank Hamilton Cushing," *Dictionary of American Biography*, ed. by Allen Johnson and Dumas Malone (New York, 1930), 630. Raymond Stewart Brandes, "Frank Hamilton Cushing: Pioneer Americanist," unpub. Ph.D. dissertation, University of Arizona, 1965 is excellent and detailed, particularly on Cushing's early years up through the Hemenway expedition. See also *Zuni: Selected Writings of Frank Hamilton Cushing*, edited and with an introduction by Jesse Green (Lincoln, University of Nebraska Press, 1979).

2. Frank Hamilton Cushing, "The Arrow,"*Proc., AAAS*, 44 (1895), 199–240.

3. Neil M. Judd, *The Bureau of American Ethnology: A Partial History* (Norman, University of Oklahoma Press, 1967), 5.

4. Detailed catalogues of the collections made at Zuni and elsewhere were published by the Bureau: James Stevenson, "Illustrated Catalogue of the Collections Obtained from the Indians of New Mexico and Arizona in 1879," including colored plates, *Second Annual Report*, Bureau of Ethnology, 1880–1881 (Washington, D.C., 1883), 311–421; James Stevenson, "Catalogue of the collections from New Mexico and Arizona in 1881," *Third Annual Report*, Bureau of Ethnology, 1881–1882 (Washington, D.C., 1884), 517–595.

5. Frank Hamilton Cushing, "My Adventures in Zuni. III," *Century Magazine*, 26 (1883), 28–47, 31; see also Parts I and II in *Century Magazine*, 25 (1882), 191–207, 500–511. All three parts were reprinted in book form with introduction by E. De Golyer (Peripatetic Press, Santa Fe, 1941).

6. Frank Hamilton Cushing to Spencer F. Baird, Aug. 2, 1880, National Anthropological Archives, Smithsonian Institution.

7. Brandes, *op. cit.*, 57–58.

8. *Ibid.*, 75, 90.

9. Sylvester Baxter, "F.H. Cushing at Zuni," *The American Architect and Building News*, XI (1882), 56.

10. Sylvester Baxter, "Some Results of Mr. Cushing's Visit," *The American Architect and Building News*, XI (1882), 195–196.

11. Sylvester Baxter, "An Aboriginal Pilgrimage," *Century Magazine*, 25 (1882), 526–527.

12. Frank Hamilton Cushing to Spencer F. Baird, undated letter written between Sept. 24, 1881 and Jan. 24, 1882. Brandes dated it Oct. 21. National Anthropological Archives.

13. Spencer Baird to John Wesley Powell, Jan. 12, 1882; Baird to Powell, undated but a response to Powell's letter of Jan. 23, 1882; Baird to Cushing, Jan. 24, 1882, all in the National Anthropological Archives.

14. Charles F. Lummis, "The White Indian," *Land of Sunshine* (later *Out West*), 12 (1900), 8–17. The article includes portraits of Cushing and five photographs of him at Zuni.

15. Frank Hamilton Cushing to F.W. Putnam, May 20, 1883, Putnam Papers.

16. Fred A. Ober, "How a White Man Became the War Chief of the Zunis," *Wide Awake* (June, 1882), 382–388; Hope Gilbert, "1882: Zuni Pilgrimage to the Atlantic Ocean," *Desert Magazine*, 24 (1961), 12–15.

17. Neil M. Judd, *op. cit.*, 63. The address to the National Academy of Sciences, although a hasty job and one of Cushing's poorest efforts, was later printed in *Popular Science Monthly*, F.H. Cushing, "The Zuni Social, Mythic, and Religious Systems," 21 (1882), 186–192.

18. Alice C. Fletcher, "Zuni: Notes on an evening spent with Frank Cushing and a Zuni friend, 5-10-1882," Unpub. MS., Papers of

Alice C. Fletcher and Francis La Flesche, National Anthropological Archives.

19. Brandes, *op. cit.*, 92.

20. Carl Resek, *Lewis Henry Morgan: American Scholar* (Chicago, University of Chicago Press, 1960), 37.

21. Sylvester Baxter, "The tenacity of Indian custom," *The American Architect and Building News*, XII (1882), 195–197.

22. Herman F.C. ten Kate made this point with reference to Cushing only in "The Indian in Literature," *Annual Report of the Smithsonian Institution*, 1921 (Washington, D.C., 1922), 507–528, 517, but John Wesley Powell and Alice Fletcher were equally important. See John Wesley Powell, "The ancient province of Tusayan," *Scribner's Monthly*, 11 (1876), 193–213 and Alice C. Fletcher, "Indian Songs: Personal Studies of Indian Life," *Century Magazine*, 47 (1894), 421–431; "Hunting Customs of the Omahas," *Century Magazine*, 50 (1895), 691–702; "Tribal Life among the Omahas," *Century Magazine*, 51 (1896), 450–461.

23. Robert C. Euler, "Introduction" to Frank Hamilton Cushing, *The Nation of the Willows* (Flagstaff, Arizona, Northland Press, 1965), 6. See also Leslie Spier, *Havasupai Ethnography*, American Museum of Natural History, Anthropological Papers, 29 (1928).

24. Triloki Nath Pandey gives a good account of the political controversies in which Cushing was involved in "Anthropologists at Zuni," *Proceedings of the American Philosophical Society*, 116 (1972), 321–337. See also Arthur Woodward, "Frank Hamilton Cushing—First War Chief of the Zunis," *The Masterkey*, 13 (1939), 172–179.

25. Eben N. Horsford, an inventor and chemistry professor in Cambridge, Massachusetts, feared from Cushing's repeated letters to him describing his "terrible suffering from dyspepsia" that Cushing might die in Zuni a martyr to science. Horsford urged Powell to recall Cushing and offered to pay the debts Cushing had incurred in building himself a large house at Zuni. (Horsford to J.W. Powell, Nov. 19, 1883, National Anthropological Archives). See also Cushing to Powell, Jan. 29, 1884, March 30, 1884, Nov. 16, 1885 (National Anthropological Archives).

26. Frank Hamilton Cushing, "A Study of Pueblo Pottery as Illustrative of Zuni Culture Growth," *Fourth Annual Report*, Bureau of Ethnology, 1882–1883 (Washington, D.C., 1886), 467–521.

27. Frank Hamilton Cushing, "Zuni Breadstuff," *The Millstone*, IX (1884), X (1885), republished as *Zuni Breadstuff*, Indian Notes and Monographs, 8 (New York, Museum of the American Indian, Heye Foundation, 1920).

28. Frank Hamilton Cushing, *Zuni Folk Tales* (New York, G.P. Putnam's, 1901).

29. Edmund Wilson, *Red, Black, Blond, and Olive: Studies in Four Civilizations: Zuni, Haiti, Soviet Russia, Israel* (New York, Oxford University Press, 1956). Dennis Tedlock evaluates Cushing's translations somewhat critically in "On the Translation of Style in Oral Narrative," *Journal of American Folklore*, 84 (1971), 114–133.

30. Alan Dundes, *The Study of Folklore* (New York, Prentice-Hall, 1965), 269. "The Cock and the Mouse" is in *Zuni Folk Tales*, 411–422.

31. Frank Hamilton Cushing, "Preliminary Notes on the Origin, Working Hypothesis, and Primary Researches of the Hemenway Southwestern Archaeological Expedition," *Seventh Congrès international des américanistes* (Berlin, 1890), 159.

32. Brandes, *op. cit.*, 130–131.

33. Frank Hamilton Cushing, "Field Notes and Journal of Explorations and Discoveries in Arizona and New Mexico During the Years

1887–1888," unpub. MS., Peabody Museum of Archaeology and Ethnology, 26.

34. Brandes, *op. cit.*, 134–152 gives many details on the Hemenway expedition including delays, events in camp, and the progress of the work.

35. Sylvester Baxter, "The Old New World, an illustrated letter from Camp Hemenway, Arizona," *Boston Sunday Herald* (April 15, 1888); Sylvester Baxter, "Archaeological Camping in Arizona," *The American Architect and Building News*, 25 (Jan. 5, 1889, 8–10; Jan. 12, 1889, 15–16; Jan. 19, 1889, 32–34; Jan. 26, 1889, 43–44), 26 (Aug. 31, 1889, 101–102; Sept. 14, 1889, 120–122).

36. Benjamin Ives Gilman and Katherine H. Stone, "The Hemenway Southwestern Expedition," *Journal of American Ethnology and Archaeology*, V (1908), 229–235. The Hemenway expedition published five volumes of this journal (1891–1908).

37. Frederick W. Hodge, "Foreword," vii–ix in Emil W. Haury, *The Excavation of Los Muertos and Neighboring Ruins in the Salt River Valley, Southern Arizona*, Peabody Museum of Archaeology and Ethnology Papers, 24 (1945).

38. Alan P. Olson, "Changing Frontiers in Southwestern Archaeology," in "Pioneers in Southwestern Anthropology; A Symposium," *Journal of the Arizona Academy of Sciences*, II (1963), 120–123.

39. E.B. Tylor, *Primitive Culture* (London, 1871), I, 1.

40. George W. Stocking, Jr., "Matthew Arnold, E.B. Tylor, and the Uses of Invention," in *Race, Culture, and Evolution* (New York, The Free Press, 1968), 69–90.

41. Alice C. Fletcher, "Frank Hamilton Cushing," *American Anthropologist*, II (1900), 367.

42. Frank Hamilton Cushing, "The Zuni Social, Mythic, and Religious Systems,"

Popular Science Monthly, XXI (1882), 186–192.

43. Sylvester Baxter, "The Father of the Pueblos," *Harper's New Monthly Magazine*, 65 (1882), 72–91, 73.

44. Frank Hamilton Cushing, *Zuni Breadstuff*, 18.

45. Frank Hamilton Cushing, "Preliminary Notes on the Origin, Working Hypothesis, and Primary Researches of the Hemenway Southwestern Archaeological Expedition," 151.

46. Sylvester Baxter, "The Old New World," *Boston Sunday Herald* (April 15, 1888); Sylvester Baxter, "Archaeological Camping in Arizona," *The American Architect and Building News*, 25 (Jan. 26, 1889), 43.

47. Sylvester Baxter, "The Bureau of Ethnology's Fifth Annual Report—I," *The American Architect and Building News*, 27 (1890), 152.

48. Frank Hamilton Cushing, "Outline of Zuni Creation Myths," *Thirteenth Annual Report*, Bureau of Ethnology, 1891–92 (Washington, D.C., 1896), 321–447, 342.

49. John Wesley Powell, "Introduction" and "Report of the Director," *Thirteenth Annual Report*, Bureau of Ethnology, lvii.

50. Frank Hamilton Cushing, "The Arrow," *Proc., AAAS*, XLIV (1895), 236.

51. Frank Hamilton Cushing, "Exploration of Ancient Key Dwellers' Remains on the Gulf Coast of Florida," *Proceedings of the American Philosophical Society*, XXXV (1896), 354; see "Discussion," 433–448.

52. Franz Boas, "The Limitations of the Comparative Method of Anthropology," *Science*, n.s. 4 (1896), 901–908, 902. A.L. Kroeber and Clyde Kluckhohn gave other examples of the use of the term "culture" in the modern technical sense in the 1890s (by J.W. Fewkes, O.T. Mason, and W J McGee) in "Culture: A Critical Review of Concepts

and Definitions," *Papers of the Peabody Museum of American Archaeology and Ethnology*, XLVII (1952), 150. Kroeber and Kluckhohn attributed the modern concept of culture to Tylor in 1871 and were puzzled as to why it seemed to disappear after the 1890s only to be defined again by Clark Wissler in 1920. They suggested that the influence of Boas may have been a factor in its disappearance.

53. George W. Stocking, Jr., "Franz Boas and the Culture Concept in Historical Perspective," in *Race, Culture, and Evolution: Essays in the History of Anthropology* (New York, The Free Press, 1968), 195–233, see excerpts 202–203 from Boas's writings in 1894 and 1911 which Stocking interprets in a different way.

54. Ronald P. Rohner, *The Ethnography of Franz Boas*, compiled and edited by Ronald P. Rohner, "Introduction" by Ronald P. Rohner and Evelyn C. Rohner (Chicago, University of Chicago Press, 1969), xxiv.

55. H.K. Haeberlin, "The idea of fertilization in the culture of the Pueblo Indians," *Memoirs*, American Anthropological Association, III (1916), 1–55, 50. Haeberlin added that he felt this to be of no scientific value, for the problem was really a psychological one.

56. Franz Boas, "In Memoriam: Herman Karl Haeberlin," *American Anthropologist*, XXI (1919), 71–74.

57. Edward Sapir, "Notes on Psychological Orientation in a Given Society," *Social Science Research Council, Hanover Conference*, I (Aug. 9–20, 1926), 238.

58. Edward Sapir, "The Unconscious Patterning of Behavior in Society," in E.S. Dummer, ed., *The Unconscious: A Symposium* (New York, Knopf, 1927), 114–142; reprinted in David G. Mandelbaum, ed., *Selected Writings of Edward Sapir in Language, Culture, and Personality* (Berkeley and Los Angeles, University of California Press, 1958), 544–559.

59. Margaret Mead, *An Anthropologist at Work: Writings of Ruth Benedict* (Boston, Houghton Mifflin, 1959), 206. See 207–209 for the importance of Sapir in Benedict's and Mead's thinking.

60. Ruth F. Benedict, "Psychological Types in the Cultures of the Southwest," *Proceedings of the International Congress of Americanists*, 23 (New York, 1930), 572–581; Ruth F. Benedict, "Configurations of culture in North America," *American Anthropologist*, 34 (1932), 1–27.

61. Franz Boas, "The Methods of Ethnology," *American Anthropologist*, XXII (1920), 311–322; Ruth Benedict, *Patterns of Culture* (Boston, Houghton Mifflin, 1934).

62. Robert H. Lowie, "Reminiscences of Anthropological Currents in America Half a Century Ago," *American Anthropologist*, LVIII (1956), 995–1016, 996. Boas presumably meant both that much of Cushing's material had not been published and that what was published was misleading. In 1897 when Cushing was under attack, Boas wrote to McGee, "Mr. Cushing has my fullest sympathy in all the trials he is undergoing . . . I have always considered him one of the frankest, most generous, open hearted and honorable men whom it was my good fortune to meet. His greatest enemy is, I take it—his genius." (Boas to McGee, Jan. 1, 1897, Boas Papers)

In "The Methods of Ethnology,"*American Anthropologist*, XXII (1920), 311–322, Boas contrasted Cushing's attempt "to explain Zuni culture entirely on the basis of the reaction of the Zuni mind to its geographical environment" with the work of "modern students" such as Benedict, Ruth Bunzel, and Elsie Clews Parsons in particular who showed the deep influence of Spanish ideas on Zuni culture and hence the importance of acculturation (p. 316). Ruth Bunzel suggested in her 1932 study of Zuni ceremonialism that some of the metaphysical glosses on the basic elements of a Zuni origin myth may have originated in Cushing's mind. (Ruth L. Bunzel, "Introduction to Zuni Ceremonialism," *Forty-Seventh Annual Report*, Bureau of American Ethnology, 1929–1930, 1932, 467–544).

63. E. Adamson Hoebel and Edward P. Dozier have made surveys of southwestern studies, and both note the conceptual innovations of Haeberlin and Benedict, although not that of Cushing. See E. Adamson Hoebel, "Major Contributions of Southwestern Studies to Anthropological Theory," *American Anthropologist*, 56 (1954), 720–727, and Edward P. Dozier, "The Pueblo Indians of the Southwest: A Survey of the Anthropological Literature and a Review of Theory, Methods, and Results," *Current Anthropology*, 5 (1964), 79–97. A different kind of survey is the very interesting one by Triloki Nath Pandey, "Anthropologists at Zuni," *Proceedings of the American Philosophical Society*, 116 (1972), 321–337 in which the Zunis recall the anthropologists (from Cushing to Bunzel) who have worked there. See also Charles J. Erasmus, *Las dimensiones de la cultura: historia de la etnología en los Estados Unidos entre 1900 y 1950* (Bogatá, 1953), 53, who discusses Haeberlin.

64. Lansing B. Bloom, "Bourke on the Southwest, IX," *New Mexico Historical Review*, XI (1936), 188–207, 204–205. John G. Bourke (1846–1896) was President of the American Folk-Lore Society at the time of his death. He kept 128 notebooks on his ethnological work which Lansing Bloom edited for publication in successive issues of the *New Mexico Historical Review*, beginning with VIII (1933).

65. Frank Hamilton Cushing, "Outline of Zuni Creation Myths, *Thirteenth Annual Report*, Bureau of Ethnology, 1891–92 (1896), 339. See also Cushing's article on "Pueblo Indians or Pueblos" in *Johnson's Universal Cyclopaedia*, VI (New York, 1895). Washington Matthews agreed that little of Christianity had been absorbed by the Zunis. See his "Review" of "Outline of Zuni Creation Myths," *Journal of American Folklore*, 9 (1896), 233–235.

66. Frank Hamilton Cushing, "Manual Concepts: A Study of the Influence of Hand-usage on Culture Growth," *American Anthropologist*, V (1892), 289–317; E.B. Tylor, *Researches into the Early History of Mankind and the Development of Civilization* (London, 1865).

67. Frank Hamilton Cushing, "Primitive Copper Working: An Experimental Study," *American Anthropologist*, VII (1894), 93–117; F.H. Cushing, "The Germ of Shoreland Pottery: An Experimental Study," *Memoirs of the International Congress of Anthropology* (Chicago, The Schulte Publishing Co., 1894), 217–234.

68. Frank Hamilton Cushing, "The Arrow," 201.

69. Eakins was as iconoclastic in his own way as was Cushing, having lost his teaching job at the Pennsylvania Academy of Fine Arts after he lifted the loin cloth on a model in order to show his female students the origin of a muscle. The first of Eakins's full length portraits was of Cushing in Zuni costume. Eakins also painted Mrs. Emily Cushing. Sylvan Schendler, *Eakins* (Boston, Little, Brown, 1967), xi, 136–138. See also Gordon Hendricks, *The Photographs of Thomas Eakins* (New York, Grossman, 1972), 152–153, 221; *Thomas Eakins: His Photographic Works* (Pennsylvania Academy of Fine Arts, Philadelphia, 1969); Lloyd Goodrich,

Thomas Eakins: His life and Work (New York, Whitney Museum of American Art, 1973).

70. Frank Hamilton Cushing, "The Arrow," 219–220.

71. Frank Hamilton Cushing, "A Preliminary examination of aboriginal remains near Pine Island, Marco, West Florida," *American Naturalist*, XXIX (1895), 1132–1135.

72. Frank Hamilton Cushing, "Exploration of Ancient Key Dwellers' Remains on the Gulf Coast of Florida," 354.

73. John Alden Mason, "Primitive Wooden Masks from Key Marco, Florida," *Archaeology*, IV (1951), 4–5; H. Newell Wardle, "The Pile Dwellers of Key Marco," *Archaeology*, IV (1951), 181–186 (Photographs by Reuben Goldberg). Marian Spjut Gilliland, *The Material Culture of Key Marco Florida* (Gainesville, University Presses of Florida, 1975), 5.

74. Alice Fletcher described these events in three letters to Putnam: July 1, 1896 (Peabody Museum Papers); June 22, 1896, July 9, 1896 (Putnam Papers).

75. J. Walter Fewkes to "Dear Hemenway," Nov. 30, 1896, Peabody Museum. Marian S. Gilliland suggests (in *The Material Culture of Key Marco Florida*, 183) that the painted shell is genuine.

76. Frank Hamilton Cushing to F.W. Putnam, Oct. 26, 1896, Nov. 21, 1896, Putnam Papers.

77. Alice C. Fletcher to Putnam, July 9, 1896, Putnam Papers.

78. Frank Hamilton Cushing, "Exploration of Ancient Key Dwellers' Remains on the Gulf Coast of Florida," 112.

79. F.H. Cushing to Putnam, Jan. 4, 1898, Peabody Museum. For an account of the AAAS and BAAS meetings, see W J McGee, "Anthropology at Detroit and To-

ronto," *American Anthropologist*, X (1897), 317–345.

80. F.W. Hodge to Emil W. Haury, Oct. 5, 1931, Peabody Museum.

81. Hodge was very critical of the way in which Cushing had managed the Hemenway expedition and in addition had a curious personal relationship to Cushing. In 1891 he married Mrs. Cushing's sister, Miss Margaret Magill, the young woman who had accompanied the Cushings to Zuni in 1882 and had traveled with the Hemenway expedition in 1888–1889. Margaret Magill was far more enthusiastic about life and travel in the Far West than was her married sister. She did a superb series of colored drawings of Zuni pots and designs, and occasionally she and Cushing went exploring together. (F.H. Cushing, "Field Notes and Journal of Explorations and Discoveries in Arizona and New Mexico During the Years 1887–1888," unpub. MS., Peabody Museum.) Why Hodge married a woman so closely associated with scientific work whose value he questioned is unclear, as is the reason for their subsequent divorce, but Hodge's hostility to Cushing was long sustained. It is only thinly disguised in the "Introduction" he wrote for Haury's book, more than fifty years after the events described.

82. John Wesley Powell, "In Memoriam, F.H.C.," *American Anthropologist*, II (1900), 367.

83. Philip Phillips, "Introduction," to Frank Hamilton Cushing, *Exploration of Ancient Key Dwellers' Remains on the Gulf Coast of Florida* (New York, AMS Press for the Peabody Museum of Archaeology and Ethnology, 1973), originally published in *Proceedings of the American Philosophical Society*, XXXV (1896).

84. Henri Ellenberger, *The Discovery of the Unconscious* (New York, Basic Books,

1970), deals mostly with Europeans but gives an indication of the great interest in psychological and psychic phenomena in the late nineteenth century. In the United States, William James was the most prominent of the inquirers into the human mind.

85. Frank Hamilton Cushing, "Oraibi in 1883," in F.H. Cushing, J. Walter Fewkes, and Elsie Clews Parsons, "Contributions to Hopi History," *American Anthropologist,* XXIV (1922), 253–268.

86. They also worked out unusual ways of dealing with him. Brandes (*op. cit.*, 128) reports an incident described in the *Saturday Evening Post* on Nov. 27, 1902 in which Mrs. Hemenway hired a secretary to sit behind a screen at Manchester-by-the-sea and take down, unbeknown to Cushing, every word of his conversation with her. After Cushing's death the material went to the Bureau of American Ethnology.

87. Frank Hamilton Cushing, "The Need of Studying the Indian in Order to Teach Him," *Twenty-Eighth Annual Report of the Board of Indian Commissioners* (Washington, D.C., 1897), 5.

88. Marvin Harris, *The Rise of Anthropological Theory* (New York, Thomas Y. Crowell, 1968), 344–347.

89. Robert H. Lowie, "Review of *The Omaha Tribe* by Alice Fletcher and Francis La Flesche," *Science*, 37 (1913), 910–915, 912.

90. J. Owen Dorsey, "Omaha Sociology," *Third Annual Report*, Bureau of Ethnology, 1881–1882 (Washington, D.C., 1884), 205–370.

91. Alice C. Fletcher to Miss Frances Mead, June 13, 1913, Peabody Museum Papers.

92. Emile Durkheim and Marcel Mauss, "De quelques formes primitives de classification: contribution à l'étude des représentations collectives," *Année sociologique,* VI (1903), 1–72; Mauss also picked up Cushing's work on "Manual Concepts." See M. Mauss, "Divisions et proportions des divisions de la sociologie," *Année sociologique,* n.s., II (1927), 106–107.

93. Claude Lévi-Strauss, *Structural Anthropology*, trans. by Claire Jacobson and Brooke Grundfest Schoepf in 1963 (Garden City, New York, Anchor, 1967), 282. Several contributors to Alfonso Ortiz, ed., *New Perspectives on the Pueblos* (A School of American Research Book, Albuquerque, University of New Mexico Press, 1972) have pointed to the importance of Cushing's work and its influence on Lévi-Strauss. See articles by Louis A. Hieb, Dennis Tedlock, and Fred Eggan.

94. A.F. Chamberlain, "In Memoriam," *Journal of American Folklore*, 13 (1900), 131.

Chapter Five
William Henry Holmes
(1846–1933)

William Henry Holmes was both an artist and a scientist. He wove these two threads together so skillfully through his long career that his friends commented on the wholeness, the near perfect quality of his life.[1] Holmes made his home and felt most at home in the nation's capital, and there for many years he was the leader of "Washington anthropology." He took on the biggest problems that the anthropology of this time had to offer, yet simultaneously one of his greatest pleasures was the sort of detailed museum work that others considered beneath them. His steady work produced a series of important studies, one of which in particular became a landmark in American anthropology. So easily did achievement and recognition come to Will Holmes, so smoothly did his life seem to flow, that the angry outburst on which he ended his career in anthropology comes all the more as a surprise. That sudden eruption of deep feeling reveals some of the previously hidden strain within Holmes himself and within the anthropological community.

Holmes's life in anthropology can be divided into three periods: his work in geology culminating in the working out of the stratigraphic method in archaeology in 1884, his studies of American Indian art and technology leading to the Loubat Prize in 1897, and finally his years up to 1920 as a reluctant leader in the profession. But first there are the years during which the Ohio farm boy, who wanted to be an artist, worked himself into the scientific world in Washington, D.C.

Holmes was born, as he liked to recall, on the same day and year as the Smithsonian Institution with which he was associated for more than fifty years. The day was December 1, 1846; the place, a farm at Short Creek in Jefferson County, Ohio. Holmes could trace his ancestors in America back seven generations to Obadiah Holmes, who had come to Boston from Lancaster County in England in about 1638. The family had moved from Massachusetts to Rhode Island, then to New Jersey, Virginia, and finally to

Ohio. Short Creek, Ohio is near Adena, the site of famous prehistoric mounds, but there is no evidence that Holmes was much interested in these or in archaeology of any kind as a youth. He had two older brothers who with his father did most of the heavy work on the farm so he was generally free to do as he pleased. He liked to draw and sketch. When he wanted paints, he squeezed berries and weeds to get red and green juice until the long trip could be made to a nearby town.[2]

The earliest art work Holmes saved, a drawing of "My Dog Studying the Fish,"[3] is dated 1865, when he was nineteen years old. It must have been around this time that he decided to try a career in art. He alternately taught school and attended the McNeely Normal School in Ohio until his graduation in 1870, while trying to find someone who would give him art lessons. Twice he was rebuffed by Ohio artists who did not want to take pupils. Then a local man who worked in Washington as a clerk in the War Department suggested that Holmes try the well-known Washington artist Theodore Kauffman. Holmes took the two hundred dollars his father had advanced him for a special course of study at the State Normal School in Salem, Massachusetts and went instead to Washington, D.C. in May of 1871.

Kauffman accepted Holmes as a pupil, and in his studio Homes met Mary Henry, the daughter of Joseph Henry, famous physicist and first secretary of the Smithsonian Institution. From her Holmes learned of the Smithsonian and decided to see it for himself. On his first visit there he was observed sketching and was invited upstairs to meet some of the Smithsonian scientists. He was asked if he would like to do illustrations for their work. Holmes accepted with enthusiasm and was soon doing drawings of fossil shells and living species of mollusks for William H. Dall and of birds for Spencer F. Baird.

Dall and Baird were the first scientists with whom Holmes came into contact, and, although he worked for them for less than a year, their influence on him was considerable.

W.H. Dall was a young naturalist who had studied briefly with Louis Agassiz and then made repeated trips to Russian America, or Alaska, as it was called after its purchase by the United States in 1867. In 1871 when Holmes first met him, Dall was working in the tower of the Smithsonian on his studies of mollusks. Subsequently he joined the United States Coast Guard and returned to Alaska where he studied the native tribes and took

William Henry Holmes

"Holmes on an ocean of 'paleoliths'"

time out to excavate a shell heap on one of the Aleutian Islands. In the shell heap Dall identified successive strata from the food remains: first an *Echinus* (shellfish) layer, then a layer of fish bones, and finally a layer of bones of large mammals. These layers, he wrote, "correspond to actual stages of development in the social history of the people who formed the shell-heaps."[4] Dall recognized that the sharp break between the first and second layers meant either a sudden incursion or more advanced peoples or a new invention which led to a change of habits. Dall's report was published in 1877. There is no evidence that Holmes read it, but he may have kept up with the work of his former employer. Seven years later Holmes made masterful use of this same stratigraphic method in work he was doing outside Mexico City, this time with ceramic shards, not with kitchen refuse such as Dall has studied.

From Spencer Baird, Holmes learned the importance of careful observation. Holmes had drawn a title page for the book Baird was writing on birds. When Baird saw it, he leaned toward it and inquired, "Well, what is the species of the bird?"[5] Holmes was so chagrined that the incident remained etched in his mind for years thereafter. He was subsequently to be famous for the accuracy of his drawings.

Holmes kept a notebook during his first year in Washington in which he recorded events of special interest, and two of these stand out in the light of his later work. In the Patent Office building where ethnological objects belonging to the federal government were kept, he came across effigies of two Indian chiefs in full dress which he thought were "hideous."[6] He later labelled this experience his first lesson in ethnology. At the Smith Gallery Holmes admired a landscape painting by Albert Bierstadt. Bierstadt was the first major landscape painter to go west, having joined an expedition exploring wagon routes through the Rocky Mountains in 1859.[7] Holmes wished ardently that he might have a chance to do likewise.

He did not have long to wait. In 1872 Henry Elliott, the official painter on F.V. Hayden's Geological and Geographical Survey of the Territories, decided instead to go on an expedition to Alaska, and Holmes was appointed to the survey in his place.

The survey which Holmes joined in 1872 had just lobbied successfully for the establishment of the first national park in the country. Ferdinand V. Hayden had gone into the Yellowstone area in 1871 with a party which included Henry Elliott, the photographer W.H. Jackson, and the painter

Thomas Moran. With the help of Moran's watercolors and Jackson's photographs, Hayden promoted the establishment of Yellowstone National Park on March 1, 1872. The Hayden Survey returned to Yellowstone in 1872 and in subsequent summers worked in Colorado. Holmes painted and sketched, he climbed mountains (at which he was very adept), and he began to learn the science of geology. He studied and drew the succession of geological strata, noting accumulations of sedimentary layers and signs of abrupt and violent disruption.[8] His observations and the reasoning based on them made him one of the co-discoverers of what later in geology came to be called "the lacolithic idea," a recognition that eruptive rocks can break through sedimentary strata.[9] By 1874 Holmes had learned enough geology in the field to be appointed assistant geologist on the survey, and in 1875 he was put in charge of the division of the survey which worked in the San Juan valley of New Mexico, Arizona, and Colorado.

The San Juan valley is the Cliff-Dweller region, and Holmes gave himself the additional assignment of examining the ancient ruins in the area. He studied lowland settlements, cave dwellings, and cliff houses and the agricultural products, pottery, and rock inscriptions associated with them. He and his party found a number of large ruins around Mesa Verde, but they missed the biggest one, Cliff Palace, which was first brought to public attention in 1888 after it had been found by the local traders Al and Richard Wetherill.[10] The 1874 expedition was Holmes's first venture into archaeology, and at the time only an interesting diversion for him, although he wrote later that he had found the relics so fascinating that it was hard to keep the geologic problems properly in mind.[11]

Holmes drew one general conclusion about the area. He thought, from the pottery and house ruins, that the cliff-dwellers were the ancestors, not of Utes and Navahos and other nomadic peoples living in the area in the nineteenth century, but of pueblo tribes in New Mexico and Arizona. Little else could be said until excavations were undertaken. Holmes surveyed and sketched on these trips; he did not do any digging. Still a geologist, he commented wistfully that "a rich reward awaits the fortunate archaeologist" who can work in this area.[12]

Holmes spent his seventh and final summer with the Hayden Survey again in Yellowstone National Park. His remarkably accurate sketches of the geological formations were beginning to be noticed, and Hayden named a mountain peak for him in recognition of his work. It was fifty years however before the full scientific harvest of the 1878 Yellowstone survey was realized. In 1929 two geologists studying Yellowstone Canyon came across Holmes's 1878 report and discovered that he had anticipated their interpretation of the geology of the area. R.M. Field and O.T. Jones called on Holmes in Washington to congratulate him and included in their published report several paragraphs from Holmes's report of 1878 and a map and section that he had drawn of the Canyon. [13] Holmes, then eighty-two, was delighted to be rediscovered as a geologist and wrote Field a characteristically wry expression of thanks. [14]

In July of 1879 Holmes left Washington for a year of art studies in Europe. He travelled in Italy and lived for a few months in the American artists' colony in Munich, but he may have been hoping for a career with an institution for he wrote his future wife from Dresden that "Prof. Mayer [sic], of the Anthropologie Museum, has given us a great lesson in Museum making, which is what we are here for." [15] This was A.B. Meyer, later Director of the Royal Zoological, Anthropological, and Ethnographical Museum in Dresden who in 1899 spent several months in the United States visiting museums from New York to Chicago. Holmes and Meyer were but two of the many museum builders and scholars who in this period went back and forth across the Atlantic observing one another's work. When some twenty-five years later Holmes went to Stuttgart for the International Congress of Americanists, he stopped along the way at fifty different museums. [16]

Holmes returned from his carefree year as an art student to a reorganized Geological Survey. In 1879 Congress had discontinued the separate and, to some extent, rival Hayden, King, and Powell surveys and in their place established the United States Geological Survey. Clarence King headed it for a year, after which John Wesley Powell, the guiding force behind the reorganization, was made Director. Holmes was named geological assistant and sent out with Major Clarence Dutton to survey the Grand Canyon of the Colorado. There he did the magnificent sketches, panoramic views, and maps for which he is justly famous. (see Plate X) The frontispiece and most of the illustrations in Clarence Dutton's *Tertiary History of the Grand Canyon District* are Holmes's work, as are the accompanying panoramas in the atlas. Wallace Stegner called it "the most beautiful book produced by any of the surveys." [17]

Stegner insisted that none of the famous survey photographers, not W.H.
Jackson or J.K. Hillers or T.H. O'Sullivan or the artist Thomas Moran,
clarified the West as Holmes did. Stegner wrote:

> A Holmes panorama cuts through the haze, it is clear to the farthest
> distance as no photograph ever is. By almost imperceptible tricks of
> contrast it emphasizes lines of stratification and the profiles of ero-
> sional forms. More impressively than any Western artist, even Moran,
> he captured the plastic qualities of rock. Look at his sketches: the ar-
> chitecture of his sedimentaries is instantly recognizable, his granite
> could be nothing else, his lava is frozen motion.[18]

Something of what Holmes himself intended he expressed in his report to
the director of the Geological Survey in 1885. He wrote:

> Illustrations are no longer to be treated chiefly as a means of embel-
> lishment; they are expected to express facts with a clearness and accu-
> racy not surpassed by the language of the letter press.[19]

The strong scholarly convention that scientific knowledge is conveyed in
the text, not in the pictures, has, however, remained unshaken. The Grand
Canyon sketches and panoramas did not find their way into Holmes's vast
and official bibliography as an acknowledged part of his scientific work.[20]

Throughout the 1880s Holmes was a geologist in charge of the illustrative
work of the Geological Survey, but he took on many other projects, some of
his own choosing and some assigned to him by John Wesley Powell. In the
spring of 1884 he left his bride, Kate Clifton Osgood, whom he had married
in the fall of 1883, to travel for two months in Mexico in a private railroad
car with three photographers, Mr. and Mrs. Chaim, and W.H. Jackson, his
old associate from the Hayden Survey. It was in Mexico that Holmes happened on a site which led him to make a fundamental advance in American
archaeology.

The Mexico City Central Railway station was on the outskirts of the city,
and it happened to be near an adobe brick factory which had open diggings
eight to ten feet deep. Holmes had observed that the Mexican museum had

Panorama from Point Sublime, Looking West

little information on the origin and chronology of the objects it exhibited, and he decided to seize this opportunity to learn what he could.

He spent several weeks at the site. The section showed two periods of occupation, and the pottery fragments were clearly accumulated with the soil and not subsequent intrusions. They were deposited in more or less continuous layers and the fragments occurring at corresponding depths had "identical character." The pottery of the lower part of the section was of an archaic type, and Holmes thought it represented an early epoch of the art of Anahuac, the central Mexican plateau. The upper part of the section contained handsome pottery like that found in the pyramid of Cholula and in the ancient graves of Costa Rica and New Granada. Holmes found two other varieties of ware in the upper part of the lower beds, finer ware than that with which it coexisted. Perhaps, he suggested, the first people to settle there, possibly the Aztecs, made the crude ware and later secured the finer ware in trade with more advanced peoples of neighboring settlements. There was also a third variety, beginning a little higher in the section, which was identical to that found in the pyramids of San Juan Teotihuacan, Texcoco, and Cholula. It was apparently the forerunner of the pottery in the upper deposits of the section. Holmes wrote in conclusion:

> It may be affirmed with certainty that the site of the City of Mexico was at one time occupied by a people in a very primitive stage of art, the remains of which art, so far as found, include nothing but fragments of an extremely rude pottery. There are no traces of tools and no indications of houses. This period of occupancy was a very long one, as it permitted the accumulation in nearly horizontal layers of at least eight feet of finely comminuted refuse.
>
> . . . far along in this period of occupancy new forms of art appeared that do not look like the work of the proper occupants of the site produced by gradual improvement, but rather like intrusive products acquired by exchange or otherwise from more cultured tribes. Again, at the end of this first period there is a horizon, pretty well marked, above which primitive forms of art do not appear.
>
> Near the base of the deposits of the second period foundations of houses are discovered in which rubble, squared stones, and adobe bricks have been used. In this part of the section we find stone imple-

ments and ceramic products of a very high order of merit. With these, and especially near the surface, there is a layer abounding in obsidian implements. This marks the last and culminating stage of Aztec art, ending in the historic period proper.[21]

Holmes here began the sophisticated use of stratigraphy in American archaeology. The first important use of stratigraphy in New World archaeology was not, as has been alleged, Manuel Gamio's work directed by Franz Boas in the Valley of Mexico in 1911 or Nels C. Nelson's work in New Mexico in 1914, but Holmes's work in Mexico more than twenty-five years earlier.[22] Before Holmes, Thomas Jefferson had recognized strata when he excavated a mound as had Jeffries Wyman and William H. Dall in their work in shell heaps. Beginning with Holmes, however, careful use of stratigraphy became the cornerstone of American work in archaeology. Holmes recognized both what its possibilities were and what was necessary in order for it to prove anything at all. He rejected Adolph Bandelier's suggestion that at Pecos and the Rio Grande a lower level which contained coiled ware but no ancient painted Pueblo ware might be evidence of a coiled pottery people antecedent to the painted ware people. Holmes pointed out that the two kinds of ware might have been made at the same time but in different places. He insisted, "Unless there is an actual super-position of the ancient painted ware upon deposits of the coiled variety, we learn nothing of chronological importance."[23]

Holmes made excellent use of stratigraphy again in a paper in 1894 on "Caribbean Influence in the Prehistoric Art of the Southern States." He wrote:

> The ceramic products bearing evidence of Caribbean influence in Florida belong to the latest pre-Columbian times—the Timuquanan-Muskhogean period—while the earlier pottery, represented in what appears to be a middle period of shell-heap deposition, affiliates with phases of the art prevalent in the Gulf States beyond the limits of supposed Carib influence.[24]

This paper was published in the *American Anthropologist* and was read widely. Daniel Brinton referred to it two years later at a meeting of the

American Philosophical Society in pointing out that Cushing was in error in thinking that Florida had been settled from the Caribbean. Holmes's ceramic studies showed that influence from the Caribbean appeared late in Florida, long after the area was first settled.[25]

Again in 1903 in his "Aboriginal Pottery of the Eastern United States" Holmes pointed the way. Clarence Moore, a Philadelphia businessman turned archaeologist, had invited Holmes to describe his collections from the mounds and shell heaps of Florida, Georgia, and Alabama. Holmes was very impressed with Moore and with the collections he had carefully gathered, and he predicted that careful study of the collection would make it possible to (1) assign the pottery to particular tribes and stocks of peoples, (2) correlate it with culture features of neighboring regions, and (3) determine chronology. As Gordon Willey has noted, this is essentially a modern view.[26]

From 1884 on Holmes repeatedly, and in prominent places, discussed his own use of stratigraphy and showed what could be done with it. Most anthropologists were aware of his work. The technique entered the mainstream of American archaeology and became in effect taken for granted. F.W. Putnam used it in interpreting the work he sponsored in the Trenton gravels, Max Uhle used it in his work in South America, and Franz Boas and Manuel Gamio used it in the Valley of Mexico.[27] Yet in 1936 looking back over his career, Franz Boas wrote:

> It is true that I have done little archaeological work myself. My own only contribution was the establishment of the sequence of archaic, Teotihuacan type and Aztec in Mexico, I believe—except Dall's work on the Aleutian Islands—the first stratigraphic work in North America.[28]

Boas made this claim twenty-five years after the fact in a heated response to an analysis of his work by A.L. Kroeber. Much ill feeling had by then passed between Boas and Holmes, and Boas's blocking out of his rival is understandable. Yet what remains is the fact that again the historical record was altered and another important American anthropologist, this time William Henry Holmes, has not gotten the credit due him.

Holmes joined the Geological Survey when he returned from the year in Europe, but he was soon drawn into Washington anthropology as it developed around John Wesley Powell. Holmes studied the collections in the National Museum and wrote monographs on aboriginal American art which were then published by the Bureau of Ethnology. The ease with which Holmes moved between the Geological Survey, the Bureau of Ethnology, and the National Museum is an indication of the close connection between them, that connection being Powell, who had taken it upon himself to organize government work in anthropology.

John Wesley Powell was the eldest son of an immigrant and itinerant Methodist preacher.[29] He was born in New York state, but the family moved west in stages through his boyhood. By the time he was eighteen, they were in Illinois. Powell picked up an education in science wherever he could and taught school until he volunteered to fight in the Civil War. He lost his right arm above the elbow at Shiloh, but he returned to duty and rose to the rank of major. He was Major Powell for the rest of his life. He made his name and reputation in daring and much publicized explorations down the Green and Colorado Rivers in 1869 and 1871 and then moved to Washington to seek support for further explorations. His ability, enthusiasm, and political acumen soon made him a leader in the scientific community in Washington, D.C. It was in his parlor that friends and colleagues, including Henry Adams, Clarence Dutton, and Captain Garrick Mallery, gathered in 1878 to form the Cosmos Club, subsequently the gathering place for Washington's intellectual elite. Powell was elected temporary president of the group, and William Henry Holmes was soon a member.[30]

Powell derived much of his political power from close relations with members of Congress. He befriended a junior congressman who had lost a leg in the war, and that man, D.B. Henderson, eventually was a member of the appropriations committee and then Speaker of the House. For thirty years Powell exchanged gloves with another long-term congressman, C.E. Hooker from Mississippi, who had lost his left arm in the battle of Vicksburg.[31] These associations stood him in good stead when he wanted something. What he wanted and got in 1879 was a massive Geological Survey and a much smaller research-oriented Bureau of Ethnology for the study of North American ethnology. The Bureau of Ethnology (after 1894 Bureau of

American Ethnology) was put under the Smithsonian Institution, but it and the Geological Survey were run by Powell.

Five years after its founding the Bureau of Ethnology was described by the visiting English anthropologist E. B. Tylor as "one of the most remarkable things I have seen in this country."[32] Here was an instituion that was doing the work of a scientific society but with the power and leverage of a government department. Tylor commented on the energy and enthusiasm which pervaded the Bureau and on its highly centralized organization, which he compared to the Jesuits. Powell had recruited all kinds of talents: office workers and field collectors with various specialities, research scholars like Holmes, and synthesizers like Powell himself who put the whole thing together along the theoretical lines laid out by Lewis Henry Morgan, whom Powell much admired.[33]

Powell also had at least informal connections with the National Museum, another branch of the Smithsonian Institution, for it housed the objects of material culture collected by his and the other government surveys. Powell and his parties alone had by 1880 gathered more than six thousand pieces of Pueblo pottery.[34]

Holmes was made Honorary Curator of Aboriginal American Ceramics in the National Museum in 1882. He had already done a comprehensive study of the "Art in shell of the ancient Americans,"[35] based on museum collections. Now he turned to pottery, making studies of "Pottery of the ancient Pueblos" and "Ancient Pottery of the Mississippi Valley," both of which were published in the *Fourth Annual Report* of the Bureau of Ethnology, along with a general essay on the "Origin and development of form and ornament in ceramic art."[36] Seventeen years later when his "Aboriginal pottery of the eastern United States"[37] was published, the projected study of the major pottery collections in the country was completed. It was, according to Gordon Willey and Jeremy Sabloff, "a major substantive contribution for it laid the groundwork of archaeological knowledge for ceramics for a large part of North America."[38]

By 1903 when the study was completed, Holmes was interested in historical problems, but when he began the work in 1882, he was less interested in questions of time and migrations than in assigning the earthenware to a particular evolutionary stage. He took his method from biology. The remains of art must be classified and assigned their proper place in the scheme of culture, "just as the naturalist has learned to treat the elements of biologic science."[39] Here the influence of his early work for Dall and Baird at the Smithsonian is apparent.

Holmes classified the objects and then evaluated them in terms of specialization of form, perfection of technique, and range of decorative motives. He ranked the pottery, considering the wheel made ware of the Mediterranean countries to be the best and below that in order came the pottery of Mexico, Central America, and Peru, then ancient Pueblo ware, then Mississippi Valley ware, and finally other prehistoric ware in the eastern United States and in central and northern Europe. Holmes was trying to do for art what Lewis Henry Morgan had done for social structure, that is, show its supposed evolution. He did the kinds of historical studies American anthropologists later concentrated on but in an offhand way, for they were preliminary questions. He really wanted to find out how art had evolved and what that meant for understanding the evolution of human culture.

When Holmes studied the engraved designs on shells, for example, he was less interested in finding out what the designs meant than in insisting that they meant *something*, that at a certain stage in the evolution of art people begin to introduce their religious and philosophical ideas. He wrote:

> I do not assume to interpret these designs; they are not to be interpreted. Besides, there is no advantage to be gained by an interpretation. We have hundreds of primitive myths within our easy reach that are as interesting and instructive as these could be. All I desire is to elevate these works from the category of trinkets to what I believe is their rightful place—the serious art of a people with great capacity for loftier works.[40]

Holmes was perceptive and careful, and he insisted on two principles in this search for the evolution of art. For him, as for Powell, the differences between culture stages were not owing to biological "race" for neither of them took any such categories seriously.[41] Repeatedly Holmes insisted that human beings seem to be "almost the same" in natural wants and capacities, and the "almost" here is a gesture in the direction of scientific caution. Physical anthropologists might come up with some innate differences between groups of people, but he thought whatever they might find would be so slight as to be negligible.

Holmes also insisted that "culture" did not travel as a package or follow a single line of development. He warned that paths of development are different, that some abilities or forms of art may decline or be lost completely, and that a high level of achievement in one area, ceramics for example, is not an adequate indicator of the culture status of a people.[42] He suggested that the early men and women who crossed the Bering Strait to populate the Americas had probably participated in the high grade of culture in Asia but had lost some of their technical skills over time as they fought for survival in harsh climates. Environment was a major factor. As the groups of people and their descendants moved south there was a "tedious but steady" advance in culture.[43] Although it took different forms in different places, Holmes hoped to be able to trace its general course.

Holmes had scarcely begun the pottery studies when he was drawn into one of the most important archaeological controversies in the United States in the late nineteenth century, the question of the mound builders. John Wesley Powell's interests were in linguistics and ethnology, not particularly in archaeology, but public interest in the prehistoric mounds on the Mississippi and Ohio Rivers soon pushed the Bureau of Ethnology in that direction. Who had built the mounds, an ancient, mysterious, and long vanished race? Or were they "merely" Indian? Heinrich Schliemann's excavations on the site of ancient Troy in Asia Minor were much in the news in the late nineteenth century, and many Americans hoped that the mounds were the New World equivalent, that America too had had an epic, even heroic past. Furthermore, if the mounds were not Indian, it was easier for white settlers moving west to argue for Indian removal.[44]

In 1881 Congress voted the Bureau of Ethnology a special appropriation for research on the mounds. Powell assigned the archaeological study of the mounds to Cyrus Thomas who in the course of his long investigation became converted to Powell's view that the mounds were the work of historic Indians. Holmes took on the collateral studies of pottery, textiles, and ornaments found associated with the mounds. He was to decide whether they were similar to Indian arts or so different as to indicate an alien tradition.

Holmes found that they were similar, that, as shown by their textiles and pottery at least, the Moundbuilders had a "status of culture" not superior to that of historic Indian tribes. In the process of reaching this conclusion Holmes invented a new and valuable research technique. Textiles were difficult to study because they were subject to rapid decay and seldom turned

up in museum collections. Holmes found that if he made clay casts of pottery shards that had textile markings, the cords of the fabric would appear
in high relief on the casts. It was a technique he borrowed from
paleobotany, and it worked very well.[45] He found that the mound builders
had used bark, grasses, and weeds in their textiles and that they kept the
meshes open by knotting. Holmes published his conclusions in 1884, but
Cyrus Thomas's final report on the mound explorations did not appear until
ten years later.[46] Then it essentially laid to rest the fanciful speculation
about the mounds. They were the work of historic Indians.

The Moundbuilder studies led Holmes into a new area of investigation,
that of textiles. He published "A Study of the Textile Art in its Relation to
the Development of Form and Ornament" in 1888, and in this he noted "the
remarkable power of this almost universally practiced art" to impose
geometric forms on design elements.[47]

Holmes made special studies of ancient Peruvian textiles and of prehistoric textiles from the eastern United States.[48] In 1890 he summarized
some of the theory he was developing in a paper which he titled "On the
Evolution of Ornament" and called in the text "the natural history of conventional ornament."[49]

Holmes suggested that the idea of ornament goes back to the pre-human
stage of our existence. Decorative or ornamental elements come from two
sources, from nature and from technique, and it was the latter, Holmes
thought, that came first. "In the primitive stages of art, technique deter-
mines what is considered beautiful."[50] When delineative subjects are introduced, they are modified by the mechanical force of the particular art
and by the aesthetic considerations which originate in the consideration of
technical forms. The textile arts of basketry and weaving were early and
widespread, and Holmes insisted on their importance as the source of
geometric motifs.

Holmes was particularly interested in certain conventional decorative
elements that occur in many "advanced cultures" and in many branches of
art: herring-bone, chevron, meander, fret, and scroll. He concluded that it
was impossible to know their exact derivation because they have developed
along different lines among different peoples. So strong is the tendency to
conventionalize and geometricize that any animal motif might by impercep-
tible steps be transformed into any one of the conventional geometric de-

signs. As a result different peoples would associate very different "ideas" with the same geometric motif.

Holmes considered the possibility of contact and borrowing between nations as an explantion for similar design elements, but he thought them less important than changes within the tradition.[51] A key factor in general in Holmes's art studies was his conviction that all art, including "aboriginal" or "primitive" art had a history, that it was not static and unchanging unless acted upon by outside forces but was constantly changing.[52] He also produced interesting and potentially testable speculations, as for example:

Nations practicing arts having pronounced technical characteristics, such as weaving and architecture, and possessing at the same time few or feeble ideographic elements, will develop a highly geometric conventional decoration, while nations practicing arts with less pronounced techniques such as modeling, sculpture, and painting, and who make ideography a prominent feature will have a system of decoration characterized by imperfectly defined conventionalism.[53]

Holmes's work was picked up by Alfred C. Haddon, the English biologist and anthropologist in his book *Evolution in Art: As Illustrated by the Life-Histories of Designs* (1895). Haddon thought realistic representations came first and were afterward conventionalized, but he liked Holmes's demonstrations of the power of conventionalization and geometrization and referred repeatedly to the studies published by Holmes and by Frank Hamilton Cushing in the *Annual Reports* of the Bureau of American Ethnology.[54]

While Holmes was making these pioneering studies of the art of American Indian nations, he was drawn into the second big archaeological question in the United States in the late nineteenth century: how valid was the accumulating evidence pointing to the existence of palaeolithic man in America?

Since 1887 when Dr. Thomas Wilson became curator of prehistoric archaeology at the National Museum, the quest for "palaeolithic man" had come to be strongly associated with that institution. Jeffries Wyman and F.W. Putnam had searched for signs of ancient man in America, but the very term they used, ancient man, indicated a more open and less European derived concept. Wilson however had come to the National Museum after having spent five years in France at Abbeville and the Dordogne valley, among the most famous prehistoric sites in Europe. He was looking for "paleoliths" analogous to those he had seen in Europe and supposedly dating from the same geological periods.[55] In 1888 he had Secretary Langley of the Smithsonian send out a circular asking that rudely shaped stones or "paleolithic implements" be collected wherever they were found and shipped to the National Museum. Soon he had nearly eight hundred to add to the nine hundred and fifty he had already collected, and there were reports of six thousand others in scattered collections around the country.[56] Wilson began his study of these in an article in the *American Anthropologist* in 1889 on "The Paleolithic Period in the District of Columbia."[57]

It was too much for Major Powell, who moved Holmes from the Geological Survey to the Bureau of Ethnology, changed his profession from "Geologist" to "Archeologist," and told him to begin work on the palaeolithic problem. Holmes was eventually to spend nearly five years on the assignment, and when he was finished, Powell called it, rightly, "the most thorough single piece of archeologic research ever conducted in America."[58]

When Holmes began his work, Thomas Wilson believed that form alone was enough to indicate age, but F.W. Putnam had cautioned in the *American Anthropologist* that to be labeled "paleolithic" an object must have come unquestionably from glacial gravels. Vertical sections must be carefully examined. "It is no longer enough," Putnam wrote, "to pick things up on the surface."[59]

Holmes went first to a quarry in the District of Columbia. He was soon convinced that the site had been an Indian workshop for flaked-stone tools. He found rejects from each stage of the process, and by striking stones one against another, he was able to reproduce most of the shapes he found. The famous "turtle-backs" were not crude tools dating back to palaeolithic or glacial times but more likely failures cast aside by historic Indians as they toiled over the production of arrowheads (see Plate IX).[60]

It was not its shape but where an object was found that indicated its age. In this Holmes agreed with Putnam, and he spoke respectfully, at first, of the Putnam-sponsored finds in glacial gravels at Trenton, New Jersey and elsewhere. Then, however, he went to inspect those sites himself.

Holmes went first to Little Falls, Minnesota, where some famous flaked quartz "palaeoliths" turned out to be surface finds.[61] Next he went to Trenton, New Jersey, where C.C. Abbott had been finding "palaeoliths" since the 1870s. By chance the city of Trenton was cutting a trench to the Delaware River through the very bluff on which finds had previously been made. Holmes stationed his assistant, William Dinwiddie, to watch carefully as the trench was cut and the gravels exposed. Dinwiddie was there for a month. No palaeoliths tumbled out of the previously undisturbed gravels. Holmes was convinced that Abbott had found nothing but Indian shop-refuse which had settled into the surface deposits of the bluff. They have made "a scheme of culture evolution that spans ten thousand years," he wrote, out of a day's work of one Indian.[62]

Holmes continued his attack in *Science* in 1893, calling the literature on palaeolithic man so hopelessly full of blunders and misconceptions that it was "a stumbling-block to science."[63] The whole question ought to be tackled only by those thoroughly versed in geology and in all early phases of human art, Holmes wrote, not admitting that this limitation would leave him nearly alone in the field.

Meanwhile Holmes continued his own meticulous studies of stone implements found in the tidewater country of Maryland and Virginia. Holmes wanted to prove that the rude stone implements had been made by historic Indians, the Algonquins and their neighbors, and that there was no evidence of an earlier race of much lower culture. To do this, he needed to account for every shaped stone he found. He began by distinguishing between workshop sites and village sites. Then he studied the workshop sites and surmised from what was rejected that the desired product was a leaf-shaped blade. Finally, he showed how, by stemming, trimming, and notching, the leaf-shaped blades were turned into the knives, spearheads, and arrow-points commonly found on Indian sites all through the area. Holmes called this the "Natural History of Flaked Stone Implements,"[64] when he presented it to a large gathering of anthropologists at the World's Columbian Exposition in Chicago in 1893.

In the *American Anthropologist* in the same year Holmes spelled out the "Distribution of Stone Implements in the Tidewater Country." He traced the various kinds of stone to their sources in the distant mountains. He showed how they had been carried by flowing streams to various deposits which when discovered became quarry sites. Once the rough stones had been worked, he found a logic in their distribution. He wrote:

other things being equal, human distribution of small things is far, of large objects near; implements of war and the chase travel far, domestic utensils remain near; improvised articles or devices are near, highly elaborated and valuable objects go far; with thoroughfares distribution is far, across thoroughfares it is near. Much-occupied sites are richly stocked with utensils, and slightly occupied spots have but few; sites near the source or sources of supply have a wealth of art, very distant ones have almost nothing; sites convenient to a plentiful supply of one material have many tools of that material, sites remote from any of the sources have a limited supply from many sources. A sedentary people will not distribute widely; wandering or semi-sedentary tribes will transport their possessions to many distant places, and sites occupied by numerous tribes in turn will have diversified art remains. It may be further noted that on sites devoted to single or simple industries the range of tools will be small and on sites where occupations are varied the range will be large, and that where peoples are varied, occupations varied, and materials varied, and time long we will have the widest range.[65]

With that background Holmes described several different sites in the Tidewater country and interpreted what was found there.

Then Holmes put the separate pieces together in a short and deceptively titled monograph, "Stone Implements of the Potomac-Tide-Water Province," published in the *Annual Report* of the Bureau of American Ethnology for the year 1893–1894.[66] In it Holmes showed by example how archaeological work ought to be done, and, by implication, he demolished the claims for palaeolithic man in the New World.

Holmes had early discovered that, as he wrote, it was almost as hard to sift the truth out of the literature as to dig the data out of the ground.[67] He was determined to change that situation. He had already corrected diverse accounts of a large monolith in Mexico[68] and had pointed out that the famous Serpent Mound in Ohio was being incorrectly restored.[69] In 1892

F.W. Putnam jocularly accused him of "annihilating paleolithic man."[70] A year later Putnam confessed that he was so driven with work on the World's Fair that he did not have time to read anything and hardly knew what was going on in the archaeological world, but when the fair was over he would catch up.[71]

Accordingly the two men defended their respective positions in 1897 at a special joint meeting of Sections E and H, Geology and Anthropology, of the American Association for the Advancement of Science. Holmes insisted that the question was not the age of man in America, for linguistic diversity showed that man had been in America for a long time. The question was whether the archaeological evidence thus far presented could stand scientific scrutiny. Putnam insisted that the evidence then being produced at Trenton by Ernest Volk could.[72] Neil Judd wrote of debates on this question that "Holmes, always quiet and reserved, argued calmly, but McGee, so tradition has it, supported his beliefs with much table-pounding."[73]

In 1898 the prestigious Loubat First Prize for the most noteworthy work in American anthropology during the previous five years went to Holmes's monograph, "Stone Implements of the Potomac-Tide-Water Province." The judges, H.T. Peck, D.G. Brinton, and W J McGee, passed over a manuscript by Frank Hamilton Cushing titled "Tomahawk and Calumet, Shield and Gorget," a paper by Walter Hoffman on the Menomini Indians, and one by Karl Lumholz on "Objective Symbolism of the Huichol Indians." They gave the runner-up award to Franz Boas for his work on "The Social Organization and Secret Societies of the Kwakiutl Indians."[74]

The Loubat award established Holmes as one of the foremost anthropologists in the country, and it put the weight of scientific opinion behind his position on palaeolithic man. Holmes continued to examine the evidence as it was brought forth: the famous Calaveras skull which had been found in a California gold mine in 1866 and a skull found in glacial gravels in Lansing, Kansas.[75] Both he thought were recent intrusions. He went to a site at Kimmswick, Missouri where mammoth and mastodon remains had been found, hoping to find traces of man in direct association with these fossil remains but found none.[76] There seemed to be no evidence that human beings had been in America during palaeolithic times, i.e., before the last ice age.

Holmes wrote with pride in his memoirs:

At the beginning of this period [his investigation of flaked stone tools]....Museum cases were filled with rudely chipped stones labelled "American Paleolithic Implements"....at the close of the period no implement or chipped stone of any kind was to be found in an American museum of repute labelled "paleolithic."[77]

As Holmes was writing these words, the kind of evidence for which he had looked in vain was found. In 1926 at Folsom, New Mexico, a flaked point was found lodged between the ribs of an extinct mammal.[78] Here at last was convincing proof of palaeolithic man. What Holmes thought about this new development is not on record. He was by then well out of anthropology.

The Loubat award made official what many people were already beginning to realize, that William Henry Holmes was a man to reckon with. George Dorsey called him in 1898 "America's greatest anthropologist."[79] During the previous twenty years Holmes had moved from geology to anthropology. For the next twenty years he was to be a reluctant leader in his new profession. Holmes did not seek honors and positions of leadership for himself, but he accepted them as they came. Even before the Loubat Prize, Holmes's achievements as an archaeologist and museum man had been recognized, beginning with the Columbian Exposition in Chicago.

The World's Columbian Exposition in Chicago in 1893 was a significant event for anthropology in the United States. Besides the official Anthropological Building, which had exhibits organized by F.W. Putnam and Franz Boas, the federal government had an anthropology exhibit in its building, representing both the National Museum and the Bureau of Ethnology and organized by Holmes.[80] The main government exhibit was based on Powell's map of linguistic families, each group being represented by figures engaged in characteristic arts and industries. There was also an exhibit of Indian mining and quarrying techniques, for which Holmes created a special quarry "group," three life-size plaster figures engaged in stone chipping and flaking. At least two important phenomena in American anthropology date from the exhibits at Chicago: the use of life-size plaster "groups" in museums and the "culture-area" concept.

O.T. Mason returned home from the Chicago Fair in 1893 to work out a scheme of eighteen American Indian culture areas extending from the Arctic to Patagonia. This was the beginning of the "culture-area" concept, subsequently developed in the United States by A.L. Kroeber and Clark Wissler, and Mason included as influences on him Major Powell's linguistic map and a paper which Franz Boas had read at Chicago based on his and Putnam's work there.[81]

The quarry group which Holmes created was the beginning of the use of life-size models in anthropology museums.[82] Holmes actually made three quarry groups, one for Chicago, one for the National Museum in Washington, D.C., and one for an outdoor site at Piny Branch outside Washington which Frank Cushing helped him set up. Subsequently F.W. Putnam and Franz Boas used life-size groups for exhibits at the American Museum of Natural History in New York, and such groups became one of the most popular methods of museum presentation.

Holmes had therefore attracted attention in Chicago as an innovative museum man, and he had given one of the most significant papers at the Congress of Anthropology held there, his "Natural History of Flaked Stone Implements." Within months of the end of the Exposition, Holmes was put in the ironic position of being called to Chicago to take charge of the rival anthropology exhibits, those assembled by Putnam and Boas which had become part of the new Field Museum. Frank Hamilton Cushing arranged a banquet in his honor as he prepared to leave Washington for Chicago, and nearly one hundred of his friends gathered for dinner and testimonials, both humorous and serious, and the presentation of an engraved loving cup.[83]

Holmes was unhappy in Chicago, in particular with the management of the Field Museum, and he left as soon as he decently could.[84] There was, however, one compensation, a three month exploring expedition to Yucatan with Mr. Allison V. Armour of Chicago, on the latter's yacht. On the expedition Holmes drew maps, ground plans, and panoramic views of many of the ancient ruins of Yucatan and Central America which were subsequently published by the Field Museum in a large volume called *Archeological Studies Among the Ancient Ruins of Mexico*. A significant feature of these drawings is that, unlike his Far West panoramas, here Holmes tampered with nature, eliminating it for the most part in order better to show the buildings. Although hastily and impressionistically done, Holmes's Mexican sketches have been found to be amazingly accurate.[85]

In October of 1897 Holmes returned to Washington to head the Department of Anthropology in the reorganized National Museum. He took up again his studies of American Indian pottery, planned museum exhibits, and in 1900 spent three months on a collecting trip in Cuba and Jamaica with Major Powell.[86]

A new era in Holmes's life began when he was appointed Powell's successor at the Bureau (see Plate VIII) three weeks after Powell's death on September 23, 1902. Holmes did not seek the position. He took it only after the anthropological community, himself included, had tried to persuade Smithsonian Secretary Samuel P. Langley to appoint W J McGee, the heir apparent. When Langley would not be moved, Holmes took the job, but he took pains to indicate his disinterestedness, asking Langley to make him "chief" rather than "director" and at a lesser salary than Powell had received.[87]

Holmes carried on the Bureau as best he could, despite a reduced budget and a full scale investigation in the summer of 1903 into the affairs of the Bureau. A major product of the Holmes years at the Bureau was the invaluable *Handbook of American Indians*. At Langley's behest a dictionary of Indian tribes was expanded to include descriptions of Indian tribes, bands, and other social units, biographies of noted Indians, and sketches of native arts and customs. Part One of Bulletin 30, the Handbook, was published in 1907, Part Two in 1910. Frederick W. Hodge was the general editor, almost everyone at the Bureau was involved in it, and there were numerous guest contributors including Alice Fletcher who wrote on "Music and Musical Instruments" and Franz Boas who wrote on "Language" and "Religion." Holmes made the greatest contribution to the *Handbook* himself, writing on more than a hundred topics.

Holmes traveled widely as head of the Bureau of American Ethnology and a senior scholar-statesman, but reluctantly, always fearful "that he should find himself a stranger in a strange land," as he expressed his feelings about a trip to Chile for the first Pan-American Scientific Congress in 1908–1909.[88] Heading for Berlin in 1904 on his way to the meeting of the Congress of Americanists at Stuttgart, he asked Franz Boas to meet him at the station and help him find his way around.[89] Throughout his long years of study of American Indian art, Holmes never attempted to observe first-hand the Indian peoples at work. Pottery, textiles, metal work, stone tools—all that Holmes knew about these arts and industries he learned from the study of the objects themselves and from his own attempts at re-producing them. Once he asked James Mooney, who was going to the Cherokee villages of western North Carolina, to find out what he could about how the Cherokee women made pottery, and Mooney duly reported back to him.[90] He never went himself. Archaeological digs where Holmes could take his associates and direct the work were one thing, but "field work," that twentieth century hallmark of social and cultural anthropology, was quite another. Perhaps the reserve and dignity for which Holmes was famous covered an insecurity that made him hesitate to go where he did not know the language, where he might feel ill at ease, and where he could not move confidently through institutional halls a recognized and respected scholar.

Holmes did not like administrative work, and it was with relief that he re-signed from the Bureau of American Ethnology in 1909 and returned to his former position as head curator of the department of anthropology in the National Museum. He planned the anthropological exhibits for the new museum building, arranging most of them according to geographical areas rather than "grade of culture" for he had come to see that the latter was complicated and uncertain at best.[91] He also worked on a *Handbook of American Antiquities*,[92] Part One of which was published in 1919 and won for Holmes the second prize in the Loubat awards of 1923. The second part was never finished.

Holmes became a member of the managing committee of the School of American Archaeology in Santa Fe in 1910 after Alice Fletcher had quar-reled with F.W. Putnam, Franz Boas, and Charles P. Bowditch over the founding of that school, and he succeeded her as chairman of the committee when she retired in 1912. The school was largely run by its director, Edgar L. Hewett, but Holmes gave it kindly encouragement from a distance and the prestige of association with his name. The parent body of the School of American Archaeology was the Archaeological Institute of America, and from 1914 on Holmes contributed frequently to its new journal *Art and Archaeology*, whose editor, Mitchell Carroll, was a Washington friend of Holmes's. Holmes did a series on "Masterpieces of aboriginal American art"[93] and served for a time as art editor of the journal.

In 1920 Holmes left the National Museum to become the first director of the National Gallery of Art, newly established as a separate part of the Smithsonian Institution. The separation was his idea. His Department of Anthropology at the National Museum had included not only archaeology, ethnology, and physical anthropology which he established in 1903 when he brought a skull collection over from the United States Army Museum and hired Aleš Hrdlička, but also technology, history, and art. The art collection was meagre after a fire in the Smithsonian building in 1865 but had been growing recently through bequests. Holmes thought it ought to be a separate and publicly recognized institution.

Holmes was seventy-four years old when he took on this new job and he stayed with it for twelve years, through an amputation of his left leg above the knee in 1926 after a sore foot developed into blood poisoning. At least one friend felt that part of the trouble came from the damage that the stone floors of the National Gallery had done to a delicate foot.[94] Holmes had two shows of his own watercolors in Washington galleries in the 1920s, but mainly he was preoccupied with bringing the National Gallery to public attention and in trying to get a separate building for it. In 1929 Congress set aside land on Pennsylvania, but no building followed. In 1931 there were rumors, verified by *Art Digest*,[95] that the Soviet Government had sold masterpieces from the Hermitage Museum in Petrograd to Andrew W. Mellon, the Secretary of the Treasury of the United States, in order to get money to finance their second Five Year Plan for economic development. Holmes watched these developments with interest, but the following year he retired and went to live with one of his two sons in Red Oak, Michigan. There on April 20, 1933 he died.

Soon afterward Andrew Mellon offered his art collection to the federal government with money for a building and maintenance. But Mellon did not want to endow an existing institution. He wanted to found his own, and he wanted it to be called the National Gallery of Art. Faced with such munificence the Congress and the Smithsonian Institution were obliging, and what had been the National Gallery of Art became on March 24, 1937 the National Collection of Fine Arts. The old name went to the new museum created by Mellon.[96] Holmes's two creations, the National Collection of Fine Arts and the National Portrait Gallery, did not have a home of their own until they were moved into the Old Patent Office building in 1968.

One last event in Holmes's life is noteworthy for it showed not only tensions within the anthropological community but also an aspect of Holmes's character previously glimpsed only in the vehemence with which he pursued the question of palaeolithic man. In 1919 Holmes wrote a resolution of censure against Franz Boas which was presented to the American Anthropological Association. The resolution was carried by a vote of twenty-one to ten, and as a result Boas was excluded from the Council of the American Anthropological Association and forced to resign from the National Reserarch Council.[97]

The immediate issue was a letter Boas had written to *The Nation* which was published on December 20, 1919, in which he questioned Woodrow Wilson's integrity as President of the United States and protested the activities of certain anthropologists in Latin America who "have prostituted science by using it as a cover for their activities as spies."[98] The explosion which this letter precipitated can be explained not only as part of the general high tide of patriotism and xenophobia which swept over the country after World War I but also as the culmination of long festering resentments against Boas. Holmes participated in both of these currents of feeling.

The careers of William Holmes and Franz Boas had been intertwined for twenty-five years, ever since Chicago in 1894 when Holmes was given the job at the Field Museum which Boas felt was his due. Subsequently Holmes had won the Loubat Prize for which Boas was runner-up. Then chance threw the two men into a close working relationship.

Franz Boas had begun to do linguistic work for the Bureau of American Ethnology before Powell's death. When Holmes became Bureau Chief, Boas had to get authorization for work to be done and pay vouchers from him. Holmes in turn had to mediate between commitments Boas had made to linguistic workers out in the field and Secretary Langley's order that all other work be dropped in order to complete the *Handbook of American Indians* as soon as possible. Occasionally the voluminous correspondence between the two men became an almost comic dialogue of challenge and response. Boas asked on February 17, 1904 why his name had not been included in the list of officers of the Smithsonian Institution printed on the back of the new Quarterly, and Holmes replied the next day, "an accident, I am sure."

Boas asked on October 29, 1904 why the Bureau linguists, John Swanton and J.N.B. Hewitt, should go over his manuscripts, and Holmes answered, "in order that they might form a more definite idea as to what you desired from them. I cannot conceive that this should be against your wishes or difficult to understand."

If Holmes did not reply immediately to a flurry of Boas letters, Boas would write, as he did on January 23, 1903 and again two years later, "Dear Sir: I have not had the pleasure of receiving a reply to my various communications."[99]

Boas was hostile and Holmes slightly condescending, as when he referred to an exhibit of designs by different Indian tribes which Boas was putting together for the Louisiana Purchase Exposition as "your little exhibit of symbols for the Exposition."[100] But they were able to work together. Holmes encouraged Boas to move ahead on his proposed *Handbook of American Indian Languages,* an updating of Powell's *Introduction to the Study of Indian Languages* (1877) and *Indian Linguistic Families* (1891), for which Boas had worked out a new method in which he classified languages by morphology rather than by vocabulary as Powell had done. Part One of his *Handbook of American Indian Languages* was published in 1911, Part Two in 1922 and 1938.[101]

Franz Boas had begun to make studies of American Indian art by 1897, and for a time Holmes and Boas acknowledged with appreciation one another's work in this area. Holmes contributed an article to the Boas Anniversary Volume in 1906, in which he bestowed mild praise on the detailed art studies which Boas and his students had been doing. Holmes took their main thesis, that an ornamental form may be given different meanings by different tribes and even by single individuals within a tribe, and put it in the wider context of his own thinking about the development and use of ornament. Holmes was not uninfluenced by Boas, for he emphasized here more than he had previously the composite character of the art of most tribes and the importance of borrowing.[102] Boas read the proofs for Holmes's *Handbook* article on "Ornament" and must have expressed his approval, for Holmes subsequently wrote him a letter of thanks, adding that he was "exceedingly pleased to know that what I have said agrees so fully with your own views."[103]

In 1916 it was Boas's turn to contribute to the Holmes Anniversary Volume, and he sent a short piece on "Representative Art of Primitive People" in which he noted Holmes's many "excellent contributions" in the *Annual Reports* of the Bureau of Ethnology.[104]

Gradually however Holmes became disturbed by developments within the anthropological community. World War I aroused his patriotism and increasingly Franz Boas aroused his ire. Holmes had been active in the National Research Council, a group of scientists who organized themselves in 1916 to give advice to the government in planning for war, and in January of 1917 he became chairman of the committee on anthropology in the National Research Council.[105] This was the sort of position Holmes was accustomed to having, where he was in effect the national spokesman for anthropology. But by 1919 the tide had turned, as Franz Boas and his students began to get more power in anthropological affairs. Holmes felt that he was being squeezed out of the National Research Council, and he saw his own loss of power as symptomatic of what was happening in the discipline as a whole.

There were other considerations. Boas had made no secret of his opposition to the war,[106] whereas Holmes was genuinely, even intensely, patriotic. He had spent most of a lifetime living in the nation's capital and working for the federal government. So involved was he in the rightness of the Allied cause that when the war was over, he arranged to have American artists paint the portraits of the leaders of the Allied nations and a tableau painting of the signing of the Versailles treaty, and these were the beginning of what came to be the National Portrait Gallery.[107]

One of the men at whom Boas's attack was directed was Sylvanus G. Morley, a young friend and former associate of Holmes's at the School of American Archaeology. Holmes had helped Morley get his appointment in 1914 as head of the Mayan archaeological project sponsored by the Carnegie Institution of Washington and had accompanied Morley in 1916 on a Carnegie Institution to Guatemala and Honduras. When on June 6, 1917 the United States formally entered the war Morley and several others began secret work for Navy Intelligence.[108] Whether or not Holmes knew of this work while it was going on, there is little doubt that for him patriotism would have ranked ahead of any presumed internationalism of science.[109]

A few days after the Boas letter appeared, Holmes wrote to F. W. Hodge:

You have doubtless seen the traitorous article by Boas in the last Nation, and I want to say to you and to Saville and others who do not favor Prussian control of Anthropology in this country that we are determined now to end the Hun regime. The position of Honorary Philologist in the Bureau of Ethnology *has been abolished,* and this, I am sure, is not the final step in the official assault upon the Hun positions.

My attitude is this. In case Boas or any of his henchmen is selected to fill the $6,000.00 position in the National Research Council, I shall resign from the Association and shall advocate the organization of a new Association which shall be American in reality. I am sure that the majority of anthropologists outside of New York will be glad to join any movement that will tend to purge the stables.[110]

The resolution of censure which Holmes wrote "in the name of Americanism as against un-Americanism" was somewhat more restrained, but the ideas were the same. The last paragraph of the resolution read:

Boas and his followers have sought to gain control of and direct anthropological researches in this country, especially those undertaken on behalf of the nation. There appears now danger that the Research Council may give this group control of researches and measures affecting the most intimate and vital interests to the nation—interests which should be entrusted to those, and those only, whose standard of citizenship is wholly above criticism.[111]

Holmes wrote the resolution, but he did not attend the meeting to vote on it. He was already on his way out of anthropology.

Holmes turned his attention in 1920 to the new National Gallery of Art. He was proud to be both first Director of the National Gallery and a member of the National Academy of Sciences, and he was pleased to be rediscovered as a geologist in 1928 when two young scientists congratulated him on his discoveries fifty years earlier. Holmes may well have begun to wonder what the fate of his anthropological work would be. In 1927 Franz Boas wrote *Primitive Art,* the closest thing that then existed to a survey of the field, and one is hard pressed to find in it any indication of the monumental contributions Holmes had made to the study of aboriginal American art. Boas referred to Holmes four times in the book, twice arguing against him on minor points and twice on major points misinterpreting him completely.[112] The next generation would know little of the work of William Henry Holmes.

Yet Holmes had been one of the first to use stratigraphy in the New World, he had solved what was perhaps the most important problem in nineteenth century archaeology in the United States, and his writings had contributed greatly to the fame of the Bureau of American Ethnology. Holmes wrote with clarity and readability unsurpassed in anthropological literature, Neil Judd wrote in 1967, adding for good measure, "There has been nothing comparable since."[113]

Notes and References

1. Microfilm of letters to William Henry Holmes written by 160 of his friends and bound together for his eightieth birthday, National Collection of Fine Arts Library.

2. John R. Swanton, "William Henry Holmes, 1846–1933," *National Academy of Sciences Biographical Memoirs*, XVII (1935), 223. Other biographical information on Holmes is in the anonymously written "Brief Biography of William Henry Holmes," *Ohio Archaeological and Historical Publications*, XXXVI (1927), 493–527.

3. William Henry Holmes, "Random Records of a Lifetime, 1846–1931," vols. I–XX, MS., Library of the National Collection of Fine Arts and the National Portrait Gallery, XVII (2). By his own account, Holmes threw away masses of material in compiling these volumes and as a result they are less informative than scholars might wish. They are useful however, for personal and family history.

4. W.H. Dall, "On Succession in the Shell-heaps of the Aleutian Islands," *Contributions to North American Ethnology*, United States Department of the Interior (Washington, D.C., 1877), I, 91. Dall also in this paper made an important criticism of

cranial studies. He found such a range of variation even within a single group of people that cranial studies seemed to him to be of little value. For Dall's life, see Paul Bartsch, "Biographical Sketch of William Healey Dall, Aug. 21, 1845–March 27, 1927," *Smithsonian Miscellaneous Collections*, 104 (Washington, D.C., 1946), 2–4.

5. "Brief Biography of William Henry Holmes," *Ohio Archaeological and Historical Publications*, XXXVI (1927), 498–499.

6. William Henry Holmes, "Doings in Washington, Selections from My Note Book, May 22, 1871," in "Random Records," XVII, Section III.

7. William H. Truettner and Robin Bolton-Smith, *National Parks and the American Landscape*, Catalogue of exhibit held in 1971 (Washington, Smithsonian Institution Press, 1972), 22.

8. William Henry Holmes, "Report on the geology of the north-western portion of the Elk Range," *Eighth Annual Report*, United States Geological and Geographical Survey of the Territories for the year 1874 (Washington, D.C., 1876), 59–71.

9. George P. Merrill, "Contributions to the History of American Geology," *Report of*

the United States National Museum, 1904 (Washington, D.C., 1906), 600.

10. Frank McNitt, *Richard Wetherill: Anasazi* (Albuquerque, University of New Mexico Press, 1957, rev. ed., 1966).

11. William Henry Holmes, "Pottery of the Ancient Pueblos," *Fourth Annual Report,* Bureau of Ethnology, 1882–83 (Washington, D.C., 1886), 315.

12. William Henry Holmes, "Report on the ancient ruins of southwestern Colorado examined during the summers of 1875 and 1876," *Tenth Annual Report,* United States Geological and Geographical Survey of the Territories for the year 1876 (Washington, D.C., 1878), 408.

13. R.M. Field and O.T. Jones, "The Resurrection of the Grand Canyon of the Yellowstone," *American Journal of Science,* 5th ser., XVII (1929), 260–278. They quote from W.H. Holmes, "Report on the geology of Yellowstone National Park," *Twelfth Annual Report,* United States Geological and Geographical Survey of the Territories for the year 1878 (Washington, D.C., 1883), II, 1–57.

14. Holmes wrote, "My dear Professor Field: Thank you for the separate of your Journal of Science article on the Yellowstone Canyon Geology. It saves me from utter extinction geologically, and at the same time puts you and Professor Jones on the map to stay." (W.H. Holmes to R.M. Field, June 3, 1929 in W.H. Holmes, "Random Records," III, 167)

15. William Henry Holmes to "Kate," Aug. 26, 1880, "Random Records," V, 9.

16. William Henry Holmes, "Report on the Congress of Americanists held at Stuttgart, Germany, August 18–23, 1904," *Smithsonian Miscellaneous Collections,* XLVII, (Washington, D.C., 1905), 391–395. See also George A. Dorsey, "Notes on

the Anthropological Museums of Central Europe," *American Anthropologist,* n.s., I (1899), 464–474; A.B. Meyer, "Studies of museums and kindred institutions of New York City, Albany, Buffalo, and Chicago, with notes on some European institutions," *Smithsonian Institution Annual Report,* 1903 (Washington, D.C., 1905), 311–608; Alice C. Fletcher, "Brief History of the International Congress of Americanists," *American Anthropologist,* XV (1913), 529–534.

17. Wallace Stegner, *Beyond the Hundredth Meridian: John Wesley Powell and the Second Opening of the West* (Boston, Houghton Mifflin, 1954), 189. The book is C.E. Dutton, *The Tertiary History of the Grand Canyon District,* with Atlas (Washington, D.C., 1882).

18. *Ibid.,* 188.

19. William Henry Holmes, "Report [of the Geologist] to the Director of the United States Geological Survey," *Sixth Annual Report,* United States Geological Survey, 1884–1885 (Washington, D.C., 1885) 96.

20. See Bibliography in John R. Swanton, "William Henry Holmes, 1846–1933," *National Academy of Sciences Biographical Memoirs,* XVII (1935), 238–252, compiled by Ella Leary, Librarian of the Bureau of American Ethnology.

21. William Henry Holmes, "Evidences of the Antiquity of Man on the Site of the City of Mexico," *Transactions of the Anthropological Society of Washington,* III (1885), 80.

22. Richard B. Woodbury, "Nels C. Nelson and Chronological Archaeology," *American Antiquity,* XXV (1960), 400–401; R.B. Woodbury, "Nelson's Stratigraphy," *American Antiquity,* XXVI (1960), 98–99; Richard E. Adams, "Manuel Gamio and Stratigraphic Excavation," *American Antiquity,* XXVI (1960), 99; Franz Boas, "Archaeological Investigations in the Valley of

Mexico by the International School, 1911–1912," *Proceedings of the Eighteenth International Congress of Americanists* (London, 1913), 176–179, reprinted in Franz Boas, *Race, Language, and Culture* (New York, The Free Press, 1940, 1968), 530–534.

23. Holmes, "Pottery of the Ancient Pueblos," 298.

24. William Henry Holmes, "Caribbean Influence in the Prehistoric Art of the Southern States," *American Anthropologist*, VII (1894), 78.

25. "Discussion," p. 433 following Frank Hamilton Cushing, "Exploration of Ancient Key Dwellers' Remains on the Gulf Coast of Florida," *Proceedings of the American Philosophical Society*, XXXV (1896), 329–432.

26. Gordon R. Willey, *Archaeology of the Florida Gulf Coast*, Introduction by Ripley P. Bullen (New York, AMS Press for Peabody Museum of Archaeology and Ethnology, 1973), 26. Holmes's comments on the collections made by Clarence Moore are in "Earthenware of Florida; Collections of Clarence B. Moore," *Journal of Academy of Natural Sciences of Philadelphia*, 2nd ser., X (1894), 105–128 and again in Holmes, "Aboriginal Pottery of the Eastern United States," *Twentieth Annual Report*, Bureau of American Ethnology, 1898–1899 (Washington, D.C., 1903), fn. 114.

27. For Putnam see W J McGee, "Anthropology at Detroit and Toronto," *American Anthropologist*, 10 (1897), 317–345.

28. Franz Boas, "History and Science in Anthropology: A Reply," *American Anthropologist*, XXXVIII (1936), 137–141, reprinted in *Race, Language, and Culture*, 307–308.

29. Two good studies of Powell (although they have little on his anthropology) are Wallace Stegner, *Beyond the Hundredth Meridian: John Wesley Powell and the Second Opening of the West* and William Culp Darrah, *Powell of the Colorado* (Princeton University Press, 1951). For Powell's anthropology, see Don D. Fowler, Robert C. Euler, and Catherine S. Fowler, "John Wesley Powell and the anthropology of the Canyon country," *United States Geological Survey, Professional Paper* no. 670 (Washington, D.C., 1969), Don D. Fowler and Catherine S. Fowler, eds., "Anthropology of the Numa: John Wesley Powell's Manuscripts on the Numic Peoples of Western North America," *Smithsonian Contributions to Knowledge*, No. 14 (Washington, D.C., 1971), and Curtis M. Hinsley, Jr., "The Development of a Profession: Anthropology in Washington, D.C., 1846–1903," unpub. Ph.D. diss., University of Wisconsin, 1976.

30. Stegner, *op. cit.*, 242.

31. Darrah, *op. cit.*, 319. Frederick W. Hodge commented on John Wesley Powell's carefully cultivated political power in a tape-recorded interview with Corinne Gilb in 1956 when Hodge was 91 years old. For this and many other comments on his contemporaries, see "Frederick Webb Hodge, Ethnologist," MS. in the National Anthropological Archives, Smithsonian Institution.

32. E.B. Tylor, "How the Problems of American Anthropology Present Themselves to the English Mind," *Transactions of the Anthropological Society of Washington*, III (1884), 92.

33. Powell wrote to Lewis Henry Morgan on May 23, 1877, "I believe you have discovered the true system of science and governmental organization among the Indians." See also Powell to Morgan on Nov. 16, 1876, May 11, 1880, and June 19, 1880, all in the Rush Rhees Library, The University of Rochester.

Powell accepted Morgan's three stages of social evolution, Savagery, Barbarism, and Civilization, and added a fourth state of his own, Enlightenment, but he was not a social Darwinist for, like Morgan, he felt that biological and social evolution were very different things. The mechanism Powell envisioned for getting from one social stage to the next was not competition and struggle, but rather increasing cooperation among human beings. (See, for example, J.W. Powell, "Competition as a Factor in Human Evolution," *American Anthropologist*, I, 1888, 297–323.) Powell kept Lester Ward, the foremost opponent of social Darwinism in the United States, in the employ of the Geological Survey as much for Ward's sociological ideas as for his skills in paleobotany, and in 1887 he sponsored a frankly socialist talk in Washington by Alfred Russel Wallace, the co-discoverer with Charles Darwin of the theory of evolution by natural selection. (Alfred Russel Wallace, *My Life: A Record of Events and Opinions*, New York, Dodd, Mead, and Co., 1905, II, 126; Richard Hofstadter, *Social Darwinism in American Thought*, Boston, Beacon Press, 1944, rev. ed., 1955, 1959, 68–72, fn. 17, 226.) Virtually no leading anthropologist in the United States in the late nineteenth century accepted social Darwinism.

34. Powell to Lewis Henry Morgan, Feb. 25, 1880, Rush Rhees Library, The University of Rochester; Richard Rathbun, "Report on the Condition and Progress of the U.S. National Museum during the year ending June 30, 1903," *Annual Report*, Smithsonian Institution, 1903 (Washington, D.C., 1905); Frank H.H. Roberts, Jr., "One Hundred Years of Smithsonian Anthropology," *Science*, 104 (1946) 119–125.

35. William Henry Holmes, "Art in shell of the ancient Americans," *Second Annual Report*, Bureau of Ethnology, 1880–1881 (Washington, D.C., 1883), 179–304. Holmes used museum materials, examined private collections, and combed the historical literature for references to shell work, including wampum.

36. William Henry Holmes, "Pottery of the ancient Pueblos," *Fourth Annual Report*, Bureau of Ethnology, 1882–1883 (Washington, D.C., 1886), 257–360; "Ancient Pottery of the Mississippi Valley," *op. cit.*, 361–436; "Origin and development of form and ornament in ceramic art," *op cit.*, 437–465. The origin of the Mississippi Valley pottery study was a request from the Academy of Science in Davenport, Iowa that Holmes help them organize the boatloads of ancient pottery which were being brought to them by Mississippi river boat captains.

37. William Henry Holmes, "Aboriginal pottery of the eastern United States," *Twentieth Annual Report*, Bureau of American Ethnology, 1898–1899 (Washington, D.C., 1903), 1–201.

38. Gordon R. Willey and Jeremy Sabloff, *A History of American Archaeology* (San Francisco, W.H. Freeman and Co., 1974), 84.

39. William Henry Holmes, "Ancient Pottery of the Mississippi Valley," 435.

40. William Henry Holmes, "Art in shell of the ancient Americans," 281.

41. For Powell's position on this, see J.W. Powell, "Museums of Ethnology and their Classification," *Science*, IX (1887), 612–614. Powell insisted that there was no necessary connection between race, language, and culture.

42. William Henry Holmes, "Ancient Pottery of the Mississippi Valley," 436; William Henry Holmes, "Ancient art of the province of Chiriqui, Colombia," *Sixth Annual Report*, Bureau of Ethnology, 1884–1885 (Washington, D.C., 1888), 54.

43. Holmes, "Art in shell of the ancient Americans," 186.

44. Robert Silverberg makes this point in his excellent *Mound Builders of Ancient America: the archaeology of a myth* (Greenwich, N.Y., New York Graphic Society, 1968).

45. William Henry Holmes, "Prehistoric textile fabrics of the United States, derived from impressions on pottery," *Third Annual Report*, Bureau of Ethnology, 1881–1882 (Washington, D.C., 1884), 393–425.

46. Cyrus Thomas, "Report on the Mound Explorations of the Bureau of American Ethnology," *Twelfth Annual Report*, Bureau of American Ethnology, 1890–1891 (Washington, D.C., 1894), 3–370. A good short study of Cyrus Thomas is Bennie C. Keel, "Cyrus Thomas and the Mound Builders," *Southern Indian Studies*, XXII (1970), 3–16.

47. William Henry Holmes, "A Study of the Textile Art in its Relation to the Development of Form and Ornament," *Sixth Annual Report*, Bureau of Ethnology, 1884–1885 (Washington, D.C., 1888), 185–252.

48. William Henry Holmes, "Textile fabrics of ancient Peru," *Bulletin 7*, Bureau of Ethnology, 1889, 17 pp.; Holmes, "Prehistoric textile art of eastern United States," *Thirteenth Annual Report*, Bureau of Ethnology, 1891–1892 (Washington, D.C., 1896), 3–46; Holmes, "Textile art in prehistoric archaeology," *American Antiquarian*, VII (Chicago, 1886), 261–266; Holmes, "Uses of textiles in pottery making and embellishment," *American Anthropologist*, n.s., III (1901), 397–403. Holmes also made a study during this period of "Ancient art from the province of Chiriqua, Colombia," *Sixth Annual Report*, Bureau of Ethnology, 1884–1885 (Washington, D.C., 1888), 13–187.

49. William Henry Holmes, "On the Evolution of Ornament. An American Lesson," *American Anthropologist*, III (1890), 145.

50. *Ibid.*, 140.

51. Holmes, "Ancient art of the province of Chiriqui," 184.

52. A recent and emphatic restatement of this position is Jean Laude, *The Arts of Black Africa*, trans. by Jean Decock (Berkeley, University of California Press, 1971).

53. Holmes, "On the Evolution of Ornament. An American Lesson," 142.

54. Alfred C. Haddon, *Evolution in Art: As Illustrated by the Life-Histories of Designs* (London, W. Scott, 1895).

55. "July 1889 meeting of Anthropological Society of Washington," *American Anthropologist*, II (1889), 226.
Note: on the spelling of "archaeology" and "palaeolithic".

Between 1888 and 1891 government scientists and the Government Printing Office began to spell these words and their derivatives without the "a" before the "e". A persuasive case has recently been made that the Latin derived "ae" form is preferable so it is used here except for titles and quotations. See John Howland Rowe, "The Spelling of 'Archaeology' " in *Anthropology Newsletter*, 16 (June, 1975), 11–12.

56. Thomas Wilson, "Results of an inquiry as to the existence of man in North America during the paleolithic period of the stone age," *Report of the United States National Museum*, 1888 (Washington, D.C., 1890), 677–702.

57. Thomas Wilson, "The Paleolithic Period in the District of Columbia," *American Anthropologist*, II (1889), 235–241.

58. John Wesley Powell, "Report," *Fifteenth Annual Report*, Bureau of American Ethnology, 1893–1894 (Washington, D.C., 1897), xcvii.

59. F.W. Putnam, "Discussion," in "Symposium on the aborigines of the District

of Columbia and the lower Potomac," *American Anthropologist*, II (1889), 268.

60. William Henry Holmes, "A Quarry Workshop of Flaked-Stone Implement Makers in the District of Columbia," *American Anthropologist*, III (1890), 1–26; Holmes, "Recent work in the Quarry Workshops of the District of Columbia," *American Anthropologist*, III (1890), 224–225.

61. In 1880 Miss Frances E. Babbitt claimed to have found flaked quartz "palaeoliths" at Little Falls, Minnesota. Holmes visited the site accompanied by N. H. Winchell, the Minnesota state geologist who had first called attention to Miss Babbitt's finds. In 1892 Holmes told the AAAS: "The explanation of the unfortunate error fallen into by the original observers is that the archaeologist identified the works of art and the geologist the geologic formations, neither thinking it necessary to determine the vital point as to whether or not the works of art were really associated with the undisturbed gravels." (William Henry Holmes, "On the So-Called Palaeolithic Implements of the Upper Mississippi," *Proceedings*, Forty-first Meeting of the AAAS, Salem, 1892, 281.) See also William Henry Holmes, "Vestiges of early man in Minnesota," *American Geologist*, XI (1893), 219–240.

62. William Henry Holmes, "Are there traces of glacial man in the Trenton gravels?" *Journal of Geology*, I (1893), 34.

63. William Henry Holmes, "Gravel man and paleolithic culture; a preliminary word," *Science*, XXI (1893), 30; Holmes, "Modern quarry refuse and the paleolithic theory," *Science*, XX (1892), 295–297.

64. William Henry Holmes, "Natural History of Flaked Stone Implements," *Memoirs of the International Congress of Anthropology* (Chicago, Schulte Publishing Co., 1894), 120–139.

65. William Henry Holmes, "Distribution of Stone Implements in the Tidewater Country," *American Anthropologist*, VI (1893), 7.

66. William Henry Holmes, "Stone Implements of the Potomac-Chesapeake Tidewater Province," *Fifteenth Annual Report*, Bureau of American Ethnology, 1893–1894 (Washington, D.C., 1897), 13–152.

67. William Henry Holmes, *Handbook of Aboriginal American Antiquities*. Part I. Bulletin 60, Bureau of American Ethnology (Washington, D.C., 1919), 12.

68. William Henry Holmes, "Monoliths of San Juan Teotihuacan, Mexico," *American Journal of Archaeology*, I (1885), 361–371.

69. W.H. Holmes, "Sketch of the great Serpent Mound," *Science*, VIII (1886), 627. See also Holmes, "Ancient Pottery of the Mississippi Valley," 402. Holmes found earth embankments that formed the head of the serpent which Squier and Davis and, following them, F.W. Putnam had missed. F.W. Putnam never acknowledged Holmes's correction, but after Putnam's death, C.C. Willoughby, his long-time associate at the Peabody Museum, admitted in a contribution to the Holmes Festschrift that Holmes's drawing of the Serpent Mound was undoubtedly the correct one. (F.W. Putnam, "The Serpent Mound of Ohio," *Century Magazine*, 1890, 871–888; C.C. Willoughby, "The Art of the Great Earthwork Builders of Ohio," *Holmes Anniversary Volume*, Washington, D.C., James William Bryan Press, 1916, 469–480, reprinted in Smithsonian Institution *Annual Report* for 1916, 489–500.)

70. F.W. Putnam to W.H. Holmes, July 5, 1892, William Henry Holmes Papers, Smithsonian Institution Archives.

71. F.W. Putnam to W.H. Holmes, April 4, 1893, William Henry Holmes Papers, Smithsonian Institution Archives.

72. F.W. Putnam, "Primitive man in the Delaware Valley," *Science*, VI (1897), 824–829. See also W J McGee, "Anthropology at Detroit and Toronto," *American Anthropologist*, 10 (1897), 317–345.

73. Neil M. Judd, *The Bureau of American Ethnology: A Partial History* (Norman, University of Oklahoma Press, 1967), 15.

74. Holmes, "Random Records," I, 83–84. See also anon., "The Loubat Prizes," *American Anthropologist*, XI (1898), 191. Le Duc de Loubat was a wealthy American born of French descent and a patron of Columbia University and of anthropology.

75. W.H. Holmes, "Preliminary revision of the evidence relating to the auriferous gravel man in California," *American Anthropologist*, n.s., I (1899), 107–121, 614–645; W.H. Holmes, "Fossil Human Remains Found near Lansing, Kansas," *American Anthropologist*, IV (1902), 747.

76. William Henry Holmes, "Report of the Bureau of American Ethnology," Smithsonian Institution *Annual Report* for 1903 (Washington, D.C., 1904), 34–48, 35.

77. Holmes, "Random Records," I, 35, 36.

78. E.N. Wilmsen, "An Outline of Early Man Studies in the United States," *American Antiquity*, 31 (1965), 172–192.

79. George Dorsey to W.H. Holmes in Holmes, "Random Records," I, 91.

80. William Henry Holmes, "The World's Fair Congress of Anthropology," *American Anthropologist*, VI (1893), 423–434, 433; John Wesley Powell, "Report of the Director," *Fifteenth Annual Report*, Bureau of Ethnology, 1893–1894 (1897), xci.

81. Otis Tufton Mason, "Influence of Environment Upon Human Industries or Arts," Saturday Lecture at the U.S. National Museum, May 2, 1896, *Annual Report*, Smithsonian Institution, 1895 (Washington, D.C., 1896) fn. 646. Mason wrote: "These culture areas should be compared with Major Powell's linguistic map, 7th Ann. Report Bur. Ethnol., with Thomas's mound maps, 12th Annual B. of E., with Bancroft's geographic areas in his Native Races of the Pacific States, but especially with Franz Boas's Anthropology of the N. Amer. Indians, Mon. Internat'l. Congress of Anthrop., Chicago, C. Hart Merriam's Geographical Distribution of Life in N. Amer., Smithsonian Report, 1891, and J. A. Allen's Geographic Distribution of N. Amer. Mammals, Bull. Am. Mus. Nat. Hist., NY. IV. The importance of biological areas for the working out of cultural areas should be noted."

82. Clipping on "Lay Figure Ethnic Groups in the National Museum," *The Sunday Star*, Aug. 24, 1913 in Holmes, "Random Records," VI, 109. The article noted: "The first of these groups was made and exhibited at the World's Fair at Chicago. . . . [W.H. Holmes] originated the idea and developed the groups."

83. Holmes kept together in "Random Records" the menu for the dinner, the seating chart, newspaper clippings about the event, and a photograph and his own drawing of the engraved loving cup. He wrote that the offer to him at Chicago was due to T.C. Chamberlin, Professor of Geology at the University of Chicago and that he had had at the same time an offer from Morris K. Jesup at the American Museum of Natural History in New York. (Holmes, "Random Records," VII, 15)

84. Holmes found when he got to Chicago that his appointment was considered tentative, and he was kept "on the ragged edge of uncertainty." (Holmes, "Random Records," VII, 32)

85. Gordon R. Willey and Jeremy Sabloff, *A History of American Archaeology*, 68;

William Henry Holmes, *Archaeological Studies Among the Ancient Ruins of Mexico* (Chicago, Publications, Field Columbian Museum, Anthropological Series, I, 1895–1897).

86. William Henry Holmes, "Report on the Department of Anthropology for the year 1899–1900," United States National Museum, *Annual Report*, 1900 (Washington, D.C., 1902), 21–29.

87. Holmes, "Random Records," IX, 7.

88. W.H. Holmes, "The first Pan-American Scientific Congress held in Santiago, Chile, Dec. 25, 1908–Jan. 6, 1909," Smithsonian Institution *Annual Report*, 1909 (Washington, D.C., 1910), 94

89. Holmes to F. Boas, Aug. 6, 1904, Franz Boas Papers.

90. William Henry Holmes, "Aboriginal Pottery of the Eastern United States," 53–56.

91. Holmes indicated his conversion to the geographical method of museum arrangement in his "Report on the Department of Anthropology for 1897–98," United States National Museum, *Annual Report*, 1898 (Washington, D.C., 1900), 19–33 and in the *Annual Report*, 1901 (1903), 253–278, *esp.* 269.

92. William Henry Holmes, *Handbook of American Antiquities*. Part I—Introduction. Bulletin 60, Bureau of American Ethnology (Washington, D.C., 1919).

93. William Henry Holmes, "Masterpieces of aboriginal American art," *Art and Archaeology*, I (1914), 1–12, 91–102, 243–255; III (1916), 71–85; IV (1916), 269–278; VIII (1919), 349–360.

94. A.S. Riggs, "William Henry Holmes," *Art and Archaeology*, XXXIV (1933), 115.

95. "The Soviet Sells," *Art Digest* (May 15, 1931), 13. Holmes kept a clipping of this in "Random Records," XI, 189. Mellon purchased "The Annunciation" by Jan van Eyck and major works by Rembrandt and Van Dyck.

96. R.P. Tolman, "Report on the National Collection of Fine Arts," *Annual Report*, Smithsonian Institution, 1937 (Washington, D.C., 1938), 35.

97. Regna Diebold Darnell, "The Development of American Anthropology 1879–1920: From the Bureau of American Ethnology to Franz Boas," unpub. Ph.D. diss. University of Pennsylvania, 1969, "Appendix V—The Boas Censure," 476–483. George W. Stocking, Jr. gives an account and an interpretation of these events in "The Scientific Reaction Against Cultural Anthropology," in *Race, Culture, and Evolution* (New York, The Free Press, 1968), 270–307.

98. Franz Boas, "Scientists As Spies," *The Nation*, CIX (Dec. 20, 1919), 797.

99. F. Boas to Holmes, Feb. 17, 1904; Holmes to Boas, Feb. 18, 1904; Boas to Holmes, Oct. 29, 1904; Holmes to Boas, Oct. 31, 1904; Boas to Holmes, Jan. 23, 1903 and a similar letter Boas to Holmes, March 10, 1905, Franz Boas Papers.

100. Holmes to Boas, April 9, 1904, Boas Papers.

101. Franz Boas, *Handbook of American Indian Languages*, Bureau of American Ethnology, Part 1. Bulletin 40, 1911; Part 2, 1922; Part 3, 1938; John Wesley Powell, *Introduction to the Study of Indian Languages* (Washington, D.C., Smithsonian, 1877); Powell, "Indian Linguistic Families of America North of Mexico," *Seventh Annual Report*, Bureau of Ethnology, 1885–1886 (Washington, D.C., 1891), 7–139.

102. William Henry Holmes, "Decorative Art of the Aborigines of North America," *Boas Anniversary Volume*, B. Laufer, ed. (New York, G. Stechert, 1906). Boas's early

art studies include "The Decorative Art of the Indians of the North Pacific Coast of America," *Bulletin*, American Museum of Natural History, IX (1897), 123–176; F. Boas, "The Decorative Art of the North American Indians," *The Popular Science Monthly* (Oct., 1903), 481; F. Boas, "Decorative Designs of Alaskan Needle-Cases: A Study of the History of Conventional Designs, based on materials in the U.S. National Museum," *Proceedings* of the U.S. National Museum, 34 (1908), 321–344.

103. Holmes to Boas, April 5, 1906, Boas Papers.

104. Franz Boas, "Representative Art of Primitive Peoples," *Holmes Anniversary Volume* (Washington, D.C., 1916).

105. William Henry Holmes, "Organization of the Committee on Anthropology of the National Research Council and its Activities for the year 1917," *American Journal of Physical Anthropology*, I (1918), 77–90.

106. George W. Stocking, Jr., "The Scientific Reaction Against Cultural Anthropology," in Stocking, *Race, Culture, and Evolution*.

107. William Henry Holmes, *The National Gallery of Art: Catalog of Collections* (Washington, D.C., 1922), 8.

108. For an account of Morley's war work, see Robert L. Brunhouse, *Sylvanus G. Morley and the World of the Ancient Mayas* (Norman, University of Oklahoma Press, 1971), 112–147.

109. Although Boas wrote in "Scientists As Spies" as if the internationalism of science were a nearly universal and inviolate convention, historically it is rather an eighteenth century ideal that has barely

managed to keep afloat through the more nationalistic 19th and 20th centuries. For an example of the complex ways in which nationalistic considerations can enter into scientific discussions and practices, see the controversy between Boas's hero in science, R. Virchow, and the Frenchman A. Quatrefages after the Franco-Prussian War in successive volumes of *Revue des cours scientifique de la France et de l'Etranger*, VII (1870), VIII (1871), 2nd ser., I (1872), II (1873).

110. William C. Sturtevant, "Huns, Free-Thinking Americans, and the AAA," *History of Anthropology Newsletter*, II, No. 1 (1975), 4–6. The letters are in the Frederick W. Hodge Papers in the Southwest Museum. Hodge was apparently not sympathetic for Holmes next wrote him: "I have your recent favor and am surprised that you should wish the continuance of the Prussian regime, the vicious, scheming minority of the association has ruled long enough, and if it is to continue I shall close my connection with anthropology for good."

111. Darnell, *op. cit.* includes the full text of the censure motion.

112. Franz Boas, *Primitive Art* (Oslo, Aschehoug, 1927; Cambridge, Harvard University Press, 1928). Holmes did not "seek the origin of all decorative art in realism" as Boas claimed (p. 15) nor did he claim that all pottery shapes came from basketry (p. 151). Holmes tended to think most decorative art comes from technique, and he argued against what he believed was Cushing's overemphasis on the importance of basketry for pottery.

113. Neil M. Judd, *The Bureau of American Ethnology: A Partial History*.

Chapter Six
Aftermath

Franz Boas entered anthropology with a background in physics, mathematics, and geography, the last a near equivalent in Germany to the natural history which was so popular in the United States. In 1883 Boas went on his first trip to Baffinland to study the Eskimos, and subsequently he spent a year in Berlin under the tutelage of Adolf Bastian, a year which was significant because it helped to shape his future work in anthropology.

Adolf Bastian (1826–1905) had one of the most prolific careers of any anthropologist or ethnographer in the nineteenth century. In 1851 he went as a ship's doctor to Austrialia, and for the next fifty years he combined frequent and extended world travels with the writing of dozens of books and hundreds of articles, based on his observations and on materials which he had collected. At intervals Bastian returned to Berlin where he founded the *Zeitschrift für Ethnologie* in 1868, the Gesellschaft für Anthropologie, Ethnolgie und Urgeschichte (with Rudolf Virchow) in 1869, and in 1886 a museum of ethnography, the Museum für Völkerkunde, in the Royal Museum of Prussia.[1] Bastian paid little attention to environment, arts, industries, or physical characteristics of peoples. He was interested in beliefs. Committed to the theory of the psychic unity of mankind, Bastian held that what human beings have in common is a restricted number of basic ideas or concepts, *Elementargedanken,* which find various expressions in various geographical provinces, but which become intermingled due to migrations and contact between peoples. In his opinion it was important to study culture contact and the history of ideas and institutions because this was the way to understand the history of civilization and also to get back to the *Elementargedanken.*[2]

Bastian was not only a prolific writer and intrepid traveler, he was also unusually effective in arousing enthusiasm for ethnography and in bringing others into the field. What F.W. Putnam was doing in the United States, Adolf Bastian did in Germany. He persuaded students, merchants, travelers, and other amateurs to collect ethnographic materials for him, and he helped them to publish their writings. A large corps of disciples gathered around Bastian at Berlin and from there went out on ethnographic missions around the world, gathering collections which were then carefully clas-

sified in his own and other museums, and writing studies which were published in scientific journals.[3] But the circle around Bastian was crowded,
and professional opportunities were few. In 1886 Franz Boas went on a field
trip to British Columbia, attended a meeting of the American Association
for the Advancement of Science at which he met F.W. Putnam, and decided to settle in the United States. In effect, Boas moved from Bastian's
circle to that of F.W. Putnam. Boas carried with him several basic tenets
quite probably derived from Bastian: a commitment to the psychic unity of
mankind, a primary interest in the mind of human beings, an historical
method which involved tracing the paths of culture contact and influence,
and the concept of geographical provinces. The latter two, in particular,
were congruent with Putnam's historical and geographical approach to anthropology, and Putnam welcomed Franz Boas into the developing science
of anthropology in the United States.

In 1886 when Franz Boas and F.W. Putnam met, the Peabody Museum
of American Archaeology and Ethnology had been in existence for twenty
years, the Bureau of Ethnology for seven. Alice Fletcher was well acquainted with the Omahas, had published several accounts of Indian ceremonies, and was lobbying for the passage of the Dawes Act for the allotment
of reservation lands. Frank Hamilton Cushing had returned to Washington,
D.C. from Zuni and was about to interest Mrs. Mary Hemenway in an archaeological expedition to the American Southwest. William Henry
Holmes had already done his stratigraphic studies outside Mexico City and
had published several studies of aboriginal American art. John Wesley
Powell had published his *Introduction to the Study of Indian Languages*
(1877), to be followed soon by his *Indian Linguistic Families North of
Mexico* (1891). Adolph Bandelier was writing the final report of his expedition to the Southwest sponsored by the Archaeological Institute of America.
Only six years before, Lewis Henry Morgan had presided over the annual
meeting of the American Association for the Advancement of Science, the
first anthropologist to be so honored. Yet less than twenty years later when
Franz Boas wrote "The History of Anthropology," he did not name any of
these persons who had been his predecessors, mentors, and colleagues,[4]
and in 1943 after Franz Boas's death Ruth Benedict wrote of him:

> He found anthropology a collection of wild guesses and a happy hunt-
> ing ground for the romantic lover of primitive things; he left it a disci-

pline in which theories could be tested and in which he had delimited possibilities from impossibilities.[5]

Robert Lowie immediately challenged Benedict's account, noting that Boas himself would not have liked it for "the notion that he was a culture hero of the type featured by aboriginal folklore, a bringer of light out of total darkness, was intensely distasteful to him."[6] But Lowie gave little convincing evidence to the contrary, mentioning among Americans important in anthropology only Lewis Henry Morgan, Daniel G. Brinton, and William Henry Holmes, the latter two with qualifications. The characterization of nineteenth century American anthropology implicit in Benedict's remarks went generally unchallenged.[7]

The situation was different in Europe, where there was a continuing tradition of appreciation of American work in anthropology. Marxists revered Lewis Henry Morgan, whose book *Ancient Society* was the foundation on which Friedrich Engels based *The Origin of the Family, Private Property and the State*.[8] Frank Hamilton Cushing's work on "Zuni Creation Myths" and on "Manual Concepts" was used by Marcel Mauss, Emile Durkheim, and Lucien Lévy-Bruhl, and the study of the Omahas by Alice Fletcher and Francis La Flesche was widely read.[9] E.B. Tylor had early appreciated the American work and the American organizations for anthropology,[10] and his praise was echoed by A.C. Haddon in a presidential address to the Royal Anthropological Institute in 1902 and by the Frenchman Marcel Mauss in a long article in *La Revue de France* in 1915.[11] Mauss lamented the state of enthnography in his own country. The problem, he felt, was the lack in France of the facilities and workers which any open air observational science needed: field workers, museums and archives for storage, exhibition, and publication, and finally teachers and professors who could instruct technicians, apprentices, and the general public in the principles of their science. Mauss had high praise for the work which was going on in Great Britain, Germany, Holland, and especially in the United States where, he wrote, a government agency and numerous museums, universities, and scientific societies produced more publications in ethnography than any other nation.[12]

Why, in the midst of such generous tribute from Europe, did American anthropologists of Boas's generation and afterward play down the American tradition? It seems likely that they were somewhat embarrassed by their predecessors and diffident about American science. They preferred to find the origins of their discipline in Europe, and in particular in a European university tradition which included mathematics and the physical sciences. The pioneers of American anthropology were for the most part informally educated. Their backgrounds were diverse. They divided their attention among many different activities and seemed to lack the commitment to scientific discipline and rigor that Boas exemplified. It was easier for Europeans to appreciate the ideas of Frank Hamilton Cushing than it was for Alfred Kroeber who at closer range found Cushing's activities an embarrassment and who characterized him disapprovingly as "intense, intuitional, neurotic, and in chronic ill health, with a streak of exhibitionism."[13] Similarly, Putnam's reputation at the end of his life was shadowed by his continuing search for signs of ancient man, Alice Fletcher's by the failure of the allotment policy for which she had worked so diligently, and Holmes's (and John Wesley Powell's) by their long allegiance to a generalized scheme of social evolution which Boas vehemently opposed.

Nathan Reingold has written perceptively of the general failure of American scientists to appreciate the institutional forms for science which had developed in the United States by 1900. What America had was a large non-elite scientific community, one in which "instead of a small number of very highly esteemed professors, there were many professors, and therefore more opportunities in science."[14] Yet Americans persisted in feeling that this was not a good thing, and they sought to emulate Europe in building prestigious laboratories for the work of a few.

American anthropologists also tended to ignore their predecessors because their science moved in new directions after 1910. Museums became less important, as the natural history approach gave way to a search for laws in anthropology comparable to those in the physical sciences. Archaeology went its own way in the Southwest, as anthropology under the influence of Franz Boas moved closer to psychology.[15] Nevertheless, the legacy of the previous forty years and of the natural history tradition in American anthropology survived. The legacy included the Bureau of American Ethnology and the anthropology section of the National Museum, the many museums and university departments of anthropology which Putnam built, and the School of American Research established by Alice Fletcher. It included the ancient monuments which had been protected and preserved, the careful methods in archaeology introduced by Holmes, and the many series of publications in which ethnographic, archaeological, and linguistic studies appeared. It included Lewis Henry Morgan's kinship studies and the tradition of field work in ethnography begun by Frank Hamilton Cushing and Alice Fletcher.

Anthropology flourished in the United States in the late nineteenth century as a variously talented group of men and women found one another and a supportive environment. Each of the major figures contributed to the development of the whole in part by taking on a special task. Putnam and Powell were organizers, Holmes (and Daniel G. Brinton) were critics of the work which was done, Morgan and Cushing were theorizers, and Alice Fletcher interpreted to the general public the importance of what they were doing. Together they created a new science, one which was related to developments in Europe, but which had unique concerns of its own. They laid the foundations on which anthropology in the United States continues to build.

Notes and References

1. T.K. Penniman, *A Hundred Years of Anthropology* (New York, William Morrow, 1974; orig. 1965), 110–115 and Robert H. Lowie, *The History of Ethnological Theory* (New York, Farrar and Rinehart, 1937) have the best brief accounts of Bastian. For Bastian's influence on Franz Boas see Jacob W. Gruber, "Horatio Hale and the Development of American Anthropology," *Proceedings of the American Philosophical Society*, 111 (1967), 5–37 and George W. Stocking, Jr., "From Physics to Ethnology," in *Race, Culture, and Evolution* (New York, The Free Press, 1968), 133–160.

2. Bastian's most famous book is also his earliest, *Der Mensch in der Geschichte; zur Begründung einen psychologischen Weltanschauung* (Leipzig, 1860). Here he used for the first time the terms "Elemen-

targedanken" and "Völkergedanken," the latter being the form that the basic ideas take among a particular people. (See Penniman, *op. cit.*)

3. Marcel Mauss, "L'ethnographie en France et à l'étranger," *La Revue de Paris* (1913), 537–60; 815–837, 546.

4. Franz Boas, "The History of Anthropology," *Science*, XX (1904), 520.

5. Ruth F. Benedict, "Appreciation," *Science*, 97 (1943), 60.

6. Robert H. Lowie, "Franz Boas, His Predecessors and His Contemporaries," *Science*, 97 (1943), 202–203, 203.

7. Exceptions to this tendency to ignore nineteenth century American work include A. Irving Hallowell's classic "The Beginnings of Anthropology in America," in Frederica de Laguna, ed., *Selected Papers*

from American Anthropolgist, 1888–1920 (1960), 1–89; Gordon Willey and Jeremy Sabloff, *A History of American Archaeology* (San Francisco, W.H. Freeman, 1974); Panchanan Mitra, *A History of American Anthropology* (University of Calcutta, 1933); and Ronald P. Rohner and Evelyn C. Rohner, "Introduction" to *The Ethnography of Franz Boas*, compiled and edited by Ronald P. Rohner (Chicago, University of Chicago Press, 1969). See also the anthology of writings up through the Boas era by Margaret Mead and Ruth L. Bunzel, *The Golden Age of American Anthropology* (New York, George Braziller, 1960).

Leslie White wrote two works highly critical of the influence of Franz Boas in anthropology, *The Ethnography and Ethnology of Franz Boas*, Texas Memorial Museum Bulletin 6 (Austin, Texas, 1963) and *The Social Organization of Ethnological Theory*, Rice University Studies, Monographs in Cultural Anthropology, 52 (4), (Houston, Texas, 1966).

8. Frederick Engels, *The Origin of the Family, Private Property and the State*, trans. by Ernest Untermann (Chicago, Charles H. Kerr, 1902). Engels ended his book with an excerpt from the end of *Ancient Society* in which Morgan warned of the danger from the unchecked growth of private property, the same excerpt with which William Henry Holmes ended his "Lewis Henry Morgan, 1818–1881," *National Academy of Sciences Biographical Memoirs*, VI (Washington, D.C., 1909), 233.

9. For Mauss and Durkheim, see Chapter 3. Lucien Lévy-Bruhl referred to Cushing and Fletcher repeatedly in *How Natives Think (Les fonctions mentales dans les societés inférieures*, Paris, 1910) authorized trans. by Lilian A. Clare (London, George Allen and Unwin, 1926).

10. E.B. Tylor, "How the Problems of American Anthropology Present Themselves to the English Mind," *Trans. of the Anthropological Society of Washington*, III (1885), 81–95.

11. A.C. Haddon, "What the United States of America is doing for anthropology," *Journal of the Royal Anthropological Institute*, 32 (1902), 8–24; Marcel Mauss, "L'ethnographie en France et à l'étranger," *La Revue de Paris*, (1915), 537–560; 815–837.

12. Mauss, *op. cit.*, 831.

13. A.L. Kroeber, "Frank Hamilton Cushing," *Encyclopaedia of the Social Sciences*, IV (1931), 657. Kroeber summed him up, "His observations were of the keenest, but almost impossible to disentangle from his imaginings."

14. Nathan Reingold, "American Indifference to Basic Research: A Reappraisal," in George H. Daniels, ed., *Nineteenth-Century American Science: A Reappraisal* (Evanston, University of Illinois, 1972), 38–62, 60.

15. Franz Boas also began the revival, along with Aleš Hrdlička and with the enthusiastic support of F.W. Putnam, of physical anthropology studies in the United States. Boas began measuring school children while he was at Clark University, and he continued this work at the World's Columbian Exposition in Chicago where Putnam put him in charge of the section on Physical Anthropology. Subsequently Boas made the longitudinal studies which showed individual differences in what he called "tempo of growth," and in 1912 he published in *American Anthropologist*, 14, pp. 530–562 his "Changes in Bodily Form of Descendants of Immigrants." Boas compared the head measurements or cephalic index of immigrant children with that of their European born

parents, and he found that in a new environment there were significant changes in the cephalic index, previously assumed to be a stable, hereditary trait. (See James M. Tanner, "Boas's Contributions to Knowledge of Human Growth and Form," in Walter R. Goldschmidt, ed., *The Anthropology of* *Franz Boas*, Memoir 89, American Anthropological Association, 1959, 76–111.) The study showed that even human anatomy was influenced by environmental factors. It was a definitive answer to the claims in the 1850s of the American school of anthropology.

Bibliography

Anonymous, "Frederic Ward Putnam,"*American Indian Magazine*, III (1915).

———, "Brief Biography of William Henry Holmes,"*Ohio Archaeological and Historical Publications*, XXXVI (1927), 493–527.

Adams, Richard E., "Manuel Gamio and Stratigraphic Excavation,"*American Antiquity*, XXVI (1960), 99.

Bandelier, Adolph F., "On the Art of War and Mode of Warfare of the Ancient Mexicans,"*Tenth Annual Report*, Peabody Museum (1877), 95–116.

———, "On the Distribution and Tenure of Land," *Eleventh Annual Report*, Peabody Museum (1878), 385–448.

———, "On the Social Organization and Mode of Government of the Ancient Mexicans,"*Twelfth Annual Report*, Peabody Museum (1879), 557–699.

———, "Historical Introduction to Studies among the Sedentary Indians of New Mexico,"*Papers of the Archaeological Institute of America*, I (1881), 1–33.

———, "A Visit to the Aboriginal Ruins in the Valley of the Rio Pecos,"*Papers of the Archaeological Institute of America*, I (1881), 34–133.

———, "Report of an Archaeological Tour into Mexico in the Year 1881,"*Papers of the Archaeological Institute of America*, II (1884), 3–326.

———, "Final Report of Investigations among the Indians of the Southwestern United States, carried on mainly in the years from 1880–1885," Parts I and II, *Papers of the Archaeological Institute of America*, American Series, III, IV (1890–1892).

Bartlett, Richard A., *Great Surveys of the American West* (Norman, University of Oklahoma Press, 1962).

Bartsch, Paul, "Biographical Sketch of William Healey Dall, Aug. 21, 1845–March 27, 1927," *Smithsonian Miscellaneous Collections*, 104 (Washington, D.C., 1946), 2–4.

Baxter, Sylvester, "The Father of the Pueblos," *Harper's New Monthly Magazine*, 65 (1882), 72–91.

———, "The Old New World, an illustrated letter from Camp Hemenway, Arizona," *Boston Sunday Herald* (April 15, 1888).

———, "Archaeological Camping in Arizona," *The American Architect and Building News*, 25 (Jan. 5, 1889, 8–10; Jan. 12, 1889, 15–16; Jan. 19, 1889, 32–34; Jan. 26, 1889, 43–44), 26 (Aug. 31, 1889, 101–102; Sept. 14, 1889, 120–122).

Benedict, Ruth, "Psychological Types in the Cultures of the Southwest," *Proceedings of the International Congress of Americanists*, 23 (1928), 572–581.

————, "Configurations of culture in North America,"*American Anthropologist*, 34 (1932), 1–27.

————, *Patterns of Culture* (Boston, Houghton Mifflin, 1934).

————, "Appreciation,"*Science*, 97 (1943), 60–62.

Beuttner-Janusch, John, "Boas and Mason: Particularization vs Generalization," *American Anthropologist*, 59 (1957), 318–324.

Bloom, Lansing B., "Bourke on the Southwest," *New Mexico Historical Review*, VIII–XI (1933–1936).

Boas, Franz, "The occurrence of similar inventions in areas widely apart,"*Science*, 9 (1887), 485–486.

————, "Museums of ethnology and their classification," *Science*, 9 (1887), 587–589.

————, *The Social Organization and Secret Societies of the Kwakiutl Indians*, Report of the United States National Museum (Washington, D.C., 1895).

————, "Rudolph Virchow's Anthropological Work," *Science*, 16 (1902), 441–445.

————, "The work of the Jesup North Pacific Expedition,"*Science*, 16 (1902), 893.

————, "Some Problems in North American Archaeology," *American Journal of Archaeology*, 2nd ser., VI (1902), 1–6.

————, "The History of Anthropology," *Science*, 20 (1904), 513–524.

————, "Some Principles of Museum Administration," *Science*, 25 (1907), 921–933.

————, ed., *Putnam Anniversary Volume* (New York, G.E. Stechert, 1909). Includes Putnam bibliography.

————, *The Mind of Primitive Man* (New York, Macmillan, 1911).

————, *Handbook of American Indian Languages*, Bulletin 40, Part I, Bureau of American Ethnology (Washington, D.C., 1911).

————, "In Memoriam: Herman Karl Haeberlin," *American Anthropologist*, 21 (1919), 71–74.

————, "Scientists as Spies," *The Nation*, CIX (Dec. 20, 1919), 797.

————, *Primitive Art* (Oslo, Aschehoug, 1927; Cambridge, Harvard University Press, 1928).

————, *Race, Language, and Culture* (New York, Macmillan, 1940).

Brand, Donald D. and Fred E. Harvey, eds., *So Live the Works of Men*. 70th Anniversary Volume honoring Edgar Lee Hewett (Albuquerque, University of New Mexico Press, 1939).

Brandes, Raymond Stewart, "Frank Hamilton Cushing: Pioneer Americanist," Ph.D. dissertation, University of Arizona (1965).

Brew, J.O., ed., *One Hundred Years of Anthropology* (Cambridge, Harvard University Press, 1968).

Brody, J.J., *Indian Painters and White Patrons* (Albuquerque, University of New Mexico Press, 1971).

Brunhouse, Robert L., *Sylvanus G. Morley and the World of the Ancient Maya* (Norman, University of Oklahoma Press, 1971).

Bunzel, Ruth L., "Introduction to Zuni Ceremonialism," *Forty-Seventh Annual Report*, Bureau of American Ethnology, 1929–1930 (Washington, D.C., 1932), 467–544.

Chinard, Gilbert, "Jefferson and the American Philosophical Society," *Proceedings of the American Philosophical Society*, 87 (1943), 263–276.

Colby, William Munn, "Routes to Rainy Mountain: A Biography of James Mooney, Ethnologist," Ph.D. dissertation, The University of Wisconsin-Madison (1977).

Croly, Mrs. J.C., *The History of the Woman's Club Movement in America* (New York, H.G. Allen & Co., 1898).

Cushing, Frank Hamilton, "Antiquities of Orleans County, New York," *Annual Report*, Smithsonian Institution, 1874 (Washington, D.C., 1875), 375–377.

———, "The Nation of the Willows," *Atlantic Monthly*, 50 (1882), 362–374, 541–559. Reprinted with "Introduction" by Robert C. Euler, *The Nation of the Willows* (Flagstaff, Arizona, Northland Press, 1965).

———, "The Zuni Social, Mythic, and Religious Systems," *Popular Science Monthly*, 21 (1882), 186–192.

———, "My Adventures in Zuni," *Century Magazine*, 25 (1882), 191–207, 500–511; 26 (1883), 28–47. Reprinted with "Introduction" by E. De Golyer, *My Adventures in Zuni* (Santa Fe, Peripatetic Press, 1941).

———, "Zuni Fetiches," *Second Annual Report*, Bureau of Ethnology, 1880–1881 (Washington, D.C., 1883), 9–45.

———, "Zuni Breadstuff," *Millstone*, 9 (1884) and 10 (1885). Reprinted as *Zuni Breadstuff*, Indian Notes and Monographs, 8 (New York, Museum of the American Indian, Heye Foundation, 1920).

———, "A Study of Pueblo Pottery as Illustrative of Zuni Culture Growth," *Fourth Annual Report*, Bureau of Ethnology, 1882–1883 (Washington, D.C., 1886), 467–521.

———, "Preliminary Notes on the Origin, Working Hypothesis, and Primary Researches of the Hemenway Southwestern Archaeological Expedition," *Seventh Congrès international des américanistes* (Berlin, 1890), 151–94.

———, "Manual Concepts: A Study of the Influence of Hand-usage on Cultural Growth," *American Anthropologist*, 5 (1892), 289–317.

———, "Primitive Copper Working: An Experimental Study," *American Anthropologist*, 7 (1894), 93–117.

———, "The Germ of Shore-land Pottery: An Experimental Study," *Memoirs of the*

International Congress of Anthropology, C.S. Wake, ed. (Chicago, The Schulte Publishing Company, 1894), 217–234.

———, "The Arrow," *Proceedings of the American Association for the Advancement of Science*, 44 (1895), 199–240.

———, "Outline of Zuni Creation Myths," *Thirteenth Annual Report*, Bureau of Ethnology, 1891–1892 (Washington, D.C., 1896), 321–447.

———, "The Need of Studying the Indian in Order to Teach Him," *Twenty-Eighth Annual Report of the Board of Indian Commissioners* (Washington, D.C., 1897), 109–115.

———, "Exploration of Ancient Key Dwellers' Remains on the Gulf Coast of Florida," *Proceedings of the American Philosophical Society*, 35 (1896), 329–448.

———, *Zuni Folk Tales* (New York, G.P. Putnam, 1901).

———, "Oraibi in 1883," with J. Walter Fewkes and Elsie Clews Parsons, "Contributions to Hopi History," *American Anthropologist*, 24 (1922), 253–268.

"In Memoriam. Frank Hamilton Cushing," by WJ McGee, W.H. Holmes, J.W. Powell, A.C. Fletcher, Washington Matthews, Stewart Culin, Joseph D. McGuire and "Bibliography of Frank Hamilton Cushing," *American Anthropologist*, 2 (1900) 354–380.

Dall, W.H., "On Succession in the Shell-heaps of the Aleutian Islands," *Contributions to North American Ethnology*, I (Washington, D.C., 1877), 41–91.

Darnell, Regna, "The Development of American Anthropology 1879–1920: From the Bureau of American Ethnology to Franz Boas," Ph.D. dissertation, University of Pennsylvania (1969).

———, "The Emergence of Academic Anthropology at the University of Pennsylvania," *Journal of the History of the Behavioral Sciences*, 6 (1970), 80–92.

———, ed., *Readings in the History of Anthropology* (New York, Harper and Row, 1974).

———, "Daniel G. Brinton," in John Murra, ed., *American Anthropology: The Early Years*. 1974 Proceedings of the American Ethnological Society (St. Paul, West Publishing Company, 1976).

———, "History of Anthropology in Historical Perspective," *Annual Review of Anthropology*, 6 (1977), 399–417.

Darrah, William Culp, *Powell of the Colorado* (Princeton, Princeton University Press, 1951).

Dexter, Ralph W., "The 'Salem Secession' of Agassiz Zoologists," *Essex Institute Historical Collections*, CI (1965), 27–39.

———, "Putnam's Problems Popularizing Anthropology," *American Scientist*, LIV (1966), 315–332.

———, "Frederic Ward Putnam and the Development of Museums of Natural History and Anthropology in the United States," *Curator*, IX (1966), 150–155.

———, "Some Herpetological Notes and Correspondence of Frederic Ward Putnam," *Journal of the Ohio Herpetological Society*, V (1966), 109–114.

———, "The Role of F. W. Putnam in founding the Field Museum," *Curator*, XIII (1970), 21–26.

———, "The Role of F. W. Putnam in Developing Anthropology at the American Museum of Natural History," *Curator*, XIX (1976), 303–310.

———, "The Impact of Evolutionary Theories on the Salem Group of Agassiz Zoologists (Morse, Hyatt, Packard, Putnam)," *Essex Institute Historical Collections*, 115 (1979), 144–171.

Dorsey, George A., "History of the Study of Anthropology at Harvard," *The Denison Quarterly*, IV (1896?), 77–97.

———, "Notes on the Anthropological Museums of Central Europe," *American Anthropologist*, I (1899), 464–474.

———, "The Development of Anthropology of the Field Columbian Museum: A Review of Six Years," *American Anthropologist*, 2 (1900), 247–265.

———, "The Anthropological Exhibits at the American Museum of Natural History," *Science*, 25 (1907), 584–587.

Dorsey, J. Owen, "Omaha Sociology," *Third Annual Report*, Bureau of Ethnology, 1881–1882 (Washington, D.C., 1884), 205–370.

Dozier, Edward P., "The Pueblo Indians of the Southwest: A Survey of the Anthropological Literature and a Review of Theory, Methods, and Results," *Current Anthropology*, 5 (1964), 79–97.

Dundes, Alan, *The Study of Folklore* (New York, Prentice-Hall, 1965).

Dupree, A. Hunter, *Science and the Federal Government* (Cambridge, The Belknap Press of Harvard University, 1957).

Durkheim, Emile and Marcel Mauss, "De quelques formes primitives de classification: contribution à l'étude de représentations collectives," *Année sociologique*, VI (1903), 1–72.

Dutton, C.E., *The Tertiary History of the Grand Canyon District*, with Atlas (Washington, D.C., 1882).

Eastman, Elaine Goodale, *Pratt, the Red Man's Moses* (Norman, University of Oklahoma Press, 1935).

Eggan, Fred, "Lewis H. Morgan and the Future of the American Indians," *Proceedings of the American Philosophical Society*, 109 (1965), 272–276.

Ellenberger, Henri, *The Discovery of the Unconscious* (New York, Basic Books, 1970).

Engels, Frederick, *The Origin of the Family, Private Property, and the State*, trans. by Ernest Untermann (Chicago, Charles H. Kerr, 1902).

Erasmus, Charles J., *Las dimensiones de la cultura: historia de la etnologia en los Estados Unidos entre 1900 y 1950* (Bogatá, 1953).

Ewers, John C., "A Century of American Indian Exhibits in the Smithsonian Institution," *Annual Report of the Smithsonian Institution* (1958), 513–552.

Field, R.M. and O.T. Jones, "The Resurrection of the Grand Canyon of the Yellowstone," *American Journal of Science*, 5th ser., XVII (1929), 260–278.

Fillmore, John C., "A Study of Indian Music," *Century Magazine*, XLVII (1894), 616–623.

Fitting, James E., ed., *The Development of North American Archaeology* (Garden City, Anchor, 1973).

Flack, J. Kirkpatrick, *Desideratum in Washington: The Intellectual Community in the Capital City 1870–1900* (Cambridge, Schenkman Publishing Company, 1975).

Fletcher, Alice C., "Sun Dance of the Ogallala Sioux," *Proceedings*, American Association for the Advancement of Science, XXXI (1883), 580–584.

———, "Observations on the Laws and Privileges of the Gens in Indian Society," *Science*, II (1883), 367.

———, "Symbolic Earth Formations of the Winnebagoes," *Science*, II (1883), 367–368.

———, "On Indian Education and Self-Support," *Century Magazine*, IV (1883), 312–315.

———, "The White Buffalo Festival of the Uncpapas," *16th Annual Report*, Peabody Museum, 3 (1884), 260–275.

———, "The Elk Mystery or Festival of the Ogallala Sioux," *16th Annual Report*, Peabody Museum, 3 (1884), 276–288.

———, "The Religious Ceremony of the Four Winds as Observed by a Santee Sioux," *16th Annual Report*, Peabody Museum, 3 (1884), 289–295.

———, "The Shadow or Ghost Lodge: A Ceremony of the Ogallala Sioux," *16th Annual Report*, Peabody Museum, 3 (1884), 296–307.

———, "The Wa-Wan, or Pipe Dance of the Omahas," *16th Annual Report*, Peabody Museum, 3 (1884), 308–333.

———, "Observations upon the Usage, Symbolism and Influence of the Sacred Pipes of Friendship among the Omahas," *Proceedings*, American Association for the Advancement of Science, XXXIII (1885), 615–617.

———, "Land in Severalty to Indians; Illustrated by Experiences with the Omaha Tribe," *Proceedings*, American Association for the Advancement of Science, XXXIII (1885), 654–665.

———, "A Letter from the World's Industrial Exposition at New Orleans, to the various Indian Tribes who are interested in Education," (Carlisle, Pa., Indian School Print, 1885).

———, "The Supernatural Among the Omaha Tribe of Indians," *Proceedings of the American Society of Psychical Research*, I (1887), 3–18.

———, *Indian Education and Civilization*, Special Report, U.S. Bureau of Education, Department of the Interior (Washington, D.C., 1888).

———, "On the Preservation of Archaeologic Monuments," *Proceedings*, American Association for the Advancement of Science, XXXVI (1888), 317.

———, "Report of the Committee on the Preservation of Archaeologic Remains on the Public Lands," *Proceedings*, American Association for the Advancement of Science, XXXVII (1889), 35–37.

———, "Leaves from my Omaha note-book," *Journal of American Folklore*, II (1889), 219–226.

———, "Phonetic Alphabet of the Winnebago Indians," *Proceedings*, American Association for the Advancement of Science, XXXVIII (1890), 354–357.

———, "Indian Messiah," *Journal of American Folklore*, IV (1891), 57–60.

———, "Hal-thu-ska Society of the Omaha Tribe," *Journal of American Folklore*, V (1892), 135–144.

———, aided by Francis La Flesche and J.C. Fillmore, "A Study of Omaha Indian Music," *Archaeological and Ethnological Papers*, Peabody Museum of American Archaeology and Ethnology, I (1893), 237–287.

———, "Music as Found in Certain North American Indian Tribes," *The Music Review* (Aug., 1893), 534–538.

———, "Politics and 'Pipe-Dancing'," *Century Magazine*, 45 (1893), 441–445.

———, "Indian Songs: Personal Studies of Indian Life," *Century Magazine*, 47 (1894), 421–431.

———, "Love Songs among the Omaha Indians," *Memoirs*, International Congress of Anthropologists, ed. by C.S. Wake (Chicago, Schulte, 1894), 153–157.

———, "Hunting Customs of the Omahas," *Century Magazine*, 47 (1895), 691–702.

———, "Tribal Life Among the Omahas," *Century Magazine*, 51 (1896), 450–461.

———, "Indian Songs and Music," *Proceedings*, American Association for the Advancement of Science, XLIV (1896), 281–284.

———, "Sacred Pole of the Omaha Tribe," *Proceedings*, American Association for the Advancement of Science, XLIV (1895), 270–280.

———, "Notes on Certain Beliefs concerning Will Power among the Siouan Tribes," *Proceedings*, American Association for the Advancement of Science, XLIV (1895), 1–4.

————, "Emblematic Use of the Tree in the Dakotan Group," *Proceedings*, American Association for the Advancement of Science, XLV (1896), 191–209.

————, "The Import of the Totem," *Science*, 7 (1898), 296–304.

————, "Indian Songs and Music," *Journal of American Folklore*, XI (1898), 85–104.

————, "A Pawnee Ritual Used When Changing a Man's Name," *American Anthropologist*, I (1899), 82–97.

————, *Indian Story and Song From North America* (Boston, 1900).

————, "Giving Thanks: A Pawnee Ceremony," *Journal of American Folklore*, XIII (1900), 261–266.

————, "Frank Hamilton Cushing," *American Anthropologist*, II (1900), 367–370.

————, "The 'Lazy Man' in Indian Lore," *Journal of American Folklore*, XIV (1901), 100–104.

————, "Pawnee Star Lore," *Journal of American Folklore*, XVI (1903), 10–15.

————, "The Significance of Dress," *American Journal of Archaeology*, VII (1903), 84–85.

———— and James Murie, *The Hako: A Pawnee Ceremony*, Twenty-Second Report of the Bureau of American Ethnology (Washington, D.C., 1904).

————, "The Indian and Nature," *American Anthropologist*, 9 (1907), 440–443.

————, "Tribal Structure: A Study of the Omaha and Cognate Tribes," *Putnam Anniversary Volume* (New York, 1909), 254–267.

———— and Francis La Flesche, *The Omaha Tribe*, Twenty-Seventh Report of the Bureau of American Ethnology (Washington, D.C., 1911).

————, "The Problems of the Unity or Plurality and the Probable Place of Origin of the American Aborigines. (A Symposium): Some Ethnological Aspects of the Problem," *American Anthropologist*, 14 (1912), 37–39.

————, "Wakondagi," *American Anthropologist*, 14 (1912), 106–108.

————, "Brief History of the International Congress of Americanists," *American Anthropologist*, XV (1913), 529–534.

————, *Indian Games and Dances with Native Songs Arranged from American Indian Ceremonials and Sports* (Boston, 1915).

————, "The Study of Indian Music," *Proceedings of the National Academy of Sciences*, I (1915), 231–235.

————, "A Birthday Wish from Native America," *Holmes Anniversary Volume* (Washington, D.C., 1916), 118–122.

————, "Nature and the Indian Tribe," *Art and Archaeology*, 4 (1916), 291–296.

————, "Prayers Voiced in Ancient America," *Art and Archaeology*, 9 (1920), 73–75.

Fowler, Don D., Robert C. Euler, and Catherine S. Fowler, "John Wesley Powell and the anthropology of the Canyon country," United States Geological Survey, *Professional Paper* no. 670 (Washington, D.C., 1969).

———, and Catherine S. Fowler, eds., "Anthropology of the Numa: John Wesley Powell's Manuscripts on the Numic Peoples of Western North America," *Smithsonian Contributions to Knowledge*, No. 14 (Washington, D.C., 1971).

Freeman, John F., "University Anthropology: Early Departments in the United States," *Kroeber Anthropological Society Papers*, 32 (1965), 78–90.

Gilbert, Hope, "He Discovered the Southwest for Americans," *The Desert Magazine*, 7 (Sept., 1944), 13–16.

———, "1882: Zuni Pilgrimage to the Atlantic Ocean," *The Desert Magazine*, 24 (1961), 12–15.

Gilliland, Marian S., *The Material Culture of Key Marco Florida* (Gainesville, University Presses of Florida, 1975).

Gilman, Benjamin Ives and Katherine H. Stone, "The Hemenway Southwestern Expedition," *Journal of American Ethnology and Archaeology*, V (1908), 229–235.

Goddard, Pliny Earle, "Facts and theories concerning Pleistocene Man in America," *American Anthropologist*, 29 (1927), 262–266.

Godoy, Ricardo, "Franz Boas and His Plans for an International School of American Archaeology and Ethnology in Mexico," *Journal of the History of the Behavioral Sciences*, 13 (1977), 228–242.

Goetzmann, William H., *Exploration and Empire* (New York, Knopf, 1966).

Goldschmidt, Walter, ed., *The Anthropology of Franz Boas*, Memoir 89, American Anthropological Association, 61 (1959).

Goldwater, Robert, *Primitivism in Modern Art* (New York, Vintage Press, 1938, rev. ed., 1966, 1967).

Goode, George Brown, "The Origin of the National Scientific and Educational Institutions of the United States," *Annual Report*, Smithsonian Institution, 1897, Part II (Washington, D.C., 1901), 263–354.

Goodrich, Lloyd, *Thomas Eakins: His Life and Work* (New York, Whitney Museum of American Art, 1973).

Gordon, Dudley C., "Lummis and the Lacey Act," *The Masterkey*, 42 (1968), 17–19.

Gould, Stephen J., "Morton's Ranking of Races by Cranial Capacity," *Science*, 200 (May 5, 1978), 505–509.

Green, Jesse, ed. and introduction, *Zuni: Selected Writings of Frank Hamilton Cushing* (Lincoln, University of Nebraska Press, 1979). Includes Cushing bibliography.

Green, Norma Kidd, *Iron Eye's Family: The Children of Joseph La Flesche* (Lincoln, Nebraska, Johnsen Publishing Company, 1969).

Gruber, Jacob, "Brixham Cave and the Antiquity of Man," in M.E. Spiro, ed., *Context and Meaning in Cultural Anthropology* (Glencoe, Ill., The Free Press, 1965).

———, "In Search of Experience: Biography as an Instrument for the History of Anthropology," in June Helm, ed., *Pioneers of American Anthropology* (Seattle, University of Washington Press, 1966).

———, ed., *The Philadelphia Anthropological Society* (Philadelphia, Temple University Publications, 1967).

———, "Horatio Hale and the development of American anthropology," *Proceedings of the American Philosophical Society*, 3 (1967), 5–37.

———, "Ethnographic Salvage and the Shaping of Anthropology," *American Anthropologist*, 72 (1970), 1289–1299.

Haddon, A.C., *Evolution in Art: As Illustrated by the Life-Histories of Designs* (London, W. Scott, 1895).

———, "What the United States of America is doing for anthropology," *Journal of the Royal Anthropological Institute*, 32 (1902), 8–24; 33 (1903), 11–23.

Haeberlin, H.K., "The idea of fertilization in the culture of the Pueblo Indians," *Memoirs*, American Anthropological Association, III (1916), 1–55.

Hallowell, A. Irving, "The Beginnings of Anthropology in America," in Frederica deLaguna, ed., *Selected Papers from the American Anthropologist, 1888–1920* (Evanston, Ill., Row, Peterson and Co., 1960), 1–96.

Harris, Marvin, *The Rise of Anthropological Theory* (New York, Thomas Y. Crowell, 1968).

Haury, Emil W., *The Excavation of Los Muertos and Neighboring Ruins in the Salt River Valley, Southern Arizona*, Papers, Peabody Museum of Archaeology and Ethnology, 24 (1945).

Haven, Samuel F., *Archaeology of the United States, or Sketches, Historical and Biographical, of the Progress of Information and Opinion Respecting Vestiges of Antiquity in the United States*, Smithsonian Contributions to Knowledge, 8 (Washington, D.C., 1856).

Hellman, Geoffrey, *Bankers, Bones and Beetles; The First Century of the American Museum of Natural History* (New York, The Natural History Press, 1969).

Hendricks, Gordon, *The Photographs of Thomas Eakins* (New York, Grossman, 1972).

Hertzberg, Hazel W., *The Search for an American Indian Identity: Modern Pan-Indian Movements* (Syracuse, Syracuse University Press, 1971).

———, "Nationality, Anthropology, and Pan-Indianism in the Life of Arthur C.

Parker (Seneca)," *Proceedings of the American Philosophical Society,* 123 (1979), 47–72.

Hinsley, Curtis M., Jr., "The Development of a Profession: Anthropology in Washington, D.C., 1846–1903," Ph.D. dissertation, University of Wisconsin (1976).

———, "Amateurs and Professionals in Washington Anthropology," in John Murra, ed., *American Anthropology: The Early Years.* 1974 Proceedings of the American Ethnological Society (St. Paul, West Publishing Company, 1976).

———, "Anthropology as Science and Politics: The Dilemmas of the Bureau of American Ethnology, 1879–1904," in Walter Goldschmidt, ed., *The Uses of Anthropology,* Special Publication of the American Anthropological Association (1979), 15–32.

——— and Bill Holm, "A Cannibal in the National Museum: The Early Career of Franz Boas in America," *American Anthropologist,* 78 (1976), 306–316.

Hodge, F.W., ed., *Handbook of the American Indians North of Mexico,* Bureau of American Ethnology, Bulletin 30 (Washington, D.C., 1907, 1910).

Hoebel, E. Adamson, "Major Contributions of Southwestern Studies to Anthropological Theory," *American Anthropologist,* 56 (1954), 720–727.

Hofstadter, Richard, *Social Darwinism in American Thought* (Boston, Beacon Press, 1944, rev. ed., 1955, 1959).

Holmes, William Henry, "Report on the geology of the north-western portion of the Elk range," *Eighth Annual Report,* U.S. Geological and Geographical Survey of the Territories, 1874 (Washington, D.C., 1876), 59–71.

———, "Report on the ancient ruins of southwestern Colorado, examined during the summers of 1875 and 1876," *Tenth Annual Report,* U.S. Geological and Geographical Survey of the Territories, 1876 (Washington, D.C., 1878), 383–408.

———, "Report on the geology of the Yellowstone National Park," *Twelfth Annual Report,* U.S. Geological and Geographical Survey of the Territories, 1878, II (Washington, D.C., 1883), 1–57.

———, "Art in shell of the ancient Americans," *Second Annual Report,* Bureau of American Ethnology, 1880–1881 (Washington, D.C., 1883), 179–305.

———, "Prehistoric textile fabrics of the United States, derived from impressions on pottery," *Third Annual Report,* Bureau of American Ethnology, 1881–1882 (Washington, D.C., 1884), 393–425.

———, "Report to the Director of the United States Geological Survey, 1884–1885," *Sixth Annual Report,* U.S. Geological Survey, 1884–1885 (Washington, D.C., 1885), 94–97.

————, "Monoliths of San Juan Teotihuacan, Mexico," *American Journal of Archaeology*, I (1885), 361–371.

————, "Evidences of the antiquity of man on the site of the City of Mexico," *Transactions*, Anthropological Society of Washington, III (1885), 68–81.

————, "Sketch of the great Serpent mound," *Science*, VIII (1886), 624–628.

————, "Textile art in prehistoric archaeology," *American Antiquarian*, VIII (1886), 261–266.

————, "Pottery of the ancient Pueblos," *Fourth Annual Report*, Bureau of American Ethnology, 1882–1883 (Washington, D.C., 1886), 257–360.

————, "Ancient Pottery of the Mississippi Valley," *Fourth Annual Report*, Bureau of American Ethnology, 1882–1883 (Washington, D.C., 1886), 361–436.

————, "Origin and development of form and ornament in ceramic art," *Fourth Annual Report*, Bureau of American Ethnology, 1882–1883 (Washington, D.C., 1886), 437–465.

————, "Ancient art of the province of Chiriqui, Colombia," *Sixth Annual Report*, Bureau of American Ethnology, 1884–1885 (Washington, D.C., 1888), 13–187.

————, "A study of the textile art in its relation to the development of form and ornament," *Sixth Annual Report*, Bureau of American Ethnology, 1884–1885 (Washington, D.C., 1888), 189–252.

————, "Textile fabrics of ancient Peru," *Bulletin 7*, Bureau of American Ethnology (Washington, D.C., 1889), 17 pp.

————, "A quarry workshop of the flaked-stone implement makers in the District of Columbia," *American Anthropologist*, III (1890), 1–26.

————, "On the evolution of ornament, an American lesson," *American Anthropologist*, III (1890), 137–146.

————, "Recent work in the quarry workshops of the District of Columbia," *American Anthropologist*, III (1890), 224–225.

————, "On the so-called palaeolithic implements of the upper Mississippi. Abstract," *Proceedings*, American Association for the Advancement of Science, XLI (1892), 280–281.

————, "Modern quarry refuse and the paleolithic theory," *Science*, XX (1892), 295–297.

————, "Distribution of stone implements in the tidewater country," *American Anthropologist*, VI (1893), 1–14.

————, "The World's Fair Congress of Anthropology," *American Anthropologist*, VI (1893), 423–434.

————, "Gravel man and paleolithic culture; a preliminary word," *Science*, XXI (1893), 29–30.

———, "Are there traces of glacial man in the Trenton gravels?" *Journal of Geology*, I (1893), 15–37.

———, "Vestiges of early man in Minnesota," *American Geologist*, XI (1893). 219–240.

———, "Natural history of flaked stone implements," in C.S. Wake, ed., *Memoirs*, International Congress of Anthropology (Chicago, Schulte Pub. Co., 1894), 120–139.

———, "Caribbean influence in the prehistoric art of Southern states," *American Anthropologist*, VII (1894), 71–79.

———, *Archaeological studies among the ancient cities of Mexico*, Publications, Field Columbian Museum, Anthropological series, I (1895–1897).

———, "Prehistoric textile art of eastern United States," *Thirteenth Annual Report*, Bureau of American Ethnology, 1891–1892 (Washington, D.C., 1896), 3–46.

———, "Stone implements of the Potomac-Chesapeake tidewater province," *Fifteenth Annual Report*, Bureau of American Ethnology, 1893–1894 (Washington, D.C., 1897), 13–152.

———, "Primitive man in the Delaware valley," *Science*, VI (1897), 824–829.

———, "Preliminary revision of the evidence relating to auriferous gravel man in California," *American Anthropologist*, I (1899), 107–121, 614–645.

———, "Report on the department of anthropology for the year 1897–1898," *Annual Report*, U.S. National Museum, 1898 (Washington, D.C., 1900), 19–33.

———, "Remarks on Frank Hamilton Cushing," *American Anthropologist*, II (1900), 356–360.

———, "Use of textiles in pottery making and embellishment," *American Anthropologist*, III (1901), 397–403.

———, "Sketch of the origin, development, and probable destiny of the races of men," *American Anthropologist*, IV (1902), 369–391.

———, "Fossil human remains found near Lansing, Kansas," *American Anthropologist*, IV (1902), 743–752.

———, "Classification and arrangement of the exhibits of an anthropological museum," *Science*, XVI (1902), 487–504.

———, "Report on the department of anthropology for the year 1899–1900," *Annual Report*, U.S. National Museum, 1900 (Washington, D.C., 1902), 21–29.

———, "Aboriginal pottery of the eastern United States," *Twentieth Annual Report*, Bureau of American Ethnology, 1898–1899 (Washington, D.C., 1903), 1–201.

———, "Report on the department of anthropology for the year 1900–1901," *Annual Report*, U.S. National Museum, 1901 (Washington, D.C., 1903), 253–278.

———, "Report of the Bureau of American Ethnology," *Annual Report*, Smithsonian Institution, 1903 (Washington, D.C., 1904), 34–48.

———, "Report on the Congress of Americanists held at Stuttgart, Germany, August 18–23, 1904," *Smithsonian Miscellaneous Collections*, XLVII (Washington, D.C., 1905), 391–395.

———, "Decorative Art of the aborigines of northern America," in B. Laufer, ed., *Anthropological Papers written in Honor of Franz Boas* (New York, G.E. Stechert, 1906), 179–188.

———, "Lewis Henry Morgan, 1818–1881," *National Academy of Sciences Biographical Memoirs*, VI (1909), 219–239.

———, "The first Pan-American scientific congress, held in Santiago, Chile, December 25, 1908–January 6, 1909," *Annual Report*, Smithsonian Institution, 1909 (Washington, D.C., 1910), 86–95; also in *Science*, XXIX (1909), 441–448.

———, "Masterpieces of aboriginal American art," *Art and Archaeology*, I (1914), 1–12, 91–102, 243–255; III (1916), 71–85; IV (1916), 269–278; VIII (1919), 349–360.

———, "Organization of the Committee on Anthropology of the National Research Council and its activities for the year 1917," *American Journal of Physical Anthropology*, I (1918), 77–90.

———, *Handbook of American Antiquities. Part I–Introduction*, Bureau of American Ethnology, Bulletin 60 (Washington, D.C., 1919).

———, "The Antiquity Phantom in American Archaeology," *Science*, LXII (1925), 256–258.

———, "National Gallery of Art," *Catalogue of Collections*, National Gallery of Art (Washington, D.C., 1922, 1926), 1–2.

Homer, William Innes, *Robert Henri and His Circle* (Ithaca, Cornell University Press, 1969).

Hoxie, Frederick E., "Beyond Savagery: The Campaign to Assimilate the American Indians, 1880–1920," Ph.D. dissertation, Brandeis University (1977).

Hrdlička, Aleš, "Skeletal Remains Suggesting or Attributed to Early Man in North America," *Thirty-third Bulletin of the Bureau of American Ethnology* (Washington, D.C., 1907).

———, *Physical Anthropology* (Philadelphia, The Wistar Institute of Anatomy and Biology, 1919).

Hough, Walter, "Alice Cunningham Fletcher," *American Anthropologist*, 25 (1923), 254-258. Includes Fletcher bibliography.

———, "William Henry Holmes," *American Anthropologist*, 35 (1933), 752–764. Includes Holmes bibliography.

Jefferson, Thomas, *Notes on the State of Virginia*, edited and Introduction and Notes by William Peden (Chapel Hill, University of North Carolina, 1955).

Judd, Neil M., *The Bureau of American Ethnology: A Partial History* (Norman, University of Oklahoma Press, 1967).

———, *Men Met Along the Trail* (Norman, University of Oklahoma Press, 1968).

Keel, Bennie C., "Cyrus Thomas and the Mound Builders," *Southern Indian Studies*, XXII (1970), 3–16.

Kidder, Alfred V., "Reminiscences in southwest archaeology, I," *The Kiva*, 25, No. 4 (1960), 1–32.

Kohlstedt, Sally Gregory, *The Formation of the American Scientific Community: The American Association for the Advancement of Science, 1848–1860* (Urbana, University of Illinois Press, 1976).

Kroeber, Alfred L., "Frederic Ward Putnam," *American Anthropologist*, XVII (1915), 712–718.

———, "Frank Hamilton Cushing," *Encyclopaedia of the Social Sciences*, IV (New York, Macmillan, 1931), 657.

——— and Clyde Kluckhohn, "Culture: A Critical Review of Concepts and Definitions," *Papers*, Peabody Museum of American Archaeology and Ethnology, XLVII (1952).

La Flesche, Francis, "Alice C. Fletcher," *Science*, 58 (1923), 115.

Laird, Carobeth, *Encounter with an Angry God: Reflections of My Life with John Peabody Harrington* (Morongo Indian Reservation, Banning, California, Malki Museum Press, 1975).

Lamb, Daniel S., "The Story of the Anthropological Society of Washington," *American Anthropologist*, 8 (1906), 564–579.

Laude, Jean, *The Arts of Black Africa*, trans. by Jean Decock (Berkeley, University of California Press, 1971).

Laufer, Berthold, ed., *Boas Anniversary Volume* (New York, G.E. Stechert, 1906).

Lawrence, D. H., "America, Listen to Your Own," *The New Republic*, 25 (Dec. 19, 1920), 68–70.

Lévi-Strauss, Claude, *Structural Anthropology*, trans. by Claire Jacobsen and Brooke Grundfest Schoepf (Garden City, New York, Anchor, 1967).

Lévy-Bruhl, Lucien, *How Natives Think (Les fonctions mentales dans les societés inférieures*, Paris, 1910), authorized trans. by Lilian A. Clare (London, George Allen and Unwin, 1926).

Liberty, Margot, ed., *American Indian Intellectuals*, 1976 Proceedings of the American Ethnological Society (St. Paul, West Publishing Company, 1978).

Lister, Florence C. and Robert H., *Earl Morris and Southwestern Archaeology* (Albuquerque, University of New Mexico Press, 1968).

Lowie, Robert H., *The History of Ethnological Theory* (New York, Farrar and Rinehart, 1937).

——, "Franz Boas, His Predecessors and His Contemporaries," *Science*, 97 (1943), 202–203.

——, "Reminiscences of Anthropological Currents in America Half a Century Ago," *American Anthropologist*, 58 (1956), 995–1016.

Lummis, Charles F., "The White Indian," *Land of Sunshine*, 12 (1900), 8–17.

——, "In Memoriam. Alice C. Fletcher," *Art and Archaeology*, XVI (1923), 75–76.

Lurie, Edward, *Louis Agassiz: A Life in Science* (Chicago, University of Chicago Press, 1960).

Lurie, Nancy O., "Women in Early American Anthropology," in June Helm, ed., *Pioneers of American Anthropology* (Seattle, University of Washington Press, 1966), 29–81.

McGee, W J, "Anthropology at Detroit and Toronto," *American Anthropologist*, X (1897), 317–345.

McNitt, Frank, *Richard Wetherill: Anasazi* (Albuquerque, University of New Mexico Press, 1957, rev. ed. 1966).

Marcou, Jules, *Life, Letters, and Works of Louis Agassiz*, 2 vols. (New York, Macmillan, 1896).

Mark, Joan, "Gentleman Enthusiasts and Lady Adventurers." *Odyssey* Magazine (1980), 16–18.

Mason, O.T., "The occurrence of similar inventions in areas widely apart," *Science*, IX (1887), 534–535.

——, "Influence of Environment upon Human Industries or Arts," *Annual Report*, Smithsonian Institution, 1895 (Washington, D.C., 1896).

Mauss, Marcel, "L'ethnographie en France et à l'étranger," *La Revue de Paris* (1915), 537–560; 815–837.

——, "Divisions et proportions des divisions de la sociologie," *Année sociologique*, n.s., II (1927).

Mead, Margaret, *An Anthropologist at Work: Writings of Ruth Benedict* (Boston, Houghton Mifflin, 1959).

—— and Ruth L. Bunzel, *The Golden Age of American Anthropology* (New York, George Braziller, 1960).

Merrill, George P., "Contributions to the History of American Geology," *Report of the United States National Museum*, 1904 (Washington, D.C., 1906).

Meyer, A.B., "Studies of museums and kindred institutions of New York City, Albany, Buffalo, and Chicago, with notes on some European institutions,"

Annual Report, Smithsonian Institution, 1903 (Washington, D.C., 1905), 311–608.

Miller, Howard S., *Dollars for Research: Science and Its Patrons in Nineteenth Century America* (Seattle, University of Washington Press, 1970).

Mitra, Panchanan, *A History of American Anthropology* (University of Calcutta, 1933).

Mooney, James, *The Ghost-Dance Religion and the Sioux Outbreak of 1890*, Fourteenth Annual Report of the Bureau of Ethnology (Washington, D.C., 1896).

Morgan, Lewis Henry, "Report to the Regents of the University, upon the articles furnished to the Indian Collection," *Third Annual Report of the Regents of the University on the condition of the State Cabinet of Natural History and the Historical and Antiquarian Collection*, rev. ed. (Albany, 1850).

———, *League of the Ho-de-no-sau-nee, or Iroquois* (Rochester, Sage and Bros., 1851).

———, *The American Beaver and His Works* (Philadelphia, J.B. Lippincott, 1868).

———, "A Conjectural Solution to the Origin of the Classificatory System of Relationship," *Proceedings of the American Academy of Arts and Sciences*, VII (1868), 436–477.

———, "Systems of Consanguinity and Affinity of the Human Family," *Smithsonian Contributions to Knowledge*, XVII (1870).

———, "Montezuma's Dinner," *North American Review*, CXXII (1876), 265–308.

———, "The Hue and Cry Against the Indians," *Nation*, 23 (1876), 40–41.

———, "Factory Systems on Indian Reservations," *Nation*, 23 (1876), 58–59.

———, *Ancient Society, or Researches in the Lines of Human Progress from Savagery through Barbarism to Civilization* (New York, Holt, 1877).

———, "The Indian Question," *Nation*, 27 (1878), 332.

———, "A Study of the Houses of the American Aborigines," *First Annual Report*, Archaeological Institute of America, 1879–80 (1880), 27–77.

———, "Houses and House-Life of the American Aborigines," in *Contributions to North American Ethnology*, IV, U.S. Geographical and Geological Survey of the Rocky Mountain Region (Washington, D.C., 1881).

Morrill, Allen C. and Eleanor D., "The Measuring Woman and the Cook," *Idaho Yesterdays*, 7 (1963), 2–15.

———, "Talmaks," *Idaho Yesterdays*, 8 (1964), 2–15.

———, *Out of the Blanket: The Story of Sue and Kate McBeth, Missionaries to the Nez Perces* (Moscow, The University Press of Idaho, 1978).

Morse, Edward S., "Frederick Ward Putnam, 1839–1915. An Appreciation," *Historical Collections of the Essex Institute*, LII (1916), 8 pp.

Moses, Lester George, "James Mooney, U.S. Ethnologist: A Biography," Ph.D. dissertation, The University of New Mexico (1977).

Murra, John V., ed., *American Anthropology: The Early Years*, 1974 Proceedings of the American Ethnological Society (St. Paul, West Publishing Company, 1976).

[Norton, Charles Eliot], "Ancient Monuments in America," *North American Review*, LXVIII (1849), 466–496.

Ober, Fred A., "How a White Man Became the War Chief of the Zunis," *Wide Awake* (June, 1882), 382–388.

Olson, Alan P., "Changing Frontiers in Southwestern Archaeology," *Journal of the Arizona Academy of Sciences*, II (1963), 120–123.

Ortiz, Alfonso, ed., *New Perspectives on the Pueblos* (School of American Research Book, Albuquerque, University of New Mexico Press, 1972).

Pandey, Triloki Nath, "Anthropologists at Zuni," *Proceedings of the American Philosophical Society*, 116 (1972), 321–337.

Parker, Franklin, *George Peabody: A Biography* (Nashville, Vanderbilt University Press, 1971).

Parkman, Mary R., *Heroines of Science* (New York, The Century Company, 1918).

Parmenter, Ross, "Glimpses of a Friendship," in June Helm, ed., *Pioneers of American Anthropology* (Seattle, University of Washington, 1966).

Penniman, T.K., *A Hundred Years of Anthropology* (New York, Wm. Morrow, 1974, orig. 1965).

Phillips, Philip, "Introduction" to Cushing, *Exploration of Ancient Key Dwellers' Remains on the Gulf Coast of Florida* (New York, AMS Press for the Peabody Museum of Archaeology and Ethnology, 1973).

Powell, John Wesley, "The ancient province of Tusayan," *Scribner's Monthly*, 11 (1876), 193–213.

———, *Introduction to the Study of Indian Languages* (Washington, D.C., Smithsonian Institution, 1877).

———, "Sketch of Lewis Henry Morgan," *Popular Science Monthly*, XVIII (1880), 114–121.

———, "Museums of ethnology and their classification," *Science*, IX (1887), 612–614.

———, "Competition as a Factor in Human Evolution," *American Anthropologist*, I (1888), 297–323.

———, "Indian Linguistic Families of America North of Mexico," *Seventh Annual Report*, Bureau of Ethnology, 1885–1886 (Washington, D.C., 1891), 7–139.

Prucha, Francis Paul, ed., *Americanizing the American Indians: Writings by the "Friends of the Indian," 1880–1900* (Cambridge, Harvard University Press, 1973).

————, ed. and introduction to D.S. Otis, *The Dawes Act and the Allotment of Indian Lands* (Norman, University of Oklahoma Press, 1973, Otis orig. 1934).

Putnam, Frederic Ward, "Jeffries Wyman, *Proceedings of the American Academy of Arts and Sciences*, II (1875), 496–505.

————, *Report upon United States Geographical and Geological Explorations and Surveys West of the 100th Meridian*, in charge of First Lieut. George M. Wheeler, Vol. VII. Archaeology (Washington, D.C., 1879).

————, "Sketch of Lewis H. Morgan," *Proceedings of the American Academy of Arts and Sciences*, IX (1882), 429–436.

————, "On Methods of Archaeological Research in America," *Johns Hopkins University Circulars*, V, No. 49 (1886), 89.

————, "Conventionalism in Ancient American Art," *Bulletin of the Essex Institute*, XVIII (1886), 155–167.

————, "The Peabody Museum of American Archaeology and Ethnology in Cambridge," *Proceedings of the American Antiquarian Society*, VI (1889), 180–190.

————, "The Serpent Mound of Ohio," *Century Magazine*, XXXIX (April, 1890), 871–888.

————, "Henry Wheatland," *Proceedings of the American Academy of Arts and Sciences*, XXXI (1896), 363–367.

————, [Discussion of Trenton deposits], *Proceedings*, American Association for the Advancement of Science, XLVI (1897), 384, 387–389.

————, "A problem in anthropology," *Science*, X (1899), 225–236.

Ray, Verne F. and Nancy O. Lurie, "The Contributions of Lewis and Clark to Ethnography," *Journal of the Washington Academy of Sciences*, 44 (1954), 358–370.

Reingold, Nathan, "American Indifference to Basic Research: A Reappraisal," in George H. Daniels, ed., *Nineteenth-Century American Science: A Reappraisal* (Evanston, University of Illinois, 1972), 38–62.

Resek, Carl, *Lewis Henry Morgan: American Scholar* (Chicago, University of Chicago, 1960).

Riggs, A.S., "William Henry Holmes," *Art and Archaeology*, XXXIV (1933), 115.

Roberts, Frank H.H., Jr., "One Hundred Years of Smithsonian Anthropology," *Science*, 104 (1946), 119–125.

Rohner, Ronald P., ed. with "Introduction" by Ronald P. Rohner and Evelyn C. Rohner, *The Ethnography of Franz Boas: Letters and Diaries of Franz Boas Written on the Northwest Coast from 1886 to 1931* (Chicago, The University of Chicago Press, 1969).

Rowe, John Howland, "The Spelling of 'Archaeology'," *Anthropology Newsletter*, 16 (June, 1975), 11–12.

Sapir, Edward, "Notes on Psychological Orientation in a Given Society," Social Science Research Council, *Hanover Conference*, I (Aug. 9–20, 1926).

——, *Selected Writings of Edward Sapir in Language, Culture, and Personality*, edited by David G. Mandelbaum (Berkeley and Los Angeles, University of California Press, 1958).

Schendler, Sylvan, *Eakins* (Boston, Little, Brown, 1967).

Silverberg, Robert, *Mound Builders of Ancient America: the archaeology of a myth* (Greenwich, New York, New York Graphic Society, 1968).

Spier, Leslie, *Havasupai Ethnography*, American Museum of Natural History, Anthropological Papers, 29 (1928).

Squier, Ephraim G. and E. H. Davis, *Ancient Monuments of the Mississippi Valley*, Smithsonian Contributions to Knowledge, I (Washington, D.C., 1848).

Stanton, William R., *The Leopard's Spots: Scientific Attitudes toward Race in America, 1815–1859* (Chicago, University of Chicago Press, 1960).

Starr, Frederick, "Anthropological Work in America," *Popular Science Monthly*, XLI (1892), 289–307.

Stegner, Wallace, *Beyond the Hundredth Meridian: John Wesley Powell and the Second Opening of the West* (Boston, Houghton Mifflin, 1953).

Stern, Bernhard, *Lewis Henry Morgan; Social Evolutionist* (Chicago, University of Chicago Press, 1931).

Stocking, George W., Jr., "Franz Boas and the Founding of the American Anthropological Association," *American Anthropologist*, 62 (1960), 1–17.

——, *Race, Culture, and Evolution* (New York: The Free Press, 1968).

——, "What's In a Name? The Origins of the Royal Anthropological Institute (1837–71)," *Man*, n.s. VI (1971), 369–391.

——, *The Shaping of American Anthropology, 1883–1911: A Franz Boas Reader* (New York, Basic Books, 1974).

——, "Ideas and institutions in American anthropology: toward a history of the interwar period," in Stocking, ed., *Selected Papers from the American Anthropologist, 1921–1945*, American Anthropological Association (Washington, D.C., 1976), 1–53.

——, "Anthropology as kulturkampf: science and politics in the career of Franz Boas," in Walter Goldschmidt, ed., *The Uses of Anthropology*, Special Publication of the American Anthropological Association (1979), 33–50.

Sturtevant, William C., "Huns, Free-Thinking Americans, and the AAA," *History of Anthropology Newsletter*, II, No. 1 (1975), 4–6.

Swanton, John R., "William Henry Holmes, 1846–1933," *National Academy of Sciences Biographical Memoirs*, XVII (1935), 238–252. Includes Holmes bibliography.

Tedlock, Dennis, "On the Translation of Style in Oral Narrative," *Journal of American Folklore*, 84 (1971), 114–133.

Thomas, Cyrus, *Report of the Mound Explorations of the Bureau of Ethnology*, Twelfth Annual Report, Bureau of Ethnology (Washington, D.C., 1894).

Thomas, Isaiah, et.al., "Origins of the American Antiquarian Society," *American Antiquarian Society Transactions and Collections*, I (1820), 17–20.

Thoresen, T.H.H., ed., *Toward a science of man: Essays in the history of anthropology* (The Hague, Mouton, 1975).

———, "Paying the Piper and Calling the Tune: The Beginnings of Academic Anthropology in California," *Journal of the History of the Behavioral Sciences*, 11 (1975), 257–275.

Topinard, Paul, "L'Anthropologie aux Etats-Unis," *L'Anthropologie* (1893), 301–351.

Tozzer, Alfred M., "Memoir of Frederic W. Putnam," *Proceedings of the Massachusetts Historical Society* (June, 1916), 8 pp.

———, "Charles Pickering Bowditch," *American Anthropologist*, 23 (1921), 353–359.

———, "Frederic Ward Putnam, 1839–1915," *National Academy of Sciences Biographical Memoirs*, XVI (1935), 125–151. Includes Putnam bibliography.

Truettner, William H. and Robin Bolton-Smith, *National Parks and the American Landscape*, Catalogue of exhibit held in 1971 (Washington, Smithsonian Institution Press, 1972).

Tylor, E.B., *Researches into the Early History of Mankind and the Development of Civilization* (London, J. Murray, 1865).

———, *Primitive Culture* (London, J. Murray, 1871).

———, "How the Problems of American Anthropology Present Themselves to the English Mind," *Transactions of the Anthropological Society of Washington*, III (1884), 92.

———, "American Aspects of Anthropology," *Popular Science Monthly*, 26 (1884), 152–168.

Urry, James, "Notes and queries on anthropology and the development of field methods in British anthropology, 1870–1920," *Proceedings of the Royal Anthropological Institute* for 1972, 45–72.

Wallace, Alfred Russel, *My Life: A Record of Events and Opinions* (New York, Dodd, Mead, and Co., 1905), 2 vols.

Walter, Paul A.F., "The Santa Fe-Taos Art Movement," *Art and Archaeology*, IV (1916), 330–338.

Washburn, Wilcomb E., "The Museum and Joseph Henry," *Curator*, 8 (1965), 35–54.

————, *The Assault on Indian Tribalism: The General Allotment Law (Dawes Act) of 1887* (Philadelphia, Lippincott, 1975).

White, Leslie A., ed., *Pioneers in American Anthropology: The Bandelier-Morgan Letters, 1873–1883*, 2 vols. (Albuquerque, University of New Mexico Press, 1940).

————, *The Ethnography and Ethnology of Franz Boas*, Texas Memorial Museum Bulletin 6 (Austin, Texas, 1963).

————, *The Social Organization of Ethnological Theory*, Rice University Studies, Monographs in Cultural Anthropology, 52 (4), (Houston, Texas, 1966).

Wilkins, Thurman, "Alice Cunningham Fletcher," in *Notable American Women, 1607–1950*, ed. by Edward T. and Janet W. James (Cambridge, Massachusetts, The Belknap Press of Harvard University, 1971), 630–633.

Willey, Gordon R., *Archaeology of the Florida Gulf Coast*, introduction by Ripley P. Bullen (New York, AMS Press for Peabody Museum of Archaeology and Ethnology, 1973; orig., 1949).

———— and Jeremy Sabloff, *A History of American Archaeology* (San Francisco, W.H. Freeman and Co., 1974).

Willoughby, C.C., "The Art of the Great Earthwork Builders of Ohio," *Holmes Anniversary Volume* (Washington, D.C., James William Bryan, 1916), 469–480.

Wilson, Dorothy Clarke, *Bright Eyes: The Story of Susette La Flesche, an Omaha Indian* (New York, McGraw-Hill, 1974).

Wilson, Edmund, *Red, Black, Blond, and Olive: Studies in Four Civilizations: Zuni, Haiti, Soviet Russia, Israel* (New York, Oxford University Press, 1956).

Wilson, Thomas, "The Paleolithic Period in the District of Columbia," *American Anthropologist*, II (1889), 235–241.

Wilmsen, Edwin N., "An Outline of Early Man Studies in the United States," *American Antiquity*, XXXI (1965), 172–192.

Woodbury, Richard B., "Nels C. Nelson and Chronological Archaeology," *American Antiquity*, XXV (1960), 400–401.

————, "Nelson's Stratigraphy," *American Antiquity*, XXVI (1960), 98–99.

Woodward, Arthur, "Frank Hamilton Cushing—First War Chief of the Zunis," *The Masterkey*, 13 (1939), 172–179.

Wyman, Jeffries, "An account of some kjoekken moeddings, or shell-heaps in Maine and Massachusetts," *American Naturalist*, I (1868), 561–584.

————, "Primitive Man," *American Naturalist*, X (1876), 278–282.

INDEX